Caring for Preschool Children

A Supervised, Self-Instructional Training Program

Volume II

Diane Trister Dodge
Derry Gosselin Koralek
Peter J. Pizzolongo

Washington, DC

Published by

Teaching Strategies, Inc.
P.O. Box 42243
Washington, DC 20015

Distributed by

Gryphon House Inc.
P.O. Box 275
Mt. Rainier, MD 20712

ISBN: 0-9602892-4-0 (Volume II)
ISBN: 0-9602892-2-4 (Two-Volume Set)

Library of Congress Card Catalog Number: 89-051192

Acknowledgments

This training program is based on several previous efforts. It draws from earlier publications and experiences of the authors, each of whom has provided training and developed materials for use in day care and other early childhood settings. The primary basis for this publication is a training program developed by the authors for the U.S. Navy and the U.S. Army Child Development Services Programs. Carolee Callen, Head of the Navy Child Development Services Branch, originally conceived of the idea of a standardized, self-instructional training program for child care staff. In 1986 the Navy contracted with Creative Associates International, Inc., a Washington, DC-based consulting firm where the authors then worked, to develop a training program and to train child care center directors to implement the program. M.-A. Lucas, Chief of the Child Development Services Division in the U.S. Army, funded an adaptation of the training program to support CDA training in Army Child Development Centers. We are indebted to these two individuals, their headquarters staff, and the staff at Army and Navy child development centers who reviewed all drafts of the materials developed under this contract and provided us with constructive and helpful suggestions that greatly improved the program.

During the development of this training program, in its original format for military child care settings and as revised and expanded in 1989, several early childhood educators worked with us and provided expert advice. In particular, we want to thank Dr. Jenni Klein, whose considerable knowledge and vast practical experience made her contributions exceptionally valuable. Dr. Joan Lombardi reviewed the training materials from the perspective of the Child Development Associate (CDA) Standards and showed us where changes and additions were needed. Her guidance was particularly useful in ensuring that the materials are consistent with the profession's standards for caregiver competencies. On individual modules, we are grateful for the expert assistance we received from Marilyn Goldhammer, Dr. Trudy Hamby, Bonnie Kittredge, Cynthia Prather, and Lillian Sugarman.

The production of a document of this size required the specialized expertise of three dedicated individuals: Martha Cooley, who edited the manuscript; Jennifer Barrett, who designed the cover and graphics; and Frank Harvey, who served as production coordinator. We are indebted to each of them for their substantial contributions.

And finally, we want to acknowledge the many teachers and trainers we have worked with over the years from whom we have learned a great deal. We have undoubtedly adapted and expanded on many of their excellent ideas; this training program is richer as a result.

It is our hope that *Caring for Preschool Children* will support the important role of teachers and trainers and that its implementation in centers across the country will have a positive impact on the quality of early childhood education programs.

Contents

Module 7
Creative

What Is Creativity and Why Is It Important?

Creativity is the ability to use one's imagination and to think of or make something original. Creative people can take an idea, a plan, or an object and adapt it to make something new. Although some people are more creative than others, everyone has creative abilities that they use on the job and at home. Artists, musicians, architects, and writers are all creative people—but so are cooks, secretaries, lawyers, plumbers, and teachers. You don't have to paint a picture or write a book to be creative. Thinking of new ways to help children learn self-help skills, making up a song to sing when it's time to pick up, or rearranging your classroom to create new interest areas are all examples of creativity. Being creative is really an attitude, a state of mind.

Children are eager learners, naturally imaginative and creative. They learn by doing and by interacting with their environment. Children who are creative are willing to try new ways of doing things. They see more than one possibility in how a toy can be used or an art material explored. They are curious about how things work and why things happen as they do. They are able to learn from their mistakes and feel good about their efforts and accomplishments.

Young children learn about the world with their senses. Everything is new to them, and they want to explore everything around them. Infants reach for mobiles because they see them hanging over their cribs. Their exploration leads them to discover that when they hit a mobile, it moves. This exploration is the beginning of creativity. Toddlers need many opportunities to develop their senses and their creativity, such as playing with water or sand, finger painting with shaving cream, or being asked open-ended questions.

As preschool children develop their motor and language skills, they can play with a wider variety of materials than they could when they were toddlers. Their play with one another is more inventive, and they can make plans and carry them through. When teachers encourage children to be creative thinkers and expose them to an interesting and stimulating environment, these children's creativity continues to grow. Their ideas may not always work and their answers may not always be "right," but when children feel that their ideas and plans are appreciated and valued, they feel good about themselves and their abilities.

The relationship between child and teacher sets the stage for creativity. When children develop a sense of trust and feel secure with their teachers, they feel free to express themselves and to explore. Teachers can support the creativity of preschoolers as they plan the daily schedule and set up the environment. A schedule that gives children time to play at their own pace, and an environment that includes interesting materials and activities, are both crucial in supporting children's creativity.

Teachers promote children's creativity by:

- arranging the learning environment to support children's creative development;

- providing a variety of activities and experiences to promote creative development;

- interacting with children in ways that encourage creative expression.

Listed below are examples of how teachers demonstrate their competency in promoting children's creativity.

Arranging the Learning Environment to Support Children's Creative Development

Here are some examples of what teachers can do.

- Set up the environment so children can easily select, replace, and care for materials and equipment. "I see you found the new zoo animals in the block area. It looks as if you're building an enclosure for them to live in."

- Provide time in the daily schedule for children to make plans and carry them out. "There are a lot of children wanting to climb up and down these big block stairs that you made. Can you figure out a way to go one at a time so the stairs don't fall and nobody gets hurt?" "We could sell tickets."

- Provide and rotate according to children's current interests a variety of materials, props, and "real" things for the children to use, including some from the children's own culture. "Indrani, your mom brought us some beautiful fabric and one of her saris from India where she was born. They are in the housekeeping area. You can show your friend how to put on a sari if you want to."

- Hang interesting pictures and objects at a child's height on the wall. Invite children to explore and enjoy the world around them. "Jim, your grandmother brought us some dancing fans to use. They are made with feathers, and I've put them on the wall in the music area where you can reach them when you want to use them."

- Provide space for children's spontaneous projects or activities, such as an empty table near the "junk" building and collage materials, or space for a puppet show or creative dramatics. "Julie, I'll help you move this big box into the library area so you and Anna can do your cat and mice puppet show for an audience."

Providing a Variety of Activities and Experiences to Promote Creative Development

Here are some examples of what teachers can do.

- Provide for "messy" open-ended activities such as water, sand and mud play, shaving cream or finger painting, face painting, or bubble blowing.

- Include a variety of music and movement activities in the daily schedule. Include songs, chants, or rhythms from cultural groups represented in your class.

- Encourage children's use of imagination by telling stories, playing make-believe, and singing songs. "After the dragon had eaten 3 tons of mashed potatoes, 2 boxes of hot dogs, and 1 carrot, what do you think he did?"

- Extend dramatic play with children. "Thank you, firefighters, for saving my house. You put out the fire so fast there's hardly any damage."

- Provide sensory experiences to stimulate children's imagination and creative expression. "You've given your baby such a sudsy bubble bath! How do you feel when you get all sudsy?"

- Provide materials with which children can do many different things, such as blocks, finger paint, playdough, clay, or water. "Jacci is using all her fingers to roll her playdough, and Anna is using her fists. What different shapes you are making!"

- Avoid using dittos or product patterns. "Alison, you'll find lots of crayons, markers, paste, paper, and scissors right here where you can reach them any time you want to use them."

Interacting with Children in Ways That Encourage Creative Expression

Here are some examples of what teachers can do.

- Respect each child's unique creative expression. "Jeremy painted a picture of the farmer. Mary painted a picture of her baby sister to send the farmer's family. They both have their own way to thank the farmer for our field trip."

- Display children's creative work attractively and respectfully. "Carlos, where would you like me to hang your picture?"

- Give children positive feedback about their creative thinking. "Wow. You made a tunnel for your hand in that wet sand! How did you do that?"

- Respect the creative process as well as the creative product. "Lenny, you've finger painted with your hands and your elbows. You have really experimented with different ways to move the paint around and to see what kinds of marks you can make."

- Ask questions that encourage creative thinking. "Raoul, what can you do to get the other children to play your game with you?"

- Let a creative product stay in place for several days so children can have repeated and lengthy creative experiences. "Yes, Lori. We'll leave up the store you made so you can play in it tomorrow."

- Know when to step back and give children time and space to explore on their own. "I'm just stopping by to say hello to your babies, Susan. Now I have to go to the grocery store."

Promoting Children's Creativity

In the following situations, teachers are promoting children's creativity. As you read, think about what the teachers are doing and why. Then answer the questions that follow.

Arranging the Learning Environment to Support Children's Creative Development

Before the children arrive, Ms. Richards checks the "junk" building area that was so actively used yesterday. She adds shoe boxes, oatmeal boxes, and wrapping paper tubes. She checks the supply of glue, paper fasteners, pipe cleaners, and twist ties on the shelf above the variety of containers. She adds more popsicle sticks, strips of fabric, and the dryer lint she has been saving. She covers the table near these shelves with butcher paper and leaves it empty.

During free play Kira works on the house she started building yesterday. Ms. Richards stops by to watch. She asks, "How's your construction coming along, Kira?" Kira smiles and tells her about the boxes she glued together. "This is the kitchen and my room and the porch." Ms. Richards nods, and asks, "What do you do on your porch?" Kira responds, "That's where my new puppy sleeps. I didn't make him yet." Ms. Richards asks, "Do you have everything you need to make your puppy?" Kira says, "I need some very soft stuff." Ms. Richards shows Kira the cotton balls, dryer lint, and yarn, and says, "Yes, puppies are very soft."

1. **How did Ms. Richards arrange the environment to promote children's creativity?**

   _____

   _____

   _____

2. **How do unstructured (or open-ended) materials promote creativity in preschool children?**

   _____

   _____

   _____

Providing a Variety of Activities and Experiences to Promote Creative Development

Mr. Lopez is reading to a group of children. The story is *Teddy Bears Go Shopping* by Susanna Gretz. He stops the story and asks the children: "What kinds of things do you like to buy at the store?" "I get cereal," says Emily. "Cookies," says Paul. "What do you think would happen if the store ran out of milk?" Mr. Lopez asks. "I'd drink water, cause I don't like milk!" answers Emily. "How could you get to the store if your car was broken?" "On the bus," says Paul. "On my bike," says Juan. "Those are both good ways to get to the store," Mr. Lopez responds. Then he continues with the story.

1. **How did the questions Mr. Lopez asked support creative thinking?**

   _____

   _____

   _____

2. **Why is story time a good opportunity to promote creativity?**

   _____

   _____

   _____

Interacting with Children in Ways That Encourage Creative Expression

It's free play time in the preschool room. Ms. Williams takes a quick look around the room to see what the children are doing. Three children are building with blocks. Ms. Williams walks over to them. Brian, Carlos, and Tameka are busy planning what they will build. "Let's build the biggest house you ever saw!" says Tameka. "Yeah," says Brian. "Okay!" says Carlos. "We'll start by taking out all the blocks," Tameka says. Ms. Williams smiles as she walks away to see what the other children are doing. When it's almost time to pick up, Ms. Williams comes back to check on the builders. "That is the biggest house I ever saw," she says. "You really worked hard building that." All three children ask, "Please, please, can we leave it up?" "Yes, you may, but how could we let everyone else know that you don't want this building taken down?" "We'll make a sign that says 'Don't knock this down.'" "Good idea. Do you have any ideas about how we could remember this building for a long time?" "Take a picture!" "With all the builders too... I'll go get the camera for you."

1. **How did Ms. Williams' response to the children's request encourage them to be creative?**

   _____

   _____

   _____

2. **How did the way Ms. Williams handled the situation support an atmosphere that promotes creativity in the room?**

   _____

   _____

   _____

Compare your answers with those on the answer sheet at the end of this module. If your answers are different, discuss them with your trainer. There can be more than one good answer.

Your Own Creativity

As adults, we sometimes confuse creativity with talent. It is important to remember that creativity is a way of thinking—an attitude that helps us explore new ways to do something, solve a problem, or achieve a goal. You don't have to be an artist to plan activities for children that encourage creativity. Understanding your own creativity and how you approach problems and new situations will help you become sensitive to creativity in young children. Recognizing how you feel when you are being creative will help you support children's efforts at trying out new ideas.

Think about the satisfaction you feel when you solve a problem while cooking, gardening, reading, talking with a friend, or helping children grow and develop. That feeling is similar to the pride that children feel when they have figured something out for themselves.

Here are some exercises you can do to help stimulate your own creative thinking.

How do you get to work each day? Can you think of an alternative route or mode of transportation to get to work?

_____

_____

_____

_____

_____

Think of some unusual ways to use a common object—for example, an egg carton, a newspaper, a pencil, or a suitcase.

_____

_____

_____

_____

_____

Think of three ways to make a sandwich without using bread.

a. _____

_____

b. _____

_____

c. _____

_____

Think of a new ending to a favorite story, movie, or book.

_____

_____

_____

_____

_____

Describe something you did with children that was very creative.

_____

_____

_____

_____

_____

These questions or similar ones can help you think of new ways to approach a problem. They can also be useful in helping children develop their creativity. Supporting children's creativity is one of your major tasks—and one that gives much satisfaction in return, as you watch children gain in self-confidence and enthusiastically explore their world.

When you have finished this overview section, you should complete the pre-training assessment. Refer to the glossary at the end of the module if you need definitions of the terms that are used.

Pre-Training Assessment

Listed below are the skills that teachers use to promote children's creativity. Think about whether you do these things regularly, sometimes, or not enough. Place a check in one of the columns on the right for each skill listed. Then discuss your answers with your trainer.

SKILL	I DO THIS REGULARLY	I DO THIS SOMETIMES	I DON'T DO THIS ENOUGH
ARRANGING THE LEARNING ENVIRONMENT TO SUPPORT CHILDREN'S CREATIVE DEVELOPMENT 1. Setting up the environment so children can easily select, replace, and care for materials and equipment.			
2. Providing enough time in the daily schedule for children to make plans and carry them out.			
3. Providing materials children can use to express their creativity in many different ways.			
4. Providing and rotating a variety of materials and props, including some from the children's own cultures.			
5. Providing space for children's spontaneous projects or activities.			
PROVIDING A VARIETY OF ACTIVITIES AND EXPERIENCES TO PROMOTE CREATIVE DEVELOPMENT 6. Including a variety of planned and spontaneous music and movement activities in the daily schedule.			

SKILL	I DO THIS REGULARLY	I DO THIS SOMETIMES	I DON'T DO THIS ENOUGH
7. Providing props and playing make-believe with children.			
8. Providing art activities such as painting, drawing, using clay or playdough, or making collages or assemblages every day.			
9. Providing sand and water play regularly.			
10. Avoiding the use of dittos or product patterns.			
INTERACTING WITH CHILDREN IN WAYS THAT ENCOURAGE CREATIVE EXPRESSION. 11. Asking open-ended questions that encourage creative thinking.			
12. Providing positive feedback about children's creative thinking.			
13. Recognizing that children are more interested in the process of creating than in the product.			
14. Displaying children's creative work attractively and where they can see it.			
15. Accepting and valuing each child's unique creative expressions.			

Review your responses, then list three to five skills you would like to improve or topics you would like to learn more about. When you finish this module you will list examples of your new or improved knowledge and skills.

_____

_____

_____

_____

_____

Now begin the learning activities for Module 7, Creative.

I. Using Your Knowledge of Child Development to Promote Creativity

In this activity you will learn:

- to recognize some typical behaviors of preschool children; and

- to use what you know about children to promote their creativity.

Young children do not have to be taught how to be creative; it is part of their natural makeup. Everything they do involves creating and re-creating. They are beginners at everything— seeing, touching, tasting, talking, crawling, climbing, building, drawing, walking, and more. Each of their actions involves exploration and discovery. Their insatiable curiosity about the wonders of the world around them motivates their explorations.

Moving from toddlerhood into the preschool period, children continue to want to reach out and physically touch their environment. The rate of growth has slowed down in three-, four-, and five-year-olds, so they have much more energy to use. Also, they don't tire as quickly and can stay involved for longer periods of time. They also have much greater control over their large muscles, and as they move through the preschool period they continue to develop their fine motor skills and eye-hand coordination.

Along with children's greatly expanding physical skills comes rapid intellectual development. As they move, dig, build, lift, climb, handle, taste, fill, empty, and manipulate, they begin to gather and use information about objects and events in their environment: "These things are different; these look and taste the same; when you put this color with this color, it looks different."

Language growth is also rapid as children learn words and use them to describe what they are seeing and experiencing. And most important of all, if the environment allows for active exploration, if materials are supplied, and if time to explore actively is allowed, children begin to develop attitudes about the creative process and their own abilities to create and learn. When children experience the challenge and joy of discovery, they also develop attitudes that allow them to stick to a task. If these attitudes are nurtured during the preschool years, they will have lasting effects on the child's entire development.

The chart on the next page lists some typical behaviors of preschool children. Included are behaviors relevant to creativity. The right column asks you to identify ways that teachers can use this information about child development to promote children's creativity. Try to think of as many examples as you can. As you work through the module you will learn new strategies for encouraging children's creativity, and you can add them to the child development chart. You are not expected to think of all the examples at one time. If you need help getting started, turn to the completed chart at the end of the module. By the time you complete all the learning activities, you will find that you have learned many ways to foster children's creativity.

Using Your Knowledge of Child Development
to Promote Creativity

WHAT PRESCHOOL CHILDREN ARE LIKE	HOW TEACHERS CAN USE THIS INFORMATION TO PROMOTE CREATIVITY
They are curious and ask many "why" questions.	
They have a strong sense of wonder.	
They learn from concrete experiences. Although they can understand explanations, they need real things to work with.	
They have their own ideas and want to carry them out by themselves.	
They want to make choices and like to feel important.	

WHAT PRESCHOOL CHILDREN ARE LIKE	HOW TEACHERS CAN USE THIS INFORMATION TO PROMOTE CREATIVITY
They enjoy dramatic play and have active imaginations.	
They are beginners at doing things and may make mistakes.	
They want to be independent, but they are sometimes still very dependent on adults.	
They pass through different developmental stages in their use of art media and materials.	
They have a wide variety of interests and skills.	

When you have finished the chart, discuss your answers with your trainer. As you proceed with the rest of the learning activities, you can refer to this chart and add examples of how teachers promote children's creativity.

II. Setting the Stage for Creativity

In this activity you will learn:

- to encourage creativity by asking children questions; and

- to interact with children in ways that promote creative thinking.

The ways in which you interact with and respond to preschool children can give children the message that creativity is valued and supported. What you say, how you ask and answer questions, and the ways in which you encourage learning through discovery all nurture creativity in children.

Asking Questions to Encourage Creativity

Asking open-ended questions is one of the best ways for teachers to encourage children to think creatively. These are questions that cannot be answered with just a "yes" or "no." They encourage children to think of many different ways to solve a problem.

For example, David and Juana, both five years old, want to play with the same doll in the house corner. Their teacher, Ms. Williams, comes over to see what's the matter.

Ms. Williams:	"How do you think you both could play with the doll?"
Juana:	"I should get it first because I'm older."
David:	"I could have the doll and Juana could have the carriage."
Ms. Williams:	"Is there anything you could do with the doll together?"
David:	"We could give her a bath."
Juana:	"I'll wash her hair and then you can give her a bottle, okay?"

Ms. Williams allowed the children to reach their own solution. Her questions encouraged them to think of a way to solve the problem for themselves.

Teachers also use questions to help preschool children discover new concepts on their own. For example, a group of children, all about three-and-a-half years old, are playing at the sand table. Ms. Williams brings over a small pitcher of water and places it near the table.

Ms. Williams:	"I've brought some water for the sand table. What do you think would happen if we added some water to the sand?"
Maddie:	"It would get all mushy."
Lloyd:	"We could make mud pies."
Emilio:	"The marbles will get buried."

A teacher's questions can also help children learn to describe the concepts they are observing.

Ms. Williams:	"Maddie, how does the sand feel with water in it?"
Maddie:	"Now it's getting all stuck to my fingers."
Ms. Williams:	"That's right, wet sand does stick to your fingers more than dry sand does."

Here are some examples of questions that encourage creative thinking:

- What do you think about...?
- What would happen if...?
- What else can we use this for?
- What else is like this?
- Is there another way to do this?
- What if we added this?
- What if we take this away?

- Why do you think this happened?
- How do you think this works?
- How did you...?
- How could you...?
- What's similar about these?
- In what ways are these different?

Interacting with Children in Ways That Promote Creative Thinking

The ways in which teachers interact with and respond to children can promote or discourage creative thinking. Carefully listening to what a child has to say and recognizing each child as an individual are crucial. Your enthusiasm for a child's efforts and success will greatly encourage his or her creativity.

For preschool children, the process of doing something is more important than the end result or product. For example, Alex (4 1/2 years), has been finger painting. He is making large circles with both hands. He has some paint on the elbow of one sleeve, which has started to slip down. Ms. Williams, pushing up his sleeve gently, says to Alex, "Just look at the enormous circles you are making. It looks as if you're enjoying that paint!" Alex smiles and makes fast small circles. Her comment reflects what Alex is absorbed in doing. She does not ask him what he is making, nor does she comment on his clothing.

Sometimes the teacher's response can help a child look at a problem in a new way. For example, Joey, who is three and a half, is in the book corner reading a book about a new baby. He has a frown on his face, which Ms. Williams notices.

Ms. Williams:	"Joey, would you like to read that book together ?"
Joey (climbing into her lap):	"This is a sad story."
Ms. Williams:	"What do you think is making the boy sad?"

Joey:	"That baby is in the way."
Ms. Williams:	"You have a new baby brother too, Joey. Can you tell me something that makes you sad about having a new brother?"
Joey:	"He cries too much and Mom gets too tired."
Ms. Williams:	"Can you think of something fun about having a new brother?"
Joey:	"Well, he smiles when I sing to him."
Ms. Williams:	"Sometimes it's hard, but sometimes it's fun to be a big brother."

In this learning activity, you will review the questions on the previous pages that can promote creativity. Use these questions with the children in your room and record the results. Read the example that follows before doing the activity.

Using Questions to Promote Children's Creativity
(Example)

In the block corner:

You said:	*"How did you get this tower to stand by itself?"*
The child said:	*"I used good blocks."*
You said:	*"I wonder what it was about those good blocks that made them stand up so well?"*

In the art area:

You said:	*"What would happen if you used some white paint on top of the red?"*
The child said:	*"I don't know."*
You said:	*"I'll leave the white paint right here in case you'd like to experiment with it."*

In the house corner:

You said:	*"What other way could you help your baby stop crying?"*
The child said:	*"I could take her for a walk."*
You said:	*"Yes, that would make her feel better. Can you think of any other ways?"*

In the table toy area:

You said:	*"What's the same about these Legos and these plastic blocks?"*
The child said:	*"They're both red."*
You said:	*"They certainly are, and what can you do with them?"*

At the sand table:

You said:	*"What do you think could grow in the sand?"*
The child said:	*"Some plants live in the sand."*
You said:	*"Yes, we saw plants growing in the sand on our field trip, didn't we?"*

In the book corner:

You said: *"This is a book about a child going to bed. What do you think he'll do before he goes to sleep?"*

The child said: *"Get a drink of water."*

You said: *"What else do you do before you go to sleep?"*

CREATIVE

Using Questions to Promote Children's Creativity

In the block corner:

You said: _____

_____

The child said: _____

_____

You said: _____

_____

In the art area:

You said: _____

_____

The child said: _____

_____

You said: _____

_____

In the house corner:

You said: _____

_____

The child said: _____

_____

You said: _____

_____

In the table toy area:

You said: _____

_____

The child said: _____

_____

You said: _____

_____

At the sand table:

You said: _____

_____

The child said: _____

_____

You said: _____

_____

In the book corner:

You said: _____

_____

The child said: _____

_____

You said: _____

_____

Discuss your questions and the children's responses with your trainer.

III. Providing a Variety of
Movement Experie

In this activity you will learn:

- to recognize how music and movement ex_
  preschoolers; and

- to provide a variety of developmentally appropriate music and _
  activities for preschoolers.

From a very early age, children respond to music. Infants smile when adults sing to them. They begin to move their bodies when they hear music, and they respond to toys that make a noise. As children grow, their interest in music continues and they begin to hum, sing, and make up chants.

As their coordination develops, they also begin to move to music: to sway, dance, bounce up and down, clap their hands, and stamp their feet. The chart below summarizes the development of musical expression in young children, beginning in infancy.

The Development of Musical Expression in Children[1]

AGE	DEVELOPMENTAL STAGE	HOW CHILDREN EXPRESS THEMSELVES MUSICALLY
Infants and young toddlers (up to 24 months old).	They learn by using their senses. They touch, smell, taste, see, and hear.	They are receptive to music. They respond by listening and singing (vocalize from approximately 6 months; sing from 18 months). They move and make sounds with materials—rattles, pots and pans, and so on.

---

[1]Adapted with permission from Stephanie Feeney, Doris Christensen, and Eva Moravcik, *Who Am I in the Lives of Children?* (Columbus, OH: Charles E. Merrill Publishing, Co., 1987), p. 269.

OR PRESCHOOL CHILDREN

AGE	DEVELOPMENTAL STAGE	HOW CHILDREN EXPRESS THEMSELVES MUSICALLY
Older toddlers and young children (24 months to 4 years old).	They continue to learn by exploring with their senses. They also discover new skills, refine their small and large muscles, and begin to see similarities and differences among objects and ideas.	They are interested in and responsive to rhythmic music. They move and sing to music. They perceive differences in musical tone and color. They sing spontaneously in play. They have a comfortable singing range. They do not match pitch when singing with others. They may sing only phrases from songs. They enjoy singing the same songs repeatedly. They respond at their own tempo. They are interested in using musical instruments.
Older children and kindergarteners (4 to 6 years).	They become more aware of concepts; their ability to express themselves through language increases.	They enjoy group musical games, elaborate songs, and singing alone. They can enjoy listening to short musical selections. They have increased singing ranges. They are increasingly accurate in matching pitch and tempo when singing in a group. They are able to synchronize movement with rhythm or a piece of music. They can identify and use simple instruments appropriately.

Music affects children's moods. Quiet, comforting music can lull children to sleep, while a march or very rhythmic music can encourage them to parade around the room and sing. Music gives children many opportunities to use their bodies and voices expressively.

Teachers don't have to be talented to provide music and movement experiences for young children. When children sing, they aren't concerned with the quality of their voices or the teacher's ability to sing; they respond to the enthusiasm and pure enjoyment of playing with sounds and moving their bodies. There are no wrong ways to sing, and children have a chance to express how they feel when listening to music. One child may find a song appealing; another may find it silly. One child may move his whole body to music while another may wave her arms while standing still. Because children naturally connect movement with music,

26

listening to music invites them to explore what their bodies can do and to become aware of their bodies in space.

Music and movement allow preschool children to develop in a number of areas, including these:

Creative Self-Expression

- Children express a wide range of emotions through music and movement activities.

- Children begin to recognize what types of music they like best.

- Children can experiment freely with music and movement.

Motor Skills

- Children become conscious of what their bodies can do. Teachers have an important opportunity to accept and appreciate individual differences.

- Children develop and practice large motor skills, including hopping, skipping, jumping, trotting, swaying, swinging, and leaping.

- Children develop and refine their small muscles when they use rhythm instruments, imitate finger plays, and use props in movement activities.

Listening Skills

- Children learn to distinguish among different sounds that instruments make; different rhythms in music; and differences in tempo, tone, and volume. This ability to distinguish contributes to the development of pre-reading skills.

Social Skills

- Children participate in many group experiences with music and movement; they learn to cooperate, take turns, and to appreciate themselves and others.

- Children learn to express themselves as individuals through music and movement. This leads to an ability to communicate their ideas, thoughts, and feelings to others.

Self-Esteem

- Children feel good about their accomplishments when the atmosphere is accepting and nonjudgmental.

- Children learn that their efforts are valued.

- Children enjoy hearing their names incorporated into songs.

Music and Movement Activities

While many different types of music and movement activities can be planned for preschool children, they generally fall into these categories: listening to music, singing, marching bands, creative movement, and musical games. Each is briefly highlighted on the next page.

Listening to Music

Listening to music can be both relaxing and enjoyable. Children should have many opportunities throughout the day to listen to different types of music: classical, jazz, rock, marches, children's songs, and folk songs. The type of music you choose will definitely affect children's behavior. Rock music at naptime will surely cause problems, while a march at clean-up time can motivate the entire group.

Music can be played during free play, as background, or as part of a particular experience. For example, try playing music during an art activity. Ask the children who are painting or drawing to do so to the music: "What does the music make you think of?" "What kinds of colors do you think are in this music?" "Does this music make you feel like painting quickly or slowly?"

Encourage children to become aware of other sounds around them. Ask them how different types of birds sing, what water sounds like when it drips or when it gushes, or how rain sounds. Play guessing games in which the children listen to sounds with closed eyes, or play music that includes various sounds that children can identify.

Invite parents who play instruments to come and play for the children. Sometimes an elementary school band or orchestra will come and play. Talk about the names of instruments and describe the sounds they make together.

Singing

It is a good idea to use songs frequently and informally as well as during a set singing time (if you have one). Children can sing every day, but this may or may not occur during a special time for singing. Some suggested times for songs follow.

- Use songs for transitions between activities—to get children ready for lunch or story time or to get them back together after free-play times for group activities. Any time the children have to wait for a short time, reduce the frustration of waiting by singing.

- Use songs ritually. Start the day with the same song; use the same song for birthdays; use the same song regularly before brushing teeth or going outside or when greeting a new child. Some children need the security of certain events that they can count on in the classroom, and they will be very quick to point out if you forget regular songs in their regular places.

- Use songs as singing games or have the children act out the stories in songs while they sing.

- Play games such as "London Bridge" and "The Farmer in the Dell." Encourage everyone to sing while they play. This may be difficult for some of the children at first.

- Act out story songs such as "The Old Woman Who Swallowed a Fly." You may want to make props for the children to use.

- Reinforce the importance of singing by making a tape of the children singing. They often love to listen to their own voices. Those who want to can sing individually as well as with the group.

- Sing the same song in different ways: loudly, softly, in a whisper, quickly, slowly, sitting, standing, marching, hopping, or with and without instruments.

- Make up your own songs with the children. They don't have to be long or complicated:

    "How are you?" "I'm fine, I'm fine."

    "What do you like to eat?" "Ice cream!"

It may be helpful to remember the following about singing with preschool children:

- Preschool children enjoy repeating songs they like.

- They like singing quick, lively songs more often than slow ones.

- They enjoy funny songs and nonsense songs.

- We all have a speaking and a singing voice. Help children become aware of this by saying the words to a song in your speaking voice, then using your singing voice for the same song.

- Preschool children's ability to carry a tune improves with practice and good listening habits.

- Preschool children do not always understand what songs are appropriate for a given situation. If they want to sing "Jingle Bells" in May or "Good Morning" before going home, join them enthusiastically.

These ideas may be useful when introducing a new song:

- Allow children to play a tape recording you have made of the new song for several days. They would probably rather hear your voice than a record of a professional singer.

- Tell a story about the new song. ("Once there was a little girl named Mary. She had a little lamb...") Use a flannel board when telling a story about the new song.

- Repeat the words for the song several times (break up the phrases if they are too long for preschoolers to remember).

- Sing the song several times, encouraging children to join you.

- Let the preschoolers sing the song several times if they seem to enjoy it.

- You should not have to "drill" the children to get them to learn a new song. If they don't pick it up easily, come back to it at a later time or forget about it if it seems too difficult.

Marching Bands

Every room should have a basic set of rhythm instruments, including:

- tambourines
- rhythm sticks
- sandpaper blocks
- bells
- triangles

- drums
- cymbals
- maracas/shakers
- clackers

Allow lots of time for the children to become familiar with the different instruments. What do they sound like? How do they make noise? Can the children make the same sounds the instruments make? Let the children know the names of the instruments. It can be fun to make up a song about the names; each child in turn can demonstrate how the instrument sounds.

To have a marching band, each child selects an instrument and marches around the room playing the instrument to different types of music. Try a march, then something slower. Put the instruments down and have the children clap to the beat or stamp their feet to the beat. You can march backward, in a circle, following a rope pattern on the floor, or in shapes. Have the children use the instruments as they stand in one place or sit in a circle on the floor.

Creative Movement

Playing different types of music encourages children to move the way the music makes them feel. Use music that is fast and slow, loud and soft, happy and sad. Once the children feel comfortable moving to music, you can add props to further stimulate their imaginations: streamers, light-weight fabric, sheets, scarves, feathers, balloons, capes, ribbons, and hula hoops.

Have the children imitate the various ways that animals walk and move. They can crawl like a snake, waddle like a duck, kick like a mule, slither like a snake, or jump like a kangaroo. This can be done to music or without music.

Have the children pretend to be the wind, the rain, snow, or thunder especially on windy, rainy, or snowy days. How do they think a car moves, or a truck, a rocking chair, a weathervane? Some children enjoy using props such as hats when they are dancing. Have the children suggest other props to use.

Musical Games

Preschool children enjoy many noncompetitive games that are set to music—for example, "The Farmer in the Dell," "Bluebird, Bluebird," and "Bingo." These games combine music, movement, and group cooperation. They are appropriate for large groups and can be played outdoors as well as in the classroom. With experience, children can begin to make up their own musical games. Try setting up a series of Hula Hoops or tires on the floor or ground; ask each child to move through the hoops or tires in a different way. The children can create a chant for what they are doing; for example, "Kim is hopping, hopping, hopping," "Jamie is a leap frog, leap frog, leap frog."

Planning Successful Music and Movement Activities

These tips may help you plan successful music and movement activities for preschool children.

- Start with music that you enjoy. Your own enthusiasm and enjoyment will influence the children.

- Have all the materials you need ready ahead of time. Be sure the record player or tape recorder is working; have the record or tape ready and the musical instruments nearby.

- Allow enough time for the activity, usually 10 to 20 minutes per planned experience. If the activity is particularly successful, allow more time to continue; if it is not working the way you planned, cut it short.

- Look for cues from the children to see if the activity is developmentally appropriate; that is, can they do what you have asked, such as hopping or skipping? If not, try an easier movement.

- Be flexible. Give the children many opportunities to respond to the music in their own way. Encouraging children to "pay attention to your body and see what it feels like doing to this music" is more flexible than saying "everyone sway back and forth to the music."

- Encourage the children to come up with new ideas for music experiences; ask them, "What else could we do to this music?"

- Provide time for music activities in small groups and for individual children to explore rhythm instruments alone.

- Encourage the children to be spontaneous with music by setting an example. If you sing "will you clean up," they will begin to do the same. Create a chant as you pass around a snack or come up with a song for getting coats on.

- Maintain a balance between teacher-planned music and movement experiences and those initiated by the children, such as singing while making playdough or rocking in the rocking boat.

- Plan music and movement activities to do outside as well as indoors.

In this learning activity you will plan and implement one music and one movement activity for the preschool children in your room. After you write your plans, implement the two activities and record what happens. Review the example on the next page before you begin.

Movement Activity Plan
(Example)

Setting: _Outdoors in the afternoon_   **Date:** _October 10_

Description of activity:

We will do a creative movement activity outdoors, singing and pretending to be falling leaves.

Materials needed:

Just the leaves outside.

What happened?

We are lying on the ground under a tree watching the leaves drift down. I started a chant: "The leaves they are falling, falling, falling." The children joined in. They jumped up, twirled around, and began falling down too. They ended up playing in the leaves.

How did this activity promote creativity?

I asked them to help make up the chant and Dean said, "I am falling, into the leaves!" Renee said, "The leaves are falling into the sandbox." I asked them where else they saw leaves falling.

Would you do this activity again? What changes would you make?

Yes. Next time I think I would do some more movements. Maybe I could have the children pretend to be the wind, or a tree, or a kite stuck in a tree.

Movement Activity Plan

Setting: _____   **Date:** _____

Description of activity:

_____

_____

_____

_____

Materials needed:

_____

_____

_____

_____

What happened?

_____

_____

_____

_____

How did this activity promote creativity?

_____

_____

_____

_____

Would you do this activity again? What changes would you make?

_____

_____

_____

_____

Music Activity Plan

Setting: _____   **Date:** _____

Description of activity:

_____
_____
_____
_____

Materials needed:

_____
_____
_____
_____

What happened?

_____
_____
_____
_____

How did this activity promote creativity?

_____
_____
_____
_____

Would you do this activity again? What changes would you make?

_____
_____
_____
_____

Discuss this learning activity with your trainer.

7

iding a Variety of Art Experiences

/ill learn:

  ͻeriences to promote children's creativity; and

  a variety of developmentally appropriate art experiences for children.

An art program for preschool children provides many opportunities for self-expression and enjoyment. Art is a relaxing activity for most children and stimulates all the senses. Most young children love to paint, draw, glue things together, or pound a lump of clay. Art encourages children to use their imaginations and create something of their own. Through art experiences, children learn to be spontaneous in using a variety of textures, shapes, and colors.

When teachers provide diverse art materials, children can make choices and try out their own ideas. They can think about ways to use materials and plan what they want to do with the materials. There is no right or wrong result; children are free to experiment.

Art is an important part of each free play period in a preschool room. Children need enough time to decide what they want to work with, to gather the materials they need, and to work. Some children like to do several paintings, one after the other; others like to work with playdough or clay for a seemingly endless amount of time. Art time should not be a rushed experience but a relaxed, comfortable time when children can really move at their own pace.

Art activities that can be offered daily include:

  • easel painting;
  • drawing with crayons, markers, or chalk;
  • creating collages with paste or glue and a variety of materials;
  • cutting or tearing paper or magazines; and
  • using clay or playdough.

Some art experiences require a teacher's supervision because the materials are very messy to use or because children need help using tools or materials safely. These art experiences might include the following:

  • finger painting;
  • weaving;
  • puppet making;
  • murals;
  • making collages with special glue or materials such as wood scraps;
  • printing; and
  • any art activity that involves using a utensil that requires adult supervision, such as melting crayons on wax paper or using knives to cut potatoes for vegetable printing.

Preschool children are usually more interested in the process of art than they are in the product. They enjoy exploring and manipulating the art materials you provide for them. They want to discover what will happen if they use the side of their crayon to make scribbles, or if they finger paint with their fists or elbows. Very young children simply enjoy the physical experience of scribbling. As they develop, they are pleased to find out that they can control what marks their crayon makes on the paper or how much glue comes out when they squeeze a bottle. As they learn to use a variety of media, they like to experiment with colors, brush strokes, textures, and combinations of shapes. It is only in the late preschool years that children begin to care about the products they have created.

There is no end to the list of art experiences that can be planned for young children. You can provide new materials each day or use the same experience for several days if the children show interest. The goal is to provide a balance of experiences: those which children can choose and do independently and those which are planned ahead of time by teachers. Several kinds of preschool art experiences are described below: drawing, painting, creating collages and assemblages, and using clay and playdough.

Drawing

All young children go through the same stages as they develop drawing skills. Children may begin drawing at different ages, but they all pass through the same stages in the same order. They develop at different rates and often repeat earlier stages at the same time as they are moving forward. A child's artistic ability develops as his or her physical and cognitive skills grow. Teachers need to understand and recognize the stages of artistic development so that they can provide appropriate materials and art experiences and respond to children's work in ways that promote creativity.

The chart that follows summarizes the developmental stages of children's art and suggests ways that teachers can promote artistic development.

DEVELOPMENTAL STAGES OF CHILDREN'S ART

STAGE	WHAT CHILDREN DO AND WHY	WAYS TEACHERS CAN PROMOTE ARTISTIC DEVELOPMENT
Early scribbles	Children make random marks on papers, walls, table tops, or anywhere else they can reach. These marks go in many directions. Children cannot control which way the marks go, but this does not bother them. They enjoy the physical motions of scribbling.	Provide large pieces of paper so children can make wide arm movements and scribble in all directions. Store crayons, paints, markers, and chalk where children can select and use them during free play.
Later scribbles	Children learn that they can control the brush or crayon and the way they are scribbling. They enjoy being able to control their scribbling. They try circles, lines, or zigzags. lhey may cover the whole paper with scribbles.	Continue to provide children with a variety of art materials. Make only positive statements about their work. Children are not trying to draw pictures. Share the children's pleasure with their new skills.
Basic shapes	Children recognize circles and ovals in their scribbles and repeat them. They make rectangles and squares by drawing parallel vertical lines, then joining them with horizontal lines at the top and bottom. They combine straight lines to make crosses.	Make sure the easels are always set up with paints and brushes. Whenever possible, allow children to paint for as long as they want to. Continue to provide materials that children can use on their own, such as paper, markers, crayons, and so on.

STAGE	WHAT CHILDREN DO AND WHY	WAYS TEACHERS CAN PROMOTE ARTISTIC DEVELOPMENT
Drawing materials	Children combine two shapes they have already made by making circles with crosses in the middle. They may make one mandala on a piece of paper or several in combination with other shapes. This is the first step toward drawing representations of animals, people, buildings, trees, or flowers.	Include finger painting on paper, cookie sheets, or a table top. Observe children and comment on the shapes they make: "You put a cross inside your circle."
Drawing suns	Children draw circles or ovals with lines coming from the outside of the shape. They don't call these suns, but adults think they look like suns. Children like the way these shapes look. They may add marks for human faces: eyes, nose, and mouth.	Continue positive comments. Don't ask "what is that?" or tell a child you like his or her "sun." Point out the shapes you see or comment on the color, size, or where they are placed on the paper.
Drawing humans	Children draw circles, then add lines from the bottom as legs and perhaps a line from either side as arms. Inside the circle, dots or lines or small circles are used for eyes, noses, and mouths. Children may add more features and perhaps clothes. They draw humans because they have earned from making mandalas and suns how to combine shapes and lines into a figure that represents a person. They are still developing a skill rather than drawing a picture, however.	Do not push children to reach this stage. They will develop this skill without your help. Just continue to provide materials, time to create, and your interest and approval.

STAGE	WHAT CHILDREN DO AND WHY	WAYS TEACHERS CAN PROMOTE ARTISTIC DEVELOPMENT
Drawing animals and trees	Children apply the skills they use to draw humans to drawing animals. Often the animals stand upright like humans. Later they will have bodies parallel with the bottom of the paper and four vertical lines for legs. Trees look like tall rectangles with circles on the top. Details such as as branches or leaves appear later.	Do not push children to reach this stage; they will do so without your help. Just continue to provide materials, time to create, and your interest and approval.
Making pictorial drawings	Children may draw several different objects on the same paper that may or may not be related to one another. They create pictures by using the shapes and figures they've already learned to draw. They teach themselves to use rectangles as doors, circles as suns, or a series of arcs as a rainbow. Size and color (if added) are not realistic, and objects are free-floating: for example, trees may appear at the top of the paper. Pictures may not be planned in advance; for example, a drop of red paint might become a sun. Children may also plan ahead, deciding to paint a picture of a boat or airplane.	Expect only a few of the preschool children in your room to reach this stage. Ask children to tell you about their pictures. Listen carefully to what they are telling you because these early pictures are the child's first use of art as communication. Be aware that the process of creating a picture is still very important, but the children are beginning to care about their products.

Painting

Children move through the same stages in painting as they do in drawing. In the beginning children are interested only in how it feels to paint. They love the way the brush feels when it slides across the paper and usually are not very interested in the color that results. This is why many first paintings look the same; they are generally a brownish-purplish color that results when the child brushes layer upon layer of color onto the paper, often using every inch of space available.

Very young children often start painting using only one color. They may start with the primary colors: red, yellow, or blue. When the children become more experienced, they will discover what happens when they combine colors. Put small amounts of paint in the jar; it's easier to control where the paint goes when there is not so much of it. It's also better for the brush because the paint shouldn't come over the level of the bristles.

Children who haven't painted before may need help learning how to hold the brush or how to wipe the brush on the jar so that paint doesn't glob on the paper. Some children are not bothered by globs or enjoy holding brushes upside down. Teachers should be available to children who request help while allowing all children to experiment and learn through trial and error.

In your observations of children painting, you may have noticed that each has a particular style and approach. Some children prefer soft brushes; others like the hard ones. Some children fill the entire paper while others leave blank areas. Some will do many paintings during the day while others may do only one. The amount of time each child spends painting will vary, as will the intensity with which they work. Some children talk to themselves as they paint; others talk with other children who are also painting. Listening to what they say can provide valuable insights into the children's feelings about what they are doing.

Gradually, children become more purposeful in their painting. They ask for specific colors to use and want to place things on the paper in specific ways. They may become concerned with drips that disrupt what they are trying to do and may be very particular about the colors they select. Eventually, they reach the stage where they plan what they want to paint.

Most four- and five-year-olds enjoy a wide range of colors. They enjoy seeing what happens when colors mix or when white paint is used to create pastels. They like using colors such as purple and black as well as the primary colors. And they may still enjoy mixing every color available to create those brownish-purplish colors that adults find hard to name!

Providing a Variety of Painting Experiences

Children enjoy painting on different types of paper, such as

- colored construction paper,
- sandpaper,
- wrapping paper,
- wallpaper samples, or
- styrofoam packing pieces (on the table rather than at the easel).

For variety, cut the paper into shapes such as circles or just into long strips. By combining different types of paints, papers, and tools for painting, teachers can provide many new art experiences for preschoolers.

Exploring Texture

- Provide paper, tempera paint, and brushes.

- Put out, in separate containers, some sawdust, sand, salt, and tempera.

- Allow the children to experiment with what different substances do to the paint and paper. They can add a substance to the paint beforehand, sprinkle it on the paper and paint over it, or sprinkle it on afterward.

- Ask children questions to stimulate their curiosity: "What will happen if...?" "What else could we add to the paint?" "What happens when you mix these two colors?"

Exploring Color

- Provide primary-colored paint (either finger paint or tempera).

- While the children are painting, add a container of white paint.

- Observe the children's reactions as they add white paint to create pastels.

- Encourage the children to try mixing other colors to see what happens.

Using Different Types of Tools

Let children experiment with tools such as these:

- rollers
- whisk brooms
- straws
- marbles

- plastic squeeze bottles
- sponges cut into shapes
- stamps
- string

Finger Painting

Finger paints are another kind of painting experience. Whenever possible, children should use finger paint directly on a formica tabletop rather than on glossy finger paint paper. This paper is expensive and usually small in size, and it generally limits the child's movements. Painting directly on the table gives the child lots of room to experiment with paint rather than making a picture. If a formica table is not available, children can paint on cafeteria trays or on a large piece of heavy plastic. If children want to have a picture of their finger paintings, any type of paper can be placed on top of their pictures and pressed down to create an imprint.

Creating Collages and Assemblages

Collage refers to the pasting of all kinds of things on a flat surface. An assemblage is a three-dimensional piece made by putting various things together. Assemblages and collages offer wonderful opportunities for creative expression. Children can use a variety of materials to create something original.

Collages can include items such as fabric scraps, ribbon, wood scraps, styrofoam, feathers, magazine pictures, and buttons. Collages can be created on a variety of papers, including cardboard, heavy corrugated paper, construction paper, or posterboard. Newsprint is not recommended because it is too thin. Computer paper can be used as long as the children are just attaching paper scraps.

After the children have made many collages, put out scissors so the children can cut pieces of paper or thin materials, such as wallpaper samples or ribbon, to the size and shape they want.

When children are given a variety of items that can be put together in unusual ways, they create imaginative assemblages. Materials to provide include these:

- items that can poke into or hold together: toothpicks, wire, wooden dowels, straws, paper fasteners, yarn, nails, pipe cleaners;

- things that can be poked into or stuck on: cork, fabric, paper, styrofoam balls, sponge fragments; and

- materials that attach to wood: tile pieces, styrofoam, wooden clothespins, dowels.

The invitation to experiment develops the child's curiosity. Thinking of what to put with what leads to skills in planning. Learning that a big piece of cork is too heavy for one toothpick to hold up is a science discovery. Trying different ways to make an assemblage stand up is practice in solving problems. Looking around at other people's creations is part of developing a sense of what art is.

Using Clay and Playdough

These materials represent yet another means for creative self-expression. Most children enjoy the feeling of manipulating clay and playdough—rolling it, pushing it, or pounding it. Older children begin to make things with clay or playdough and may enjoy using clay that hardens or can be baked into a permanent form. Plasticine has different qualities than clay has; it often needs softening up through manipulation and will not dry out in the air.

Clay and playdough offer children different experiences. Playdough is usually more pliable than clay. Many teachers like to make playdough with children. Children have as much fun making playdough as they do using it. When you make your own playdough, you can vary the texture, amount, and color. Playdough can be stored in sealed plastic bags or in coffee tins lined with plastic and placed in the refrigerator. Here are two playdough recipes that are popular with teachers.

Traditional Playdough

2 cups of flour
1 cup of salt
2 tablespoons of oil
1 cup of water with food coloring

Children can help prepare this recipe. Mix all the ingredients together and then knead the dough.

A Smoother Variety of Playdough

> 2 cups of flour
> 1 cup of salt
> 1 tablespoon of cream of tartar
> 2 tablespoons of oil
> 1 cup of water with food coloring

Mix the ingredients and heat in a pan, stirring constantly, until the dough pulls away from the sides of the pan and forms a lump. Then knead the dough. Store in a plastic bag or container in the refrigerator.

There are two types of clay appropriate for young children: soft modeling clay, which does not harden and dry out, and clay that can be baked or just left to harden by itself. The first type is good when children want to manipulate the clay and perhaps make balls, snakes, or different shapes. Soft clay is also fun to use with rolling pins, cookie cutters, or tongue depressors. Clay that hardens can also be painted and the resulting creations saved. Both types should be available to preschool children.

Clay and playdough should be available each day and kept on shelves where children can reach them. Store clay and playdough in individual containers so that more than one child can play at the same time. Children can work at tables or use cafeteria trays on the floor. Children will also enjoy making and working with other modeling mixtures, such as cornstarch and water, sawdust mixtures, baker's clay, and so on.

Planning Successful Art Activities

The suggestions below may be helpful in planning successful art activities.

- Match art materials and activities to the children's abilities. Observe often to find out which children can cut with scissors, roll out playdough, or glue small pieces onto something else.

- Be flexible. When an art experience doesn't turn out the way you planned it, adjust to the children's interests. If they would rather punch holes than make sewing cards, let them do that. You can make sewing cards another day.

- Set up in advance. Make sure you have all the materials you will need before the children arrive. Also make sure there are enough materials to go around.

- Continue a planned art experience for more than one day if the children are interested. A mural started on Monday can stay up until the end of the week or longer.

- Allow individual children to continue their art while the rest move to other activities. Some children become very involved in their art and need more time.

The list on the next page includes art materials that you or the children's parents can collect. These materials can be used for many different art experiences.

Art Materials to Collect for the Preschool Room[2]

Natural Items

Acorns
Dried flowers
Dried herbs
Driftwood
Feathers
Pine cones
Seeds
Shells
Stones and pebbles

Sewing Items

Beads
Braid
Buttons
Cotton balls
Hooks and eyes
Large plastic needles
Macrame twine
Ribbon
Shoelaces
Snaps
Spools
Thread
Yarn

Kitchen/Laundry Items

Aluminum foil
Bleach bottles
Bottle tops
Candles
Cellophane paper
Coffee cans
Corks
Egg cartons
Grocery packages
Juice cans
Milk containers
Paper bags
Paper plates and cups
Paper doilies
Paper towels
Parchment
Plastic wrap
Popsicle sticks
Steel wool pads
String/rope
Toothpicks

Building materials (any size scraps)

Linoleum
Masonite
Metal pieces
Nails
Tiles
Wallboard
Wire mesh
Wood scraps

Miscellaneous

Business cards (old or used)
Cardboard tubes
Clock parts
Confetti
Containers of any kind
  (e.g., baby food jars,
    margarine tubs)
Glitter
Hangers
Hole punch
Marbles
Paint rollers
Paper clips
Pipe cleaners
Shoe boxes
Stamp pads and stamps
Stapler and staples
Styrofoam or other packing
  materials
Tongue depressors
Wire
Wooden beads
Wooden dowels

Fabrics (any size scraps)

Burlap
Canvas
Corduroy
Cotton
Denim
Felt
Fur (fake)
Gloves (old)
Hats (old)
Lace
Leather
Oilcloth
Socks (old)
Terrycloth

---

[2]Reprinted from Diane Trister Dodge, *The Creative Curriculum for Early Childhood* (Washington, DC: Teaching Strategies, Inc., 1991).

In this learning activity you will observe one child as he or she participates in art activities over a period of three days. Next, on the basis of your observations, you will select, plan, and implement an art experience that matches this child's developmental level. Review the examples below and on the next page; then begin the activity.

Observing a Child's Art Experiences
(Example)

Child: *Ronnie*   **Age:** *4 years*   **Dates:** *October 7-9*

ART EXPERIENCE	TIME	WHAT HAPPENED
Day One *Drawing with markers on computer paper*	*10 minutes*	*Ronnie used blue and red markers. He made circles and spirals. Then he left his paper on the table.*
Easel painting outside	*20 minutes*	*He used a fat brush and red paint. First he made a big circle at the top of the paper. He made some long vertical lines. He switched to black paint and made some horizontal lines. He stood back so the brush just reached the easel and made some dots. He finished by using red again, going all over the paper. He took down his paper and asked me to hang it up to dry.*

Planning An Art Experience
(Example)

Art Experience: _Sponge painting_   **Date:** _March 12_

Why have you selected this experience?

Ronnie likes the way it feels to paint. I think he'd like to use a different tool—a sponge instead of a brush to make dots.

What materials are needed?

Three pie pans; three colors of tempera paint; three sponges cut up into small pieces; large pieces of paper.

How many children can be involved at one time?

Four

When will you try this experience?

During afternoon free play

Results of the art experience:

I set up the activity and waited to see if any children would come over by themselves. Three children came and had fun making sponge paintings. Then Ronnie came over. He used the sponge to make lines on his paper. Then he smeared them all together. He didn't make dots by himself, so I suggested that he might try to use the sponge like he uses the brush at the easel. He tried it but went back to making lines.

Observing a Child's Art Experience

Child: _____   Age: _____   Dates: _____

ART EXPERIENCE	TIME	WHAT HAPPENED
Day One		
Day Two		

ART EXPERIENCE	TIME	WHAT HAPPENED
Day Three		

Planning an Art Experience

Art Experience: _____   Date: _____

Why have you selected this experience?

_____

_____

_____

_____

What materials are needed?

_____

_____

_____

_____

How many children can be involved at one time?

_____

When will you try this experience?

_____

Results of the art experience:

_____

_____

_____

_____

How did you encourage creativity among children?

_____

_____

_____

_____

_____

_____

Discuss this learning activity with your trainer.

V. Using Sand and Wat

In this activity you will learn:

- to promote children's creativity throu
- to plan developmentally appropriate act

CARING FOR PRE

Sand and water pl
either indoors o
separate activi
children are

Creative

Presch
sand
to

Preschool children are naturally drawn to sand and
materials and can use them in many imaginative ways.
exploration, and experimentation. They are pleasing to look
them can be a soothing, relaxing activity for preschool children.

One of the reasons that children enjoy sand and water play is that they can u
the materials do what they want them to. When children play with sand and wate,
discover and observe many things, including these:

- how properties change (for example, adding things to sand and water and how
  sand and water look when viewed through an object such as a magnifying glass
  or clear plastic cup);

- how water changes (it freezes, melts, cools things down, evaporates);

- how water changes other things (it makes sand soggy);

- water is absorbed by other materials in different ways (blotters, cork, styrofoam,
  paper towels, etc.);

- some objects float in water and others don't;

- reflections and ripples can be observed in water;

- water does not stay in one place;

- water levels rise and fall;

- some things dissolve in water (salt, food coloring) and others don't (objects);

- sand does many things (pours, sifts, builds);

- sand has a distinct texture (it can be fine or coarse, dry or wet);

- volume and capacity vary (containers hold different amounts of sand and water);

- sand and water can be measured; and

- water takes the shape of the object it is poured into.

---

[3] Adapted from Diane Trister Dodge, *The Creative Curriculum for Early Childhood* (Washington, DC:
Teaching Strategies, Inc., 1991).

...ay are important activities in the preschool classroom. They can be located ...outdoors when the weather is mild. Although sand and water play are ...ties, they are similar in many ways. When playing at sand and water tables, ...developing many skills.

Self-Expression

...ool children like to experiment with water and sand. They find out what happens when ...gets wet and what happens when food coloring is added to water. There are many ways ...pour sand and water, many things to observe. Most important, there are no right or wrong ...ays to play with sand or water. Playing with these media encourages children to ask questions, which enhances their creativity.

Socialization

Preschool children typically play at the sand and water tables in a group. They practice skills such as sharing, cooperating, planning, compromising, and problem solving.

Development of Small Muscles

Almost everything preschool children do with sand and water helps develop their small muscles. Pouring, sifting, scooping, digging, and so on are all ways of refining small muscle skills.

Opportunities for Language Development

Preschool children naturally talk with one another when they are playing with sand and water. Their vocabulary expands as they learn names for what they are observing, and they learn to describe the many concepts they discover.

Sand and water tables can also become settings for dramatic play.

- Soapy water leads to bathing dolls and washing doll clothes.

- Children make drinks and "potions" to sell or use in a variety of ways.

- Boats, water paddles, and tubing lead to play about boats and water travel.

- Children make sand castles, tunnels, mountains, and lakes.

- Transportation toys such as small cars and dump trucks encourage dramatic play with sand. Children make roads, rivers, buildings, and volcanoes.

- Children make and sell or "eat" mud pies or cakes.

There are many props that preschool children enjoy using with sand and water. You can collect the items listed on the next page or ask parents to bring them to the center.

Sand Only	Both Sand and Water	Water Only
Muffin tins	Clear marbles	Paintbrushes
Cookie cutters	Pebbles and rocks	Spray bottles
Seashells	String	Food coloring
Feathers	Funnels	Siphons
Sifters	Pots and pans	Water wheels
Tweezers	Buckets and bowls	Boats
Shovels	Scales	Troughs
Molds	Measuring cups	Squeeze bottles
Sprayers (to wet sand)	Measuring spoons	Eggbeaters
Small cars and trucks	Scoops	Whisks
Dump trucks	Small containers	Soap (liquid, solid,
Sticks and seed	Strainers of different sizes	and flaked)
Rolling pins	Ladles	Vegetable dyes
Rakes	Sieves	Plastic straws
Whisk brooms	Cork	Plastic tubing
	Nesting cups	Eyedroppers

To vary the children's experiences, the sand table can also be filled with sawdust, large wood shavings, or other natural materials.

Expanding Children's Sand and Water Play

After giving children many opportunities to experiment with sand and water, teachers can create learning experiences that encourage children to discover new skills and concepts on their own.

- Start with basic props and observe children's play to see when new props are needed; for example, when children are experimenting with how to fill a bottle, introduce a funnel.

- Present materials to children sequentially; for example, first dry sand and then wet, or first clear water and later colored or soapy water.

- Provide different surfaces that children can pour water on, such as wax paper, a blotter, a sponge, or plastic.

- Provide objects that can be used to conduct sink or float experiments.

- Provide a series of cans with holes punched in them so that children can see how long it takes for the different cans to empty.

- Provide materials that are proportional, such as measuring cups or nesting cups.

In this learning activity you will plan and implement a sand or water activity for preschool children. After you write your plan, implement the activity and record what happens. Review the example on the next page before you begin.

Sand or Water Activity Plan
(Example)

Setting: _Indoors at the water table during free play_   **Date:** _November 9_

Description of activity:

I will provide various sizes and shapes of blue colored ice to float in the water table as "icebergs" in an ocean.

Materials needed:

I will have ice that I froze in plastic bags, in cups, in pie tins, and in ice cube trays. It will be frozen from blue-colored water, to resemble icebergs. I will have a box of salt. I will fill the water table with cold water. I will have toy boats nearby.

What happened?

I brought in a tub of ice chunks. I asked the children what would happen when we put the ice in the water table. "It will go down to the bottom." "It will float." "It will be cold." "Let's see," I said. As the ice floated, we tried to see how much was on top of the water and how much was under the water. We put our boats in the water, and the children steered into and around the icebergs. "A real ocean is salty," I said. I showed them the salt container and they poured some in the "ocean" and some on the ice. They found they could stick pieces of ice together with salt.

How did the experiment promote creativity?

The children handled the ice, estimated how much was above and below the water (lots, a little), discovered that ice floats and is hard to sink. They experimented and discovered that ice changes when you put salt on it.

Would you do this experiment again? What changes would you make?

I would do this again. Next time I would have the children help me make the ice shapes by putting water in ziplock plastic bags and putting the bags in or over different shaped objects, and putting them in the freezer or outside in the winter. I would put pictures of icebergs, glaciers, frozen lakes and rivers on the wall by the water table.

Sand or Water Activity Plan

Setting _____   Date: _____

Description of activity:

_____
_____
_____
_____

Materials needed:

_____
_____
_____
_____

What happened?

_____
_____
_____
_____

How did the experiment promote creativity?

_____
_____
_____

Would you do this experiment again? What changes would you make?

_____
_____
_____
_____

Discuss this learning activity with your trainer.

Summarizing Your Progress

You have now completed all of the learning activities for this module. Whether you are an experienced teacher or a new one, this module has probably helped you develop new skills in promoting preschoolers' creativity. Before you go on, take a few minutes to summarize what you've learned.

- Turn back to Learning Activity I, Using Your Knowledge of Child Development to Promote Creativity, and add to the chart specific examples of what you learned about promoting children's creativity during the time you were working on this module. Compare your ideas to those in the completed chart at the end of the module.

- Next, review your responses to the pre-training assessment for this module. Write a summary of what you learned and list the skills you developed or improved.

_____

_____

_____

_____

_____

_____

_____

_____

_____

_____

_____

_____

If there are topics you would like to know more about, you will find recommended readings listed in the orientation, which can be found in Volume I.

Your final step in this module is to complete the knowledge and competency assessments. Let your trainer know when you are ready to schedule the assessments. After you have successfully completed these assessments, you will be ready to start a new module. Congratulations on your progress so far, and good luck with your next module.

Answer Sheets

Promoting Children's Creativity

Arranging the Learning Environment to Support Children's Creative Development

1. **How did Ms. Richards arrange the environment to promote children's creativity?**

   a. She provided an interesting variety of construction materials and fasteners.

   b. She prepared an inviting open space near the materials.

   c. She provided space for storage of partially-finished ongoing projects.

2. **How do unstructured (or open-ended) materials promote creativity in preschool children?**

   a. There is no right or wrong way to use the materials.

   b. The children may use the materials in a variety of ways—for example, simply enjoying the process of connecting pieces, creating moving parts, or creating representational structures such as buildings or space shuttles.

   c. Children use their imaginations, creating expressions that are unique and relevant to their own lives.

Providing a Variety of Activities and Experiences to Promote Creative Development

1. **How did the questions Mr. Lopez asked support creative thinking?**

   a. They were all open-ended questions; there were no wrong or right answers.

   b. They encouraged the children to think and to express their ideas and feelings.

2. **Why is story time a good opportunity to promote creativity?**

   a. Children are eager to participate in storytelling.

   b. Stories can be changed around or given different endings. Children are given a chance to be creative by responding to open-ended questions.

Interacting with Children in Ways That Encourage Creative Expression

1. **How did Ms. Williams' response to the children's request encourage them to be creative?**

   a. She asked them for possible solutions to the problem.

   b. She respected their suggestions and valued what they had to say.

2. **How did the way Ms. Williams handled the situation support an atmosphere that promoted creativity in the room?**

   a. She encouraged the children to think of ways to preserve their building through writing signs and taking photographs.

   b. She created an environment in which the children felt comfortable making suggestions and thinking of ways to solve a problem.

CREATIVE

Using Your Knowledge of Child Development
to Promote Creativity

WHAT PRESCHOOL CHILDREN ARE LIKE	HOW TEACHERS CAN USE THIS INFORMATION TO PROMOTE CREATIVITY
They are curious and ask many "why" questions.	Build on children's eagerness to know. Provide a variety of objects for them to explore and examine, both indoors and outdoors. Respect their questioning. Extend their thinking with follow-up materials and activities (books, props, filmstrips).
They have a strong sense of wonder.	Provide many opportunities for seeing, touching, handling, tasting, and smelling. Take time when children want to stop, look, and listen, and teach them to do this. Awareness and sensitivity go hand in hand with creativity.
They learn from concrete experiences. Although they can understand explanations, they need real things to work with.	Give children plenty of firsthand experiences, providing words as you go along. Let them try things over and over. Help children make connections between what they are doing and what they already know. Imagination builds on these connections.
They have their own ideas and want to carry them out by themselves.	Give children raw materials with which to express their ideas—paints, crayons, sand, water, clay, blocks, and dramatic play props. Give positive feedback for their original ideas for doing things (for instance, how to handle clean-up time) as well as for ideas expressed in their artwork. Ask questions to help them elaborate on their ideas and extend their thinking.
They want to make choices and like to feel important.	Provide a wide variety of choices and opportunities for success. Avoid competitive activities with winners and losers. Give children plenty of positive feedback. Display their creative work.
They enjoy dramatic play and have active imaginations.	Provide a wide variety of props and plenty of time and space. Be sure that play and pretend opportunities are open-ended. Allow children to make up their own rules: "You be the mother and I'll be the little kitten."

WHAT PRESCHOOL CHILDREN ARE LIKE	HOW TEACHERS CAN USE THIS INFORMATION TO PROMOTE CREATIVITY
They are beginners at doing things and may make mistakes.	Be patient about children's "messes." Allow plenty of time and chances to try things again and again. Toying with objects and ideas is part of the creative process.
They want to be independent, but they are sometimes still very dependent on adults.	Provide emotional support, such as a smile or a hug to communicate "I like you." Tell children when you like their ideas. Independence, which is necessary for creative thinking, grows from feeling secure.
They pass through different developmental stages in their use of art media and materials.	Learn about these stages so you will know what to expect, what media to choose, and how to guide individual children. Provide several choices of art materials daily. Keep records of children's progress and developmental stages.
They have a wide variety of interests and skills.	Provide for these differences in the daily program. One child can finish painting while others move to story time. Accept children's individual approaches to and use of materials, music, and language. Teach children to value differences by accepting all their work.

Glossary

Closed question	A question for which there is only one right answer.
Creativity	An attitude or way of looking at things that involves being willing to try out new ways of doing something and realizing that there is more than one way to solve a problem.
Flexibility	Willingness to change the way one does something or to try a new approach when making something or completing a task.
Open-ended question	A question that can be answered in many ways.
Problem-solving	The process of thinking through a problem and coming up with one or several possible solutions.
Self-esteem	A sense of worth; a good feeling about oneself and one's abilities. Someone with strong self-esteem feels respected, valued, and able to do things successfully and independently.
Unstructured materials	Materials that can be used in many different ways.

Module 8
Self

What Is Self-Esteem and Why Is It Important?

Self-esteem is a sense of one's own worth. People with self-esteem are proud of who they are and what they can do. People who have self-esteem feel:

- **connected** to others—to friends and to our families;

- **respected** and **valued** by others; and

- **powerful**—able to do things on our own.

Our self-esteem comes from daily experiences that confirm who we are and what we are capable of doing. If most of these experiences are good, our self-esteem grows. If most of these experiences are bad, we wonder if there is something wrong with us. Our self-esteem is lowered.

From birth, children begin developing a sense of self. Some of their feelings toward themselves may be positive, and some may be negative. These feelings will affect their entire adjustment to life—their ability to play, to relate to others, and to learn. And these feelings are strongly influenced by other people—family, friends, and teachers.

You are a very important person to the children in your program. In the course of daily life at the center—as you help a child build with blocks or share the task of setting up tables for a snack—you are helping children develop positive feelings about themselves. Because the children you care for are young, they are just beginning to develop ideas about themselves. Through your relationships with the children in your care, you support the development of self-esteem that will help these children throughout their lives.

Building children's self-esteem involves:

- developing positive and supportive relationships with each child;

- helping children accept and appreciate themselves and others; and

- providing children with opportunities to feel successful and competent.

Listed below are examples of how teachers demonstrate their competence in building children's self-esteem.

Developing a Positive and Supportive Relationship with Each Child

Here are some examples of what teachers can do.

- Know what each child is able to do and show that you think each child is special. "Danny, will you be my helper today and set the tables?"

- Understand that it's hard for children to say good-bye to their parents and be there to ease the pain. "It's hard to say good-bye to Daddy. He feels sad too. He'll be back to get you later."

- Identify and deal with children's feelings. "I know you want to play with the truck now. It's hard to wait. What would you like to do until it's your turn?"

- Use gentle contact—a hug, a touch, a lap to sit on—to show you care.

Helping Children Accept and Appreciate Themselves and Others

Here are some examples of what teachers can do.

- Show by what you say and do that you respect each child. "Martha, I see you used four different colors in your picture."

- Include in the room pictures and toys that reflect the ethnic backgrounds of the children.

- Avoid sexist remarks such as "little girls don't" or "boys always do."

Providing Children with Opportunities to Feel Successful and Competent

Here are some examples of what teachers can do.

- Encourage children to dress themselves even if this takes a long time. "You worked hard to zip your coat."

- Accept mistakes as natural. "Oh, the paint spilled. Let's get a sponge and clean it up."

- Select materials that children are ready to master. Comment on their success. "You put that puzzle together all by yourself! I bet you feel good."

- Repeat activities so children can master skills and experience success.

Building Self-Esteem

In the following situations teachers are building children's self-esteem. As you read each one, think about what the teachers are doing and why. Then answer the questions that follow.

Developing Positive and Supportive Relationships with Each Child

It's free play time in the preschool room. Ms. Kim is playing with some children in the house corner. She tells the children she has to leave to catch her plane, and now she is walking over to the block corner to see what the builders are doing. On her way she passes the easels where Shawn is painting a picture. Shawn is smiling and seems very happy with his work. He steps back from the easel to look at his picture. Ms. Kim stops to talk with him. "Shawn, would you like some help hanging your picture?" "Okay," he answers. They each hold one side of the picture and hang it up on the line. Ms. Kim points to the picture and says, "I see you have used a lot of blue paint, and it looks like you used the side of the brush to make those marks. Last week I also noticed you using a lot of blue paint. I like that color a lot." Shawn smiles and says, "Yeah, I like blue. I'm going to paint another blue picture." He goes back to the easel to start another picture. Ms. Kim resumes her walk to the block corner.

1. How did Ms. Kim build a positive and supportive relationship with Shawn?

_____

_____

_____

2. How did Ms. Kim build Shawn's self-esteem?

_____

_____

_____

Helping Children Accept and Appreciate Themselves and Others

Jerry places a wooden block on the tower he is building. "Look, I did it!" he calls to Mr. Lopez. "That's a very tall tower you've built," says Mr. Lopez, bending down for a closer look. Jerry smiles proudly. Just then, Sandy walks by, swinging her arms. Crash! Jerry's tower tumbles to the floor. "No!" shouts Jerry. He lifts his arm to hit Sandy. "Jerry," Mr. Lopez says, reaching up to stop Jerry's swing. "I know you're angry, but I won't let you hit Sandy. *Tell* her how you feel." Jerry turns to Sandy and says, "Don't knock down my building! Be careful."

67

1. **What feelings did Jerry have in the block corner?**

   _____

   _____

   _____

2. **How did Mr. Lopez help Jerry learn how to express his feelings in appropriate ways?**

   _____

   _____

   _____

Providing Children with Opportunities to Feel Successful and Competent

During free play time, four-year-old Mark tells Ms. Williams that he wants to work at the puzzle table. Ms. Williams says, "Mark, which puzzle do you want to do?" Mark selects a new truck puzzle that has 18 pieces. After 10 minutes Ms. Williams notices that Mark is no longer at the puzzle table, but the truck puzzle is still on the table with many of its pieces lying next to it. Ms. Williams finds Mark in the book corner. She says, "Mark, it looks like that new truck puzzle was hard to do. Come back to the puzzle table. Let's work on the puzzle together. New puzzles with lots of pieces are hard to do at first. I bet after you try a couple of times you'll be able to do it alone." Mark and Ms. Williams talk about the puzzle pieces—where the wheels belong, the cab of the truck, the driver, and so on—until the entire puzzle is put together.

1. **Why do you think Ms. Williams encouraged Mark to come back to complete the puzzle?**

   _____

   _____

   _____

2. **How did Ms. Williams support Mark in feeling positive rather than negative about himself?**

   _____

   _____

   _____

Compare your answers with those on the answer sheet at the end of this module. If your answers are different, discuss them with your trainer. There can be more than one good answer.

Your Own Self-Esteem

Self-esteem is very important to all of us. Growing up, we have many experiences that help shape our feelings about ourselves. Often, we learn to value who we are and what we can do. Yet in each situation our self-esteem is tested. In situations where we feel capable and trusted, we do well. Our self-esteem is high. In other situations we may feel less skillful. We are unsure of what support we will get. If we fail, our self-esteem may suffer.

Think of times when you have felt really good about yourself. Perhaps you had some of the following feelings.

- You felt good about an accomplishment. "Look at this closet. It took me all day, but now I know where to find everything."

- You were ready to accept responsibilities. "I'll organize the staff party."

- You were independent. "I haven't been there before, but I have a map and I'll find it."

- You didn't give up easily. "This reading assignment is really hard to understand. I think if I take notes, I'll get the important points."

- You weren't afraid to express your feelings. "I felt hurt when you questioned my word."

You also probably can remember times when you felt bad about yourself. Your self-esteem was at a low. Perhaps you had some of these feelings.

- You put yourself down. "Oh, I'm so stupid. I can never get it right."

- You felt powerless. "I don't have any idea what I'm supposed to do. I'm hopelessly lost."

- You avoided difficult situations. "I'm not going to work if she's there today."

- You blamed others. "How could I help it? He didn't tell me where the paint was."

- You felt that no one valued you. "They'll never pick me."

A teacher with low self-esteem may tend to pass on these feelings to the children in his or her care. As we have been taught, so we tend to teach. "I'm stupid" and "I can't" easily become "you're stupid" and "you can't."

It is important to focus on building your own self-esteem and to remember people who have helped you achieve positive feelings about yourself. How were you helped to feel sure of yourself and able to try new things? And how can you pass on those positive feelings to the children you care for? Many different people in your life have encouraged your self-esteem. Think back to a teacher you had in school who made you feel especially good about yourself. Picture yourself in the classroom. Respond to the questions below.

What did the teacher do or say to build your self-esteem?

_____

_____

_____

_____

How did you feel about yourself at the time?

_____

_____

_____

_____

How has this experience affected how you feel?

_____

_____

_____

_____

Self-esteem makes people happier and more productive. Your feelings about yourself influence your behavior as you care for children each day. The more capable and positive you feel about your skills as a teacher, the more rewards you will have from your profession. The children you care for will sense that you are a positive person, and that will help them to feel good also.

When you have finished this overview section, you should complete the pre-training assessment. Refer to the glossary at the end of this module if you need definitions of the terms that are used.

Pre-Training Assessment

Listed below are the skills that teachers use to build children's self-esteem. Think about whether you do these things regularly, sometimes, or not enough. Place a check in one of the columns on the right for each skill listed. Then discuss your answers with your trainer.

SKILL	I DO THIS REGULARLY	I DO THIS SOMETIMES	I DON'T DO THIS ENOUGH
DEVELOPING A POSITIVE AND SUPPORTIVE RELATIONSHIP WITH EACH CHILD 1. Observing children to learn about each child's needs, strengths, and interests and providing the right kinds of materials and activities.			
2. Talking to children about their feelings so they can learn to understand and express their emotions.			
3. Showing children in many ways that they are cared for.			
4. Spending individual time with each child every day.			
5. Planning the day's activities so each child can use and practice his or her special skills.			
6. Helping each child feel comfortable about making the transition from home to the center.			

SKILL	I DO THIS REGULARLY	I DO THIS SOMETIMES	I DON'T DO THIS ENOUGH
HELPING CHILDREN ACCEPT AND APPRECIATE THEMSELVES AND OTHERS 7. Expressing pleasure and interest in words and actions to help children feel good about who they are and what they can do.			
8. Including homelike materials and activities in the room and pictures of families so children can feel secure.			
9. Helping children learn to use words to let each other know what they want and how they feel.			
10. Modeling positive ways to talk and act to let other people know that you care about them.			
11. Letting children know that they are liked even when they are unhappy or angry.			
PROVIDING CHILDREN WITH OPPORTUNITIES TO FEEL SUCCESSFUL AND COMPETENT 12. Offering help to children learning new skills until they can manage on their own.			
13. Allowing children to learn from their mistakes, without making them feel bad, and encouraging them to solve their own problems.			

SKILL	I DO THIS REGULARLY	I DO THIS SOMETIMES	I DON'T DO THIS ENOUGH
14. Repeating games or activities so children can master skills and feel successful.			
15. Including a wide variety of materials in the room to meet the diverse needs of different children.			
16. Letting children do as much as possible for themselves, providing help only when asked or when a child is very anxious.			

Review your responses, then list three to five skills you would like to improve or topics you would like to learn more about. When you finish this module, you will list examples of your new or improved knowledge and skills.

_____

_____

_____

_____

_____

_____

_____

_____

_____

_____

_____

_____

_____

_____

Now begin the learning activities for Module 8, Self.

I. Using Your Knowledge of Child Development to Build Self-Esteem

In this activity you will learn:

- to recognize some typical behaviors of preschool children; and

- to use what you know about children to build their self-esteem.

Eric Erikson, a child development theorist, described the preschool years as the stage in which children develop **initiative**. The word brings to mind active and curious children ready to learn. How much initiative children have depends a lot on their past experiences. As infants, they learned to **trust** their world. If adults responded to their needs consistently and caringly, they learned that they were valued. As toddlers, they asserted their independence and **autonomy**. If adults nurtured their independence within acceptable limits, they felt good about their growing abilities. Preschool children have developed many skills they can use to get along in the world. If you encourage them to explore, to expand their skills, and to learn, they will show initiative. Their self-esteem will grow as their knowledge and skills increase.

Most preschool children talk a lot. They usually know many words, and they can express their ideas. They often ask "why" and "what" and "how" because they want to know more about their world. Preschool children tend to be social. They play with other children and may develop strong friendships. They notice how people are alike and different, and they are curious about these differences. Dramatic play is a favorite activity. You can learn a lot about how children feel about themselves and what is important to them by watching them play.

Sometimes adults try to push children into academic learning too early. They teach letters and numbers so children will be "ready" for first grade. If preschool children are pushed to do things before they are ready, they will experience failure and their self-esteem will suffer. The appropriate curriculum for them is one that helps them learn through play.

Learning what preschool children are like at this stage of development can help you provide an appropriate child development program. In a good program, children can succeed easily and feel good about themselves. In this way they develop self-esteem.

The chart on the next page identifies some typical behaviors of preschool children. Included are behaviors relevant to the development of self-esteem. The right column asks you to identify ways that teachers can use this information about child development to build self-esteem. Try to think of as many examples as you can. As you work through the module you will learn new strategies for building self-esteem, and you can add them to the child development chart. You are not expected to think of all the examples at one time. If you need help getting started, turn to the completed chart at the end of the module. By the time you complete all the learning activities, you will find that you have learned many ways to build children's self-esteem.

Using Your Knowledge of Child Development to Build Self-Esteem

WHAT PRESCHOOL CHILDREN ARE LIKE	HOW TEACHERS CAN USE THIS INFORMATION TO BUILD SELF-ESTEEM
They are eager to please adults.	
They may be afraid of loud noises, the dark, animals, or some people.	
They can feed and dress themselves.	
They are usually toilet trained and can ask to go to the bathroom.	
They like to help in the routines of the room.	
They like to play make-believe and act out roles.	
They can take turns and share but don't always want to.	
They use a large vocabulary to express themselves but may also stutter or use "baby talk."	

WHAT PRESCHOOL CHILDREN ARE LIKE	HOW TEACHERS CAN USE THIS INFORMATION TO BUILD SELF-ESTEEM
They have strong emotions.	
They may express anger and jealousy physically.	
They have lots of physical energy.	
They want to make decisions for themselves.	
They like to try new things and to take risks.	
They are beginning to explore and understand what it means to be a boy or a girl.	
They may have difficulty making the transition from home to school.	

When you have finished the chart, discuss your answers with your trainer. As you proceed with the rest of the learning activities, you can refer back to the chart and add examples of how teachers can build self-esteem.

II. Getting to Know Each Child

In this activity you will learn:

- to observe preschool children carefully and regularly; and

- to use this information to build self-esteem.

One of the easiest ways to learn about a child is to observe and write down what that child does over a short period of time. You will be surprised how much you can learn just by watching and noting everything you see.

One purpose of a brief observation is to learn more about the child so you can use the information to build self-esteem. Because every child is different, how you build self-esteem will depend on what you know about each child. For example, during an observation you may notice that a child who usually forgets to hang up his smock finally remembers. You can tell him later that you liked the way he remembered to hang up his smock—and thus reinforce his positive feelings about himself.

To complete a careful five-minute observation of a preschool child, arrange a time when you will have no other responsibilities. Other teachers in the room can take over for you. You will want to find a time when you know the child will be awake and doing something interesting. Use index cards or a notebook to jot down everything you see, including:

- where the child is in the room;

- what the child does; and

- what the child says.

Later, review your notes and share the information collected with your colleagues so you can plan ways to build on the child's skills, respond to the child's interests, and address the child's needs. You and your colleagues can establish a system so you can each conduct regular observations of each child.

In this learning activity you will do a five- to ten-minute observation of one child. Begin by reading the example of an observation of four-year-old Billy. Then choose a child to observe for a short period (five to ten minutes) during indoor or outdoor play or at mealtime. During the observation, make quick notes about what the child does and says and his or her facial expressions.

After you complete the observation, go back to it when you have time. Add any details you left out. Read over your observation and think about what you learned about the child. Write down any ideas that come to mind regarding ways to build that child's self-esteem. Then answer the questions on the blank form that follows the example.

Getting to Know a Child
(Example)

Child: _Billy_   **Age:** _4 years, 3 months_   **Date:** _January 10_

Setting: _Free playhouse corner_   **Time:** _10:45 a.m._

Observation notes

Billy is alone. He puts on the firefighter hat and raincoat. He says, "I have to make my lunch and eat it fast. I have to get to the fire station in a hurry." He gets pots from the shelf and puts them on the stove. He puts playdough pieces in the pots. He stands at the stove and sings a song:

> *Firefighter, Firefighter, put on your boots!*
> *Firefighter, Firefighter, put on your coat.*

He removes the pots from the stove, puts the playdough on plates, and sits at the table smiling. He pretends to eat, puts the dishes in the sink, and quickly walks to the block corner.

What do you think the child was feeling? Describe behavior that tells you how the child was feeling.

Billy smiled and sang as he played. He appears to be happy today. He feels good about cooking his lunch and being a firefighter.

What did you learn about the child?

Billy seems to enjoy acting out roles. He is thinking about cooking for himself. He pretended he was a firefighter preparing to go to work. He is happy when he is busy. Also, he memorized a song.

How can you use this information to build self-esteem?

I can put additional firefighter props in the house corner and block area. I can sing the firefighter song with him. Also, I can mention during circle time that Billy seems to like this song. I can talk with him during free play about things a firefighter does. I can include him in our next cooking project. I can watch to see when he might be ready to include other children in dramatic play.

Getting to Know a Child

Child: _____   Age: _____   Date: _____

Setting: _____   Time: _____

Observation Notes

_____

_____

_____

_____

_____

_____

_____

_____

_____

_____

What do you think the child was feeling? Describe behavior that tells you how the child was feeling.

_____

_____

_____

_____

_____

_____

What did you learn about the child?

_____

_____

_____

_____

_____

_____

_____

How can you use this information to build self-esteem?

_____

_____

_____

_____

_____

_____

_____

_____

_____

_____

It would be helpful to repeat this activity for another five-minute period with the same child to collect more information. Plan to observe each child in your group over the next few weeks. Discuss your observations and how you plan to use the information you have collected with a colleague who also cares for these children.

III. Responding to Each Child as an Individual

In this activity you will learn:

- to keep track of what one child does over a five-day period to learn about the child's interests, strengths, and needs; and

- to use what you learn to respond in ways that build self-esteem.

Preschool children develop self-esteem when they feel accepted and supported by their teachers. They learn to feel good about being a boy or a girl. They know they are a member of a family. And often they know that they belong to an ethnic group.

Preschool children are very active and curious. They have many skills that they use each day to take care of themselves and to help in the room. They also use their skills at play and learn new ones as they develop physically and mentally. Preschool children are good thinkers. When teachers let them solve their own problems, these children can use their thinking skills and feel good about their successes.

All children grow at their own pace. In your group there are children at many different levels. By playing with and observing each child, you get to know individual strengths and needs. This information helps you provide materials and activities that will allow each child to feel successful. These successes in turn help build each child's self-esteem.

You also want to find out what each child likes to do. For example, in Learning Activity II, Getting to Know Each Child, the teacher watched Billy in the house corner and saw that he liked to pretend to cook. She used that information to plan some food-preparation activities that would include Billy. Planning activities that you know a child will enjoy helps build self-esteem.

In this learning activity you will discover more about what one child likes to do and how this child learns and tries out new skills. You will then use the information to encourage the use of these skills to build self-esteem.

Review the example that follows. Then select a child in your group to focus on over a five-day period. Keep handy a pencil and something small to write on (index cards work well). Jot down notes as you observe the child. Use your notes to answer the questions on the blank form.

Responding to Each Child as an Individual
(Example)

Child: _Cynthia_   **Age:** _2-1/2 years_   **Dates:** _March 3-7_

WHAT DID YOU LEARN ABOUT THIS CHILD?	HOW CAN YOU USE THIS INFORMATION TO BUILD SELF-ESTEEM?
What does this child like to do when he or she arrives at the center? *Quiet activities. Looks through books in the reading area. Puts together puzzles in the table toys area.*	*Read to her. Encourage her interest in books and provide more difficult puzzles as her skills improve.*
How does this child act when he or she is feeling good? *Smiles often. Giggles at funny stories. Plays with her close friends in the house corner (this is new for her).*	*Laugh with her. Provide new props for her to use in the house corner with her close friends.*
Who are the children this child likes to play with? Does the child invite them to play, or do other children invite him or her? *Kim and Joey. She waits to be asked, then joins in. All three are quiet children— Cynthia is the most quiet.*	*Set up activities for the three of them, such as playing with new props in the block area.*
What new skills has this child recently learned? *Playing with other children, sharing toys and props to act out roles.*	*Comment on how she's playing with other children. At the beginning of the year she mostly played alone. Now she likes to play with one or two children. I'll encourage that, especially in the house corner.*

WHAT DID YOU LEARN ABOUT THIS CHILD?	HOW CAN YOU USE THIS INFORMATION TO BUILD SELF-ESTEEM?
What are this child's self-help skills (zipping, buttoning, tying laces, setting the table, cleaning up toys, etc.)? *She's always done things for herself. She buttons, zips, laces, loves to be a helper, is very organized about cleaning up. She's learning to twist her laces, trying to make a knot.*	*Let her do as much for herself as possible. I'll ask her to help other children learn to zip and button. We'll use the lacing board to make knots.*
What does this child like to do outdoors? *She plays quietly in the sandbox, sometimes with Kim and Joey. She says she likes riding the trike but rarely asks for a turn.*	*Comment on her group play in the sandbox. I'll be sure she gets a turn on a trike each day, and give her words to tell another child she wants to use the trike next.*
What does this child do very well? *She remembers the stories that have been read to her and can repeat them as she looks through a book.*	*Sit with her while she's reading and ask questions such as these: "What happened? How did the story end? Is there another way the story could have ended?"*
What does this child like to do at the end of the day? *Same as at the beginning—read and play with puzzles. Sometimes she "reads" to Kim and Joey, who get pretty tired by the end of the day and ask Cynthia to read to them.*	*Ask her to "read" to a small group of children. Let her read or play alone when she wants to.*

Responding to Each Child as an Individual

Child: _____   Age: _____   Date: _____

WHAT DID YOU LEARN ABOUT THIS CHILD?	HOW CAN YOU USE THIS INFORMATION TO BUILD SELF-ESTEEM?
What does this child like to do when he or she arrives at the center?	
How does this child act when he or she is feeling good?	
Who are the children this child likes to play with? Does the child invite them to play, or do other children invite him or her?	
What new skills has this child recently learned?	

WHAT DID YOU LEARN ABOUT THIS CHILD?	HOW CAN YOU USE THIS INFORMATION TO BUILD SELF-ESTEEM?
What are this child's self-help skills (zipping, buttoning, tying laces, setting the table, cleaning up toys, etc.)?	
What does this child like to do outdoors?	
What does this child do very well?	
What does this child like to do at the end of the day?	

Discuss your observations and plans for using the information with your trainer.

IV. Helping Children Deal with Separation

In this activity you will learn:

- to observe how individual preschool children react to separation;

- to communicate with children in ways that help them deal with their feelings about separation; and

- to provide an environment that helps children deal with their feelings about separation.

When children separate from their parents, they often express strong feelings. Anger, guilt, sadness, relief, fear, and happiness are among the feelings that both child and parent may feel and show. Separation is a lifelong process and an important part of growing up. Each day parents, children, and teachers have opportunities to learn better ways to cope with their feelings about separation.

Children who have high self-esteem are more able to feel safe and comfortable when away from their families. These children have learned that they will be all right while their Mommy or Daddy is away. A teacher can help children by telling them that it is all right to be upset and that the teacher will be there to help. "I know you are sad when Mommy leaves. I will help you."

In addition to letting children know that you understand their feelings and are there to help them, you can also make the center seem as much like home as possible. Encourage parents to have children bring some special item from home. A blanket or stuffed animal, for example, will help each child feel secure. Pictures of the children's families can also remind them of their parents even when they are away. Familiar cooking activities make the center more homelike. Children can use dress-up clothes and props to role-play situations where people leave and come back. This make-believe activity helps them handle their fearful feelings.

How preschool children experience separation is closely tied to their stage of development. Children at this stage are able to create a mental picture of their absent parents. When they were younger, they could not do this. Also, preschool children can understand their teacher's explanation of where their Mommy or Daddy have gone and when they will be back to pick them up. They often express their feelings about separation—in their art or other play activities, or in the books they chose to "read." Teachers can support these healthy ways of coping with separation by giving children lots of time for art and for books such as *Goodnight Moon* and *The Runaway Bunny* by Margaret Wise Brown, or *Ira Sleeps Over* by E. Waber— three favorites.

Some preschool children have great difficulty separating from their parents. These difficulties may be expressed in different ways.

- Vanessa stopped sucking her thumb last year but began again when she started coming to the center. Thumb-sucking helped her feel better about missing her Mommy.

- Felipe seemed to adjust easily to his new life at the center. Felipe's mother reported that he had been wetting his bed at night. Felipe's separation fears were expressed in his familiar home rather than at the center.

- Four-year-old Cheryl has been dressing herself since she was two-and-a-half. She has been coming to the center for three weeks. Her mother says that Cheryl tells her in the morning, "I can't get my clothes on today, so I can't go to school." Cheryl knows that she can't go to the center if she doesn't have clothes on.

- Peter brought his large teddy bear to the center today. He has been carrying it around all day. It's so big that it gets in the way of anything he tries to play with. His teddy bear reminds him of home and his parents.

Teachers can help children such as these overcome their separation difficulties. They can tell children that they understand how they feel: "I know you miss your Mommy today." They can remind children when Mommy will be back: "Mommy will pick you up this afternoon after our snack time." Teachers can make sure that children and parents say good-bye, even if the child cries. It is easier to deal with open feelings than ones that are bottled up inside.

Teachers can also remind all the children about the routines of their days at the center. A predictable order of events gives a sense of security, and by understanding this order, children are better able to understand when their parents will return to take them home.

While at the center, preschool children should be encouraged to help—to pour juice, set tables, clean up, and so on. As they gain self-confidence by successfully doing such helping activities, they will also learn to cope with separation. They will feel important and valued where they are, even though their parents are absent.

Occasionally, children revert to infant-like behaviors in reaction to being separated from their families. Thumb-sucking or wetting are typical of such behaviors. Teachers need not pay undue attention to them; criticizing or focusing heavily on them will only make the child who uses them feel bad about himself or herself.

The classroom should always be welcoming but not overwhelming. A room with attractive, inviting materials helps children cope with separation; too many materials can simply confuse children. Pictures of the children's families, hung on the wall at the children's eye-level, help make the center more like home. Teachers can make a parent mailbox so children can "write" letters to their parents during the day. Teachers' visits to the children's homes also can help children deal with separation. The teacher can see the child's home environment, how the child behaves in a different setting, how the parents interact with the child, the role of siblings, and so on. After a home visit from the teacher, many children feel more connected to the center and more comfortable spending time there.

In this learning activity you will think of ways to help individual children cope with separation. First, review the example that follows. Then choose two children in your care whom you think are very different from each other. Use what you have learned in this module and what you know about these children to complete the questions on the blank chart.

	Child: _Tony_ Age: _3-1/2 years_	Child: _George_ Age: _4 years_
How does this child say good-bye to his or her parents in the morning?	*He holds on to his mother for a few minutes. She helps him hang his coat in the cubby and sits with him in the book area until she leaves for work.*	*His father asks him what he's going to play with first. George usually says "the blocks" and takes his father to the block corner. His father watches for a few minutes and says goodbye.*
What kinds of make-believe do you see this child playing?	*Usually scenes from home—cooking, cleaning. Sometimes he plays grocery store—that's where his mother works.*	*He likes to be a police officer, directing traffic. Sometimes he's a daddy in the house corner.*
How does this child use art materials to express his or her feelings?	*He likes "soothing art" —he finger-paints carefully and smoothly.*	*He's quick. He makes broad brush strokes up and down and side to side when he's angry or sad.*
How do you know this child is thinking about his or her family?	*He talks about his mother at the store and his father on the airplane (when he is traveling for work).*	*He doesn't talk about his family very much. When we talk about our families at group time, he joins in.*
How does this child help with routines in the room?	*He likes to set the table —he's very serious about his work.*	*Table-setting doesn't interest George—he gets bored before he's done. He does well with the cots at naptime.*
How could you help this child deal with separation?	*Read to him after his mother leaves and at the end of the day. Get him to try water play when he's sad.*	*Ask him about things he does with his parents and sisters. Use family pictures to talk about them—where they are when George is at the center.*

Helping Children Deal with Separation

	Child: _____ Age: _____	Child: _____ Age: _____
How does this child say goodbye to his or her parents in the morning?		
What kinds of make-believe do you see this child playing?		
How does this child use art materials to express his or her feelings?		
How do you know this child is thinking about his or her family? How does this child help with routines in the room?		
How could you help this child deal with separation?		

Discuss your responses with your trainer.

V. Using Caring Words That Help Build Self-Esteem

In this activity you will learn:

- to use caring words to let preschool children know they are respected and understood; and

- to use caring words to help children learn to accept themselves and others.

Preschool children are able to use words to describe what they think and feel. Some children are very good at using words; others need your help. Teachers are verbal models for preschool children. Children listen to what you say and try to understand your meaning. The words you use teach them a lot about who they are. When those words are caring, they help build a child's self-esteem.

Talking with children in ways that build self-esteem requires two special skills. First, a teacher must listen carefully and then determine what the child is really saying through words and/or actions—and what he or she is feeling. By looking at and listening to a child and thinking about your own experiences, you can often tell how the child feels. Second, a teacher must respond so that the child knows that he or she is understood and respected.

> One teacher watched and listened to four-year-old James, who was new at the center. James looked at the paintings around the easel area and said, "These sure are ugly pictures." The teacher said, "We let children paint all kinds of pictures here. Everyone paints in their own way, and everyone can hang up their pictures if they want to."

This teacher knew that James was worried about how his paintings would turn out. He wondered if his pictures would be acceptable. His way of expressing his worry was to call the pictures on the wall ugly. In this situation the teacher listened carefully to what James said and figured out what he was feeling. She responded to him in a way that showed that she understood that he was feeling worried and that she respected his concern about being able to paint.

Another person who had not developed skills in listening and talking with preschool children might have said, "These pictures aren't ugly. It isn't nice to say that about the other children's work." This statement would make James feel bad. It would also leave him still worried about his own ability to paint pictures.

When you greet children each morning, you set the tone for their day. By saying something special about each child, you show that you notice and care for each one. Your caring words are also important to the parents who bring their children to your room.

Using caring words takes some practice. It may be a while before new ways of talking to children feel natural. You will be rewarded when the children you care for let you know how much better they feel because of your understanding and care.

During the day you have many opportunities to talk to the children you care for. In this learning activity you will read "Children's Self-Esteem, The Verbal Environment" and several examples of how teachers can use caring words in different situations. Then you will write down what you might say in typical situations to build a child's self-esteem.

Children's Self-Esteem, The Verbal Environment[1]

Young children continually gather information about their value as persons through interactions with the significant adults in their lives (Coopersmith, 1967; Swayze, 1980). This process begins in the home but very quickly extends to the educational settings in which children participate. Thus family members, caregivers and teachers serve as the mirror through which children see themselves and then judge what they see (Maccoby, 1980). If what is reflected is good, children will make a positive evaluation of self. If the image is negative, children will deduce that they have little worth; they are sensitive to the opinions adults have of them and often adopt these as their own.

In the classroom, teachers convey either enhancing or damaging attitudes that frequently are manifested in what they say to children and how they say it. Such manifestations may or may not be the result of conscious decisions on their part. Yet teacher verbalizations are a key factor in the degree to which children perceive themselves as worthy and competent or the opposite (Kostelnik, Stein, Whiren & Soderman, 1988). Consider the following scenario:

Imagine that you are invited to visit an early childhood program in your community. You arrive early and are asked to wait in the classroom until the youngsters return from a field trip. Surveying your surroundings, you notice brightly colored furniture comfortably arranged, sunlight softly streaming through the windows, children's art work pleasingly displayed and a large, well-stocked aquarium bubbling in a corner. You think to yourself, "What a pleasant environment for children."

Just then, a child bursts into the room sobbing. She is followed by an adult who scolds, "Maria, stop that bawling." As the other youngsters file in, you hear another child exclaim, "When do we get to take our projects home?" An adult snaps, "Why can't you listen. I just said they stay here until tomorrow."

Your favorable impression is ruined. Despite the lovely physical surroundings, the way in which adults are talking to children has made the setting uninviting. You wonder whether children could ever feel good about themselves under such circumstances. What you have overheard has made you privy to an invisible but keenly felt component of every program—the verbal environment.

THE VERBAL ENVIRONMENT

Adult participants in the early childhood setting create the verbal environment. Its components include words and silence—how much adults say, what they say, how they speak, to whom they talk and how well they listen. The manner in which these elements are enacted dictates children's estimations of self-worth. Thus verbal environments can be characterized as either positive or negative.

Characteristics of the Negative Verbal Environment
Negative verbal environments are ones in which children are made to feel unworthy, incompetent, unlovable or insignificant as a result of what adults say or do not say to them. Most practitioners can readily identify the most extreme illustrations: adults screaming at children, making fun of them, swearing at them or making them the target of ethnic slurs. Yet there are less obvious, more common adult behaviors that also contribute to negative verbal environments:

1) *Adults show little or no interest in children's activities because they are in a hurry, busy, engrossed in their own thoughts and endeavors, or tired.* Whatever the reason, they walk by children without comment and fail to acknowledge their presence. When standing near children, they do not talk with them and respond only grudgingly to children's attempts to initiate an interaction. In addition, grownups misuse time designated for interaction with children by talking more with their colleagues than the youngsters. Rather than paying attention to children, most of the adult's time is spent chatting with other adults. Children interpret these behaviors as obvious signs of disinterest.

2) *Teachers pay superficial atten-*

Marjorie J. Kostelnik, Laura C. Stein and Alice P. Whiren are faculty members in the Department of Family and Child Ecology, Michigan State University, East Lansing.

---

[1]Reprinted by permission of Marjorie J. Kostelnik, Laura C. Stein, Alice P. Whiren, and the Association for Childhood Education International, 11141 Georgia Avenue, Suite 200, Wheaton, MD. Copyright © 1988 by the Association.

tion to what children have to say. Instead of listening attentively, they ask irrelevant questions, respond inappropriately, fail to maintain eye contact or cut children off. Occasionally they simply ignore the communication altogether, saying nothing, thus treating the children as if they were not present.

3) *Adults speak discourteously to children.* They interrupt children who are speaking to them, as well as youngsters who are talking to one another. They expect children to respond to their own requests immediately, not allowing them to finish what they are doing or saying. Their voice tone is demanding, impatient or belligerent; they neglect such social courtesies as "Excuse me," "Please" and "Thank you." In addition, their remarks often make children the butt of a group joke. Young children attend as much to the sarcastic tone of voice as to the meaning of words and are not able to appreciate the intended humor.

4) *Teachers use judgmental vocabulary in describing children to themselves and others.* Typical demeaning labels include "hyper," "selfish," "greedy," "uncooperative," "motor mouth," "stubborn," "grabby" and "klutzy." Adults say these words directly to children or to another person within the child's hearing. In either case, youngsters are treated as though they have no feelings or are invisible or deaf.

5) *Staff members actively discourage children from talking to them.* They tell children that what they are doing or saying is uninteresting or unimportant and that they should be doing or talking about something else. Thus youngsters hear admonishments like: "All right, already! I'm sick of hearing about your troubles with Rhonda; find something else to talk about." Or, "I don't want to hear one more word about it. Not one peep!" Sometimes adults put children off by saying, "Hush," "Not now" or

"Tell me about it later." The "later" seldom comes.

6) *Grownups rely on giving orders and making demands as their number-one means of relating to children.* Their verbalizations consist of directions ("Sit in your chair") and admonishments ("No fighting," "Everybody get your coats off and settle down for lunch," "Stop fooling around"). Other comments that are positive in tone or content are relatively scarce.

7) *Adults ask questions for which no real answer is expected or desired.* Typical queries might include: "What do you think you're doing?" "Didn't I tell you not to stomp in the mud?" "When will you ever learn?" Regardless of how children respond, their answers are viewed as disrespectful or unwelcome. Children soon learn that these remarks are not a real invitation to relate to the adult.

8) *Caregivers use children's names as synonyms for the words "no," "stop" or "don't."* By barking out "Tony" or "Allison" as a reprimand, adults attack the essence of the child's being, thereby causing children to associate the most personal part of themselves with disapproval and rejection. When using this tactic adults fail to describe the objectionable behavior or to clarify the reason for the negative tone of voice, thus leaving children with the notion that something is inherently wrong with them as persons.

9) *Teachers use baby talk in giving information or directions.* Instead of clearly stating, "Ruth and Toby, please put the puzzles in the puzzle rack," adults confuse and demean children by saying, "We need to put the puzzles in the puzzle rack," when they have no intention of assisting. Other kinds of baby talk involve using the diminutive form of a name (*Jackie* instead of *Jack*), even though the child and the parents prefer the other. These may be combined in particularly exaggerated ways, as when one

caregiver pursed her lips and squealed in a high pitch, "How are we today, Jackie? Shall we quit crying and ride the horsie?" Such messages define children as powerless and subservient; these statements are never used between persons of equal status.

10) *Adults dominate the verbal exchanges that take place each day.* They do all the talking and allow children little time to respond either to them or their peers. Feeling compelled constantly to query, inform or instruct, they bombard children with so much talk that youngsters have few opportunities to initiate conversations on topics of their own choosing. This leaves children feeling rushed and unsatisfied.

All of the preceding verbal behaviors convey to children adult attitudes of aloofness, disrespect, lack of acceptance and insensitivity. Such encounters tend to make children feel inadequate, confused or angry (Hoffman, 1963). A different set of circumstances exists in programs characterized by a positive verbal environment.

Characteristics of the Positive Verbal Environment

In a positive verbal environment, adult words are aimed at satisfying children's needs and making children feel valued. When speaking to children, adults focus not only on content but also on the affective impact their words will have. Adults create a positive verbal environment when their verbal exchanges with children have the following attributes:

1) *Adults use words to show affection for children and sincere interest in them.* They greet children when they arrive, take the time to become engaged in children's activities and also respond to their queries. In addition, they make remarks showing children they care

about them and are aware of what they are doing: "You've been really working hard to get the dinosaur puzzle together." "You seem to be enjoying that game." They laugh with children, respond to their humor and tell chidlren they enjoy being with them.

2) *Adults send congruent verbal and nonverbal messages.* When they are showing interest verbally, they position themselves near the child at a similar height from the floor, maintain eye contact and thoroughly pay attention. Other actions, such as smiling or giving a pat, reinforce praise and words of positive regard. Incongruent messages, such as following through on a limit while smiling or pinching a child's cheek hard while giving praise, are avoided.

3) *Adults extend invitations to children to interact with them.* They may say, "Here's a place for you right next to Sylvia" or "Let's take a minute to talk. I want to find out more about your day." When children seek them out, grownups accept the invitation enthusiastically: "That sounds like fun." "Oh good, now I'll have a chance to work with you."

4) *Teachers listen attentively to what children have to say.* They show their interest through eye contact, smiling and nodding. They encourage children to elaborate on what they are saying by using such statements as "Tell me more about that" or "Then what happened?" Moreover, adults pause long enough after making a comment or asking a question for children to reply, giving them time to gather their thoughts before responding. Such reactions make children feel valued and interesting.

5) *Adults speak courteously to children.* They refrain from interrupting children and allow them to finish what they are saying, either to the adult or another child. The voice tone used by adults is patient and friendly, and social amenities

such as "Please," "Thank you" and "Excuse me" are part of the verbal interchange.

6) *Adults use children's interests as a basis for conversation.* They speak with them about the things youngsters want to talk about. This is manifested in two ways. First, they follow the child's lead in conversations. Second, they bring up subjects known to be of interest to a particular child based on past experience.

7) *Adults plan or take advantage of spontaneous opportunities to talk with each child informally.* In the course of a day, children have many chances to talk with adults about matters that interest or concern them. Eating, toileting, dressing, waiting for the bus, settling down for a nap and just waiting until the group is called to order are treated as occasions for adult-child conversation. Adults do not wait for special, planned time to talk with youngsters.

8) *Teachers avoid making judgmental comments about children either to them or within their hearing.* Children are treated as sensitive, aware human beings whose feelings are respected. Discussions about children's problems or family situations are held in private between the appropriate parties.

9) *Adults refrain from speaking when talk would destroy the mood of the interaction.* When they see children deeply absorbed in activity or engrossed in conversation with one another, staff members allow the natural course of the interaction to continue. In these situations they treat silence as a sign of warmth and respect and refrain from too much talk at the wrong time.

10) *Grownups focus their attention on children when they professionally engage with them.* They put off housekeeping tasks and personal socializing so that they are fully available for interaction with children. When possible, adults involve children in maintenance tasks

and interact with them. In a positive environment, adults are available, alert and prepared to respond to children.

Importance of a Positive Verbal Environment

Positive verbal environments are beneficial both to the children and the adults who participate in them. In such an atmosphere, children get the message that they are important. This enhances their self-perceptions of competence and worth (Openshaw, 1978). Additionally, children's self-awareness increases as they have opportunities to express themselves, explore ideas and interact spontaneously with other children and adults (Kostelnik et al., 1988). These conditions also increase the likelihood that youngsters will view the adults in the program as sources of comfort and support. As a result, adults find it easier to establish and maintain rapport with the children. This in turn makes youngsters more receptive to the social learnings adults wish to impart to them (Baumrind, 1977; Katz, 1977). These include rules, customs and how to get along with other people.

In sum, adult behaviors that characterize a positive verbal environment are synonymous with those commonly cited as representing warmth, acceptance, respect and empathy (Coletta, 1977; Gazda, 1977; Rogers, 1961). All four of these components contribute to the relationship-building process and provide the foundation for constructive child growth and development.

Establishing a Positive Verbal Environment

Few helping professionals would knowingly act in ways that damage children's self-esteem. Observations of early childhood settings, however, show that frequently adults unintentionally slip into verbal patterns that produce the negative verbal environment described here (Kostelnik, 1978, 1987). Recent interviews with day care, Head Start, preprimary and elementary school teachers point to three common reasons why this occurs (Kostelnik, 1987):

•Adults fail to consciously consider the impact their words have on children.

•Adults get caught up in the hurried pace of the job and think they cannot take the time to have more positive verbal interactions with the children.

•Adults are not used to thinking before speaking and, as a result, say things they do not really mean and talk in ways they do not intend.

Over the years it has become increasingly clear that positive verbal environments do not happen by chance. Rather, their creation is the resu¹t of purposeful planning and implementation. Those who are successful in their efforts first recognize the characteristics of the positive verbal environment and th᾿ .1 incorporate the corresponding behaviors into their interactions with children. The steps for achieving these results are listed below:

1) *Familiarize yourself with the features of both positive and negative verbal environments.* Reread the guidelines presented here. Think about situations from your experience that illustrate each one.

2) *Listen carefully to what you say and how you say it.* Consider how children may interpret your message. If you catch yourself using habits that are poor, correct them on the spot. Ask colleagues to give you feedback about how you sound, or carry a tape recorder with you for a short period of time as a means of self-observation.

3) *Make a deliberate decision to create a positive verbal environment.* Select one characteristic and think

of how to integrate it into your daily routine. Practice such simple strategies as using children's names in positive situations, showing your pleasure in their company or inviting children to elaborate on what they say. Try these techniques one at a time, until they become second nature to you. As you become more proficient, gradually increase the number of techniques you use.

4) *Keep track of the positive verbal behaviors that you use.* Ask a colleague to help you identify positive verbal characteristics and determine how often you use them. As you substitute more positive approaches to verbal interaction for the negative ones, you will have a record of your success. Self-improvement is easier to recognize when short evaluations are carried out periodically.

5) *Give recognition to other staff members who are attempting to improve the verbal environment for children.* Words of approval and encouragement are as important to adults as they are to children. Progress toward any goal is made easier when others recognize both effort and achievement.

What adults say to children conveys to them messages of competence or inadequacy. Through their verbalizations teachers create a climate in their classroom that is called the verbal environment, a key factor in the degree to which children develop high or low self-esteem. Such environments are characterized as either positive or negative. Continual exposure to a negative verbal environment diminishes children's self-esteem, whereas exposure to a positive verbal environment enhances children's self-awareness and perceptions of self-worth. To ensure that the verbal environment is a positive one, teachers should consider carefully what they say to children and make purposeful attempts to follow the guidelines

cited in this article. The outcome of these efforts is a classroom in which children feel good about themselves and see the teacher as a positive presence in their lives.

References

Baumrind, D. (1977). Some thoughts about childrearing. In S. Cohen & T. J. Comiskey (Eds.), *Child Development: Contemporary Perspectives.* Itasca, IL: F. E. Peacock.

Coletta, A. J. (1977). *Working together: A guide to parent involvement.* Atlanta: Humanics.

Coopersmith, S. (1967). *The antecedents of self-esteem.* Princeton, NJ: Princeton University Press.

Gazda, G. M. (1977). *Human relations development: A manual for educators* (2nd ed.). Boston: Allyn & Bacon.

Hoffman, M. L. (1963). Parent discipline and the child's consideration of others. *Child Development 34,* 573-595.

Katz, L. G. (1977). What is basic for young children? *Childhood Education 54*(1), 16-19.

Kostelnik, M. J. (1978). *Evaluation of a communication and group management skills training program for child development personnel.* Unpublished doctoral dissertation, The Pennsylvania State University.

Kostelnik, M. J. (1987). *Development practices in early childhood programs.* Keynote Address, National Home Start Day, New Orleans, LA.

Kostelnik, M. J., Stein, L. C., Whiren, A. P., & Soderman, A. K. (1988). *Guiding children's social development.* Cincinnati, OH: Southwestern.

Maccoby, E. E. (1980). *Social development—Psychological growth and the parent-child relationship.* New York: Harcourt Brace Jovanovich.

Openshaw, D. K. (1978). *The development of self-esteem in the child: Model interaction.* Unpublished doctoral dissertation, Brigham Young University, Provo, UT.

Rogers, C. R. (1961). *On becoming a person.* Boston: Houghton Mifflin.

Swayze, M. C. (1980). Self-concept development in young children. In T. D. Yawkey (Ed.), *The self-concept of the young child.* Provo, UT: Brigham Young University Press.

Using Caring Words
(Example)

What do you say when a child calls another child or an adult a name, such as fat or stupid?

"We don't call people names here, Carol. We just use each other's real names. Kevin is not stupid, and neither are you. Kevin is playing in his own way. You may play in your own way. Both ways are fine."

What do you say when a child knocks down something another child is building or tries to destroy another child's work?

"Scott, you have just knocked down the building that Monica worked so hard to build. It's okay to be angry but it's not okay to destroy someone else's work. Monica, you need to tell Scott how you feel. Tell him you don't like it when he knocks down your buildings. Scott, if you are angry at Monica about something you must use your words, not your feet."

What do you say when a child hurts or bites another?

"Trish, it's okay to be angry with people. But I'm not going to let you hit or bite Paul, and I'm not going to let him hurt you, either. You can tell him how you feel. Say, 'I'm angry with you, Paul. I don't like what you did.'"

What do you say when a child expresses a fear of monsters?

"There are no monsters here at the center or at home, only on TV, in books, and in make-believe. They are not for real so they can't hurt you. It's okay to be scared, but we won't let anything bad happen to you."

What do you say when a child makes fun of another child's work?

"Jerry, we let children paint all kinds of pictures in this center. Children may hang their pictures wherever they choose. When you finish yours, you can show me where you want it to be. Your picture is special because you made it, and Pamela's is special too because she made it."

What do you say when a child is sad because his or her mommy or daddy went to work and left him or her?

"Mommy has to go to work. It's hard when she leaves you. She goes to work to get money to buy clothes and food for you because she loves you and wants to take good care of you. After you wake up and have a snack, she'll be here to take you home."

What do you say when a child's parent is away traveling for work?

"Daddy did not go away because of anything you did wrong or because of anything you thought or said. Daddy's job needs him to be somewhere else for a while. He will not forget you while he is gone. He'll love you no matter where he is. He will come back as soon as he can."

What do you say when a child wants your attention and you are busy?

"Greg, I know you want me to watch you on the monkey bars, but right now I'm over in the tree house. You need to wait five minutes until I can come there, or you can come join us in the tree house."

What do you say when a child has a new sibling in the house and expresses jealousy?

"Sometimes it's hard to have to share Mommy with a new baby. Maybe you think Mommy loves the baby more than you because she has to do all those things for the baby, like changing diapers. When you were a baby Mommy did these same things for you. Mommy still loves you, too, as four-year-old Justin. You don't have to be like a baby for Mommy to love you. I bet you feel good about being able to do so many things because you are four."

What do you say when a mother and father separate and one parent leaves the home?

"Daddy/Mommy did not leave home because of anything that you did wrong or because of anything you thought. Sometimes grown-ups have problems, too, and decide they can't live in the same house together. But you did not make it happen. Mommy and Daddy both love you, and they will both still take good care of you."

Using Caring Words

When playing with a child:

_____

_____

_____

_____

When a child is upset or angry:

_____

_____

_____

_____

When a child is hurt:

_____

_____

_____

_____

When (add your own here):_____

_____

_____

_____

_____

Saying goodbye at the end of the day:

_____

_____

_____

_____

Share your words with your trainer. You could also display your caring words in your room
to help you get used to using them.

VI. Providing the Right Kind of Support
for Children

In this activity you will learn:

- to use what you know about each child to predict how he or she will approach a new situation; and

- to use what you know about children to help them experience success.

As a teacher you spend much of your day doing things for children that they cannot do for themselves. It is important, however, to recognize when children are ready to help themselves and to provide many opportunities for them to be and feel successful and competent. A teacher does this by helping three-year-old Sara climb up the slide while holding her hand, by encouraging four-year-old Andy to try a puzzle he's never done before, or by putting some plastic knives next to the peanut butter and crackers so all the children can make their own snacks. Children feel good about themselves when they can practice skills they already have and learn new skills in a safe and accepting environment.

Each child develops according to a personal clock. Each child has his or her own style, capacity to learn, and fears. As a teacher you need to provide an environment that both challenges and supports each child in your care. You use your knowledge of children's individual capabilities and limitations to provide the right kind of support and guidance as children approach new tasks. This allows children to acquire new skills in a way that builds their self-esteem.

One of the hardest things to know is when to offer help to a child learning a new skill, and when to withdraw this support gradually so that the child can manage on his or her own. Teachers need to observe children closely so they can learn which ones need their hands held, which need words of encouragement, and which simply need a teacher to wave or smile at them as they practice a new skill.

In this learning activity you will use your knowledge of each child's strengths, needs, and temperament to develop a plan for introducing something new to the group. This could be a piece of equipment, a new toy, or a new routine. Using your knowledge of the children in your care, you will predict how they will react to the new situation. Begin by reviewing the example that follows.

Providing the Right Kind of Support
(Example)

Situation:

Our center recently purchased an indoor climber. I know that the reactions of the children in the group to the new piece of equipment will be as varied as their abilities to climb and jump.

CHILDREN	PREDICTED REACTION	SUPPORT METHODS
Joey and Cheryl	*Curiosity will lead them to approach the climber. They may be timid about trying it.*	*Discussion at circle time with pictures of the equipment to start the discussion.*
Bonita and Dean	*They will be excited and may take too many chances.*	*Showing pictures at circle time and talking about what children can do on the climber. Teaching safety limits. Constant guidance and encouragement to play safely.*
Marguerite and Lloyd	*They will take a long time to adjust to the new climber. Circle time discussion may make them more fearful.*	*Talking to children individually and reassuring them that when they want to use the climber, I will be right there with them for as long as they need me.*

Providing the Right Kind of Support

Situation:

_____

_____

_____

CHILDREN	PREDICTED REACTION	SUPPORT METHODS

Discuss your completed chart with a colleague who also works with these children.

VII. Providing an Environment That Builds Self-Esteem

In this activity you will learn:

- to recognize how the physical environment of the room affects the development of self-esteem; and

- to choose materials, toys, and activities in your room to help build self-esteem.

The environment of your room—its furniture and toys, along with the activities you plan—can help build a child's self-esteem. As a teacher you are the most important factor in the environment. Your caring relationship with each child is what promotes self-esteem. The children who grow to trust you will be free to explore and learn from their environment—and to trust themselves as well.

How can the environment build self-esteem? First, the furniture and equipment must be the right size, sturdy, and safe enough for the children. If preschool children can't reach the things they need—puzzles, crayons, and so on—they will feel frustrated and angry. If a climber is too large for children to use safely on their own, you will constantly have to be there to help. The children will learn that they have to depend on an adult, and this will not help their self-esteem. The more they can explore the environment on their own, the more proud they will be of themselves. Their self-esteem grows with their increasing independence.

Toys and materials should be appropriate for the age group of the children. If the toys are broken or too simple to be of interest, the children will become frustrated or bored. Too many toys can make preschool children confused. Too few can lead to fights or boredom. Toys or materials that are for older children will make children feel like failures. The key is to provide the right number of toys that will interest the children in your care. Many opportunities to experience success with materials and toys will increase their self-esteem.

Everything should have a place in a preschool room. Each place can be labeled with a picture on a low shelf so that the children can find and return the things they need. This helps children learn to make choices for themselves and to take care of their environment.

The activities you plan can also help build self-esteem. Knowing what will interest preschool children at each stage of their development will help you plan activities that are right for them. Because you know each child, you have discovered the special interests of each one. When you plan activities you know will interest a child, you are saying to that child, "You are important to me and I know you will like this."

The children you care for will change a lot while they are in your room. Every day they are learning new skills and developing new interests. To build self-esteem, you will need to change the environment, materials, and activities to reflect these new abilities and interests.

Preschool children are developing skills in many areas. They are beginning to:

- put puzzles together;

- paint and draw pictures they can name;

- solve problems with blocks;

- enjoy listening to stories;

- make up their own stories; and

- share their feelings and experiences.

Sometimes adults expect too much from preschool children. When they see a child successfully complete a five-piece puzzle, they put out one with twenty-five pieces. When a child can paint at the easel with one color, they think he or she can handle five colors. If you put out toys and materials that are too difficult, children are likely to fail. This lowers their self-esteem. Materials and activities must be selected with care to ensure success.

It is always a good idea to build on the skills of a particular child—to help him or her achieve success in new areas on the basis of skills he or she has already mastered. Of course, all children fail at some tasks or activities, at some point; no child does everything right the first time or even the second time. The environment should be set up to encourage experiments, so that children will want to keep trying. Their efforts should meet with success often enough that they will respond favorably to new challenges, confident that they can succeed.

In this learning activity you will think about how the children in your room develop self-esteem by using materials in the environment. Review the example and complete the blank chart that follows.

Providing an Environment That Builds Self-Esteem
(Example)

TYPICAL TOYS OR MATERIALS	WHAT CHILDREN DO	HOW THIS BUILDS THEIR SELF-ESTEEM
Pegboards and pegs	*Fill the whole board with pegs* *Put a row of each color* *Make patterns (red, yellow, red, yellow, etc.)*	*They find it an easy activity that ensures success* *They are developing fine motor skills* *They are proud of what they can do*
Playdough	*Pound it, roll it* *Make impressions in it* *Make things with it (meatballs, snakes, cookies, cake)* *Mix colors together*	*It feels good* *It is soothing to play with* *They can easily succeed with it* *They like to show others what they can make with it*
Wagon	*Pretend it is a truck* *Attach it to a trike and give a friend a ride* *Load it with toys and pull it around the play yard* *Sit in it and ask a teacher for ride*	*They can use their gross motor skills* *They can have fun with a friend* *It feels good to be strong* *They like to get some one-on-one time with a teacher*

Providing an Environment That Builds Self-Esteem

TYPICAL TOYS OR MATERIALS	WHAT CHILDREN DO	HOW THIS BUILDS THEIR SELF-ESTEEM

Discuss your chart with a colleague or your trainer.

Summarizing Your Progress

You have now completed all of the learning activities for this module. Whether you are an experienced teacher or a new one, this module has probably helped you develop new skills for building children's self-esteem.

Before you go on, take a few minutes to summarize what you've learned.

- Turn back to Learning Activity I, Using Your Knowledge of Child Development to Build Self-Esteem, and add to the chart specific examples of what you have learned about building self-esteem while you were working on this module. Read the sample responses on the completed chart at the end of this module.

- Next, review your responses to the pre-training assessment for this module. Write a summary of what you learned and list the skills you developed or improved.

_____

_____

_____

_____

_____

_____

_____

_____

_____

_____

_____

_____

_____

If there are areas you would like to know more about, you will find recommended readings listed in the orientation, which can be found in Volume I.

Your final step in this module is to complete the knowledge and competency assessments. Let your trainer know when you are ready to schedule the assessments. After you have successfully completed these assessments, you will be ready to start a new module. Congratulations on your progress so far, and good luck with your next module.

Answer Sheets

Building Self-Esteem

Developing a Positive and Supportive Relationship with Each Child

1. How did Ms. Kim build a positive and supportive relationship with Shawn?

 a. She took time to talk with him on her way to the block corner.

 b. She stated that she liked the color blue without making judgments about his work.

2. How did Ms. Kim build Shawn's self-esteem?

 a. She gave him one-to-one attention while they hung his picture.

 b. She let him know that she remembered he had used blue paint last week, too.

Helping Children Accept and Appreciate Themselves and Others

1. What feelings did Jerry have in the block corner?

 a. Pride

 b. Frustration

 c. Anger

2. How did Mr. Lopez help Jerry learn how to express his feelings in appropriate ways?

 a. He told Jerry he understood what Jerry was feeling.

 b. He helped Jerry not to hit by holding his arm.

 c. He reminded Jerry to tell Sandy how he felt.

Providing Children with Opportunities to Feel Successful and Competent

1. Why do you think Ms. Williams encouraged Mark to come back to complete the puzzle?

 a. She didn't want him to feel badly about not being able to finish something he started.

b. She wanted him to feel good about working hard to complete a task.

2. **How did Ms. Williams support Mark in feeling positive rather than negative about himself?**

a. She helped him finish the puzzle.

b. She stayed with him until it was finished.

c. She reassured him that after a few more times he could do it on his own.

Using Your Knowledge of Child Development
to Build Self-Esteem

WHAT PRESCHOOL CHILDREN ARE LIKE	HOW TEACHERS CAN USE THIS INFORMATION TO BUILD SELF-ESTEEM
They are eager to please adults.	Suggest things for children to do, play with them, and help them clean up so they know that you are pleased with what they do.
They may be afraid of loud noises, the dark, animals, or some people.	Take children's fears seriously, telling them that you will make sure that nothing bad happens to them so that they will feel that it's all right to have fears.
They can feed and dress themselves.	Let children do as much as possible for themselves because this helps them feel good about their skills. Help them only when asked or when an adult's help would calm an anxious child and lead to success.
They are usually toilet trained and can ask to go to the bathroom.	Set up a system so children can use the toilet with little supervision. If they forget to wash their hands, remind them until they remember for themselves.
They like to help in the routines of the room.	Ask children to do things they are able to do so they can feel needed and important.
They like to play make-believe and act out roles.	Provide many props and time for children to role play. Encourage them to act out their feelings about themselves, their families, and others. This kind of play helps children learn who they are.
They can take turns and share but don't always want to.	Praise children when they share with others and help them when it is difficult to share.
They use a large vocabulary to express themselves but may also stutter or use "baby talk."	Wait patiently for children to get their words out so they feel good about expressing themselves.

WHAT PRESCHOOL CHILDREN ARE LIKE	HOW TEACHERS CAN USE THIS INFORMATION TO BUILD SELF-ESTEEM
They have strong emotions.	Help children talk about how they feel and reassure them that all their feelings are all right to have.
They may express anger and jealousy physically.	Help children manage their strong feelings through outlets such as working with clay and using a punching bag. Give them words to use when they are angry.
They have lots of physical energy.	Provide many ways for children to use their bodies so they are not frustrated or forced to wait for long periods of time.
They want to make decisions for themselves.	Give children many opportunities to make choices and decisions (for example, where they want to sit for lunch).
They like to try new things and to take risks.	Allow them to attempt new things safely and praise their efforts so they will continue to try new things.
They are beginning to explore and understand what it means to be a boy or a girl.	Help children feel good about their gender. Read books that reinforce the belief that gender should not play a role in determining what a person can and cannot do.
They may have difficulty making the transition from home to school.	Remind children that their parents will come back at the end of the day. Encourage parents to bring photographs of themselves to hang in the room. When children feel sad because their parents are away, try to get them involved in a soothing activity, such as water play.

Glossary

Autonomy

Independence; the stage when children develop the ability to make choices and to have control over their own actions.

Environment

The complete makeup of a classroom, including furnishings, toys, and planned activities.

Initiative

Self-motivation; the stage when preschool children display high energy and newly acquired skills to explore their world actively.

Observation

The act of watching systematically what a child says and does to learn more about that child. The information gained from observation is used to plan activities that address the child's needs, strengths, and interests.

Self-esteem

A sense of worth; a good feeling about oneself and one's abilities. Someone with strong self-esteem feels connected to others, respected and valued, and able to do things successfully and independently.

Separation

The process children go through as they grow up and become independent from their parents. Children often have strong feelings about separating from their families, and teachers can help children understand and express these feelings.

Temperament

The nature or disposition of a child; the way a child responds to and interacts with people, materials, and situations in his or her world.

Trust

The stage when infants develop deep feelings of comfort and confidence because their basic needs are met promptly, consistently, and lovingly.

Module 9
Social

What Is Social Development and Why Is It Important?

Social development refers to the way children learn to get along with others and to enjoy the people in their lives. As children develop socially, they learn to share, cooperate, take turns, and negotiate with other children and adults. Children's social development is strengthened when they have secure relationships with their parents and teachers, when they have many opportunities to play with other children, and when they feel good about themselves. Although they may argue and fight, most children really enjoy playing with others. They learn to cooperate so that play can continue.

Social development begins when an infant responds to a familiar voice or the special touch of a parent or teacher. It continues as toddlers first enjoy playing alongside each other and as preschool children learn to play in groups. Young children spend a lot of time engaged in dramatic play. They try out different roles, practice their social skills, and learn to take turns being the cook, the firefighter, or the baby.

Teachers play an important role in promoting children's social development. Through their relationships with adults, cnildren learn what behaviors are accepted in society. As a teacher, you let children know that they are loved and accepted; you meet their needs as consistently and promptly as possible. This gives children a sense of security, which helps them feel safe as they learn how to get along with other children and adults. In addition, you provide an environment where children can spend time alone or play with others. You also help children learn to respect the rights of others, so that everyone can enjoy the benefits of being part of a group. And you help them understand their feelings and show them accepted ways to express these feelings.

Children need to move from having relationships with their parents and teachers to making friends with their peers. Part of your job is ensuring that there are plenty of opportunities for children to choose what they want to do, and who they want to play with, during their days at the center.

Promoting children's social development involves:

- helping children learn to get along with other members of the group;

- helping children understand and express their feelings and respect those of others; and

- providing an environment and experiences that help children develop social skills.

Listed on the following page are examples of how teachers demonstrate their competence in promoting children's social development.

Helping Children Learn to Get Along with Other Members of the Group

Here are some examples of what teachers can do.

- Encourage children to help each other. "Peter, if you ask him, I think Todd might help you carry the sawhorse outside."

- Include enough time for free play in the daily schedule so children can choose to play with special friends during activities. "Jane, I see you and Donna are working together at the woodworking bench."

- Model positive ways to interact with others. "Ms. Kim, I have an extra pair of gloves you can wear when we go on our walk."

- Help children find solutions to their conflicts. "You both want to play with the helicopter. How can you share it or take turns using it?"

Helping Children Understand and Express Their Feelings and Respect Those of Others

Here are some examples of what teachers can do.

- Identify some of your own feelings when appropriate. "This beautiful, sunny day makes me feel very happy."

- Accept children's feelings while helping them control their actions. "I know you're angry when John grabs the truck. You can tell him you're angry, but I can't let you hurt him."

- State what you think children are feeling when they are having trouble expressing their emotions. "I wonder if you are having a bad day because you miss your mom a lot when she goes away on a trip."

- Give children words they can use to express how they feel. "Tell Michael that you don't like it when he takes things out of your cubby."

- Read stories that help children deal with their feelings about friendship, sharing, handicaps, and other similar topics. One good book is *Alexander and the Terrible, Horrible, No-Good, Very Bad Day* by Judith Viorst. "Can you think of a time when you had a 'terrible, horrible, no-good, very bad day'?"

Providing an Environment and Experiences That Help Children Develop Social Skills

Here are some examples of what teachers can do.

- Plan activities that encourage cooperation. "The plants in our garden are very dry. Joan, Nancy, and Patty, can you please help carry water to the garden?"

- Establish and maintain classroom rules that help children learn social skills. "Derek, there's only room for four children at the easels. Would you like to do something else while you are waiting for your turn?"

- Extend children's dramatic play by joining in for a while. "Dr. Jones, thank you for fixing my broken arm. I'll see you next month when you take off the cast."

- Encourage cooperation rather than competition. "Let's help the block builders put away the blocks. Then the room will be cleaned up and we can all go outside together."

- Provide a variety of props that children can use for dramatic play. "Mr. Lopez, when you put the old muffin tin in the house corner, Jackie and Kia began playing bakery."

Promoting Children's Social Development

In the following situations, teachers are promoting the social development of preschool children. As you read each one, think about what the teachers are doing and why. Then answer the questions that follow.

Helping Children Learn to Get Along with Other Members of the Group

At free play time Ms. Frilles is sitting at a table encouraging Paula to try a more difficult puzzle than the one she usually does. While Paula picks another puzzle from the shelf, Ms. Frilles stands up and looks around the room to see what everyone else is doing. She sees Sally and Gina, two good friends, playing in the house corner. They are each waving their arms and look very angry. Ms. Frilles walks over to the house corner to listen to the argument. The children are playing restaurant and both girls want to be the waitress. Ms. Frilles says to them, "I ate in a restaurant last week. There were so many customers they needed two waitresses." Then she steps back. The girls look at each other, then Sally says, "Let's sit the dolls in the chairs. Then we can both be waitresses." Ms. Frilles said, "That's good thinking, girls. You found a way to have fun together." Ms. Frilles then goes back to see how Paula is doing on the puzzle.

1. **How did Ms. Frilles help the girls learn to get along with each other?**

_____

_____

_____

2. **How did Ms. Frilles help the girls feel good about solving their problem?**

_____

_____

_____

Helping Children Understand and Express Their Feelings and Respect Those of Others

The children in Ms. Kim's class are outside, engaged in a variety of activities. Ms. Kim is walking around the play yard to watch and listen to the children. Travis, Felipe, and Karen are working together to make roads and tunnels in the sandbox. Peter and Dean are painting at the easels, which are set up in a shady spot. Maddie and Peter are at the bottom of the ladder to the slide. Maddie begins to climb the ladder, then stops. Peter, who is next in line, tells her to "hurry up," places his hand on her back, and pushes her. Maddie turns around and pushes him back. Ms. Kim quickly walks over to the slide and talks to the children. "Maddie, I think you might be feeling a little scared about going down the slide, so you are taking your time climbing up the ladder. Peter, I think you might be feeling impatient because you want to have your turn on the slide. I can't let you push each other. You can both use your words to tell each other how you feel. Maddie, you can go first, tell Peter how you feel." Ms. Kim stays with the children while they tell each other how they feel. Maddie steps down off the ladder so Peter can have his turn while she takes a little more time to conquer her fears. As Ms. Kim walks away, she turns back and hears Peter encouraging Maddie to come down the slide, "It's really fun, Maddie. You won't hurt yourself!"

1. **How did Ms. Kim let the children know that she understood and respected their feelings?**

_____

_____

_____

2. **How did Ms. Kim help the children express their feelings?**

_____

_____

_____

Providing an Environment and Experiences That Help Children Develop Social Skills

The children are getting ready to go outside. "Where's your other shoe?" Mr. Lopez asks Becky. "I lost my shoe," she says. "I've looked everywhere." Jerry and Sally, jackets on, ready to go out, are standing by the door. "We have to find Becky's shoe before we go outside," Mr. Lopez explains. "Jerry and Sally, will you two help Becky find her shoe? Then we can all get outside faster." They agree and begin searching. "Here it is," they call. "It was under the pillows." Jerry holds the shoe up proudly and hands it to Mr. Lopez, who gives it to Becky so she can put it on. "Thank you both for helping," he says. "Who would like to help carry this big bag of balls? Now, if we all work together we can carry it outside." The three children help Mr. Lopez lift the bag. "We are all ready now," he announces. "I like it when we work together to help each other."

1. **How did Mr. Lopez turn the daily routine of getting ready to go outside into an experience that helped the children develop social skills?**

_____

_____

_____

2. What social skills did the children learn as they prepared to go outside?

_____

_____

_____

Compare your answers with those on the answer sheet at the end of this module. If your answers are different, discuss them with your trainer. There can be more than one good answer.

Your Own Social Development

Adults use social skills every day. When you yield to another car in traffic, share your lunch with a colleague who forgot hers, or wait for your turn to offer your opinion at a staff meeting, you are using the social skills you learned as a child and will continue to use throughout your life.

Sometimes you find yourself in situations where you need to use your social skills to adapt to a new group of people. Perhaps you just joined a choir or started a new exercise class. In both of these situations you use social skills to get to know the other group members and to adjust to the group's accepted ways of doing things.

Some adults find it very difficult to adjust to new situations. Although this difficulty may stem from their personalities, perhaps these adults never really learned, when they were children, how to get to know new people.

Young children learn about how society expects them to behave by watching adults interact with each other as well as with children. Therefore, it is very important that children see their teachers working cooperatively, sharing feelings and ideas, having friendly conversations, and enjoying each other's company. Sometimes teachers are so busy that it's hard for them to find time to be "friends"—but when teachers model social behaviors for children, everyone benefits. The teachers can feel positive about their jobs and the people they work with, and the children can gain a more complete picture of their teachers. They see adults working out problems, sharing happy experiences, and cooperating throughout the day.

Think about how you and your colleagues model social skills. Give some examples below.

Sharing:

_____

_____

_____

Cooperating:

_____

_____

_____

Taking turns:

_____

_____

_____

Solving problems:

_____

_____

_____

Helping:

_____

_____

_____

Appreciating each other:

_____

_____

_____

Showing concern:

_____

_____

_____

Social development is an ongoing process. As adults, we continue to learn about ourselves and ways of relating to others. Your social skills help you enjoy working as part of a team that provides a valuable service to children and families. These are skills that you refine each day, on the job and elsewhere.

When you finish this overview section, you should complete the pre-training assessment. Refer to the glossary at the end of this module if you need definitions for the terms that are used.

Pre-Training Assessment

Listed below are the skills that teachers use to promote the social development of preschool children. Think about whether you do these things regularly, sometimes, or not enough. Place a check in one of the columns on the right for each skill listed. Then discuss your answers with your trainer.

SKILL	I DO THIS REGULARLY	I DO THIS SOMETIMES	I DON'T DO THIS ENOUGH
HELPING CHILDREN LEARN TO GET ALONG WITH OTHER MEMBERS OF THE GROUP 1. Observing and listening to children's conversations to learn how each child relates to others.			
2. Suggesting roles for children to play so they can be involved with their peers.			
3. Encouraging children to help each other.			
4. Including enough time for free play in the daily schedule so children can decide with whom they want to play.			
5. Encouraging children to solve their own conflicts.			
HELPING CHILDREN UNDERSTAND AND EXPRESS THEIR FEELINGS AND RESPECT THOSE OF OTHERS 6. Reminding children to use words to let others know how they feel.			
7. Providing a variety of dramatic play props so children can work through their fears and other feelings.			

SKILL	I DO THIS REGULARLY	I DO THIS SOMETIMES	I DON'T DO THIS ENOUGH
8. Providing opportunities for children to make rules and set limits.			
9. Identifying your own feelings when appropriate so children can learn about expressing feelings.			
10. Verbally expressing children's feelings for them when they are not able to use words to express their feelings.			
PROVIDING AN ENVIRONMENT AND EXPERIENCES THAT HELP CHILDREN DEVELOP SOCIAL SKILLS 11. Providing duplicates of favorite toys so children don't feel too much pressure to share.			
12. Giving children a concrete way to know when it will be their turn to do something—for example, by using a timer or a clock.			
13. Providing duplicates of certain dramatic play props, such as firefighters' hats, to encourage group play.			
14. Planning special group projects, such as painting a mural, which children can work on together.			
15. Creating prop boxes with materials related to an experience the children have shared, such as a field trip or a nature walk.			

SOCIAL

Review your responses, then list three to five skills you would like to improve or topics you would like to learn more about. When you finish this module you will list examples of your new or improved knowledge and skills.

_____

_____

_____

_____

_____

_____

_____

_____

_____

_____

Now begin the learning activities for Module 9, Social.

I. Using Your Knowledge of Child Development to Promote Social Development

In this activity you will learn:

- to recognize some typical behaviors of preschool children; and

- to use what you know about preschool children to promote their social development.

Young infants are entirely dependent on the adults who care for them. Through their interactions with the adults who diaper, feed, comfort, and talk to them, infants learn to trust their caregivers. This trust is the beginning of the child's social development.

Children begin learning how to play very early in life. Adults help infants learn by rolling a ball back and forth, playing peek-a-boo, or holding a rattle where a baby can reach for it. By the time they are toddlers, children are becoming experts at play. Play allows toddlers to work out problems, make choices, find out what they like to do, and begin making contacts with other children.

By the time children are preschoolers, they have learned a lot about accepted behaviors. Most are eager to imitate how adults get along with each other. Most enjoy being with other people.

Preschool children spend a lot of time playing with their peers. They learn from each other and imitate what they see each other do. As preschool children develop socially, they become less dependent on adults. They usually want to spend time with children their own age.

Most young children enjoy pretending to be someone else. The house corner provides a setting and props that help children take on other roles. By pretending to be a mother, a baby, a television character, or a firefighter, children are trying to make sense of their world. These dramatic play opportunities also help children develop social skills. To play with others, they must take turns, negotiate, share, and cooperate.

The chart on the next page lists some typical behaviors of preschool children. Included are behaviors relevant to social development. The right column asks you to identify ways that teachers can use this information about child development to promote social development. Try to think of as many examples as you can. As you work through the module you will learn new strategies for promoting social development, and you can add them to the child development chart. You are not expected to think of all the examples at one time. If you need help getting started, turn to the completed chart at the end of this module. By the time you complete all the learning activities, you will find that you have learned many ways to promote social development.

Using Your Knowledge of Child Development
to Promote Social Development

WHAT PRESCHOOL CHILDREN ARE LIKE	HOW TEACHERS CAN USE THIS INFORMATION TO PROMOTE SOCIAL DEVELOPMENT
They can understand some rules and limits.	
They are learning to share and take turns.	
They like to imitate adult activities.	
They carry on conversations with other children, in pairs or in groups.	
They may exclude other children from their play.	
They are moving from parallel to cooperative play.	
They continue to need opportunities for solitary play.	

WHAT PRESCHOOL CHILDREN ARE LIKE	HOW TEACHERS CAN USE THIS INFORMATION TO PROMOTE SOCIAL DEVELOPMENT
They ask a lot of questions.	
They begin to develop friendships.	
They can learn to adapt to a variety of different settings and enjoy visiting new places.	
They are gaining an awareness of the larger community.	
They want adults to like them.	

When you have completed as much as you can do on the chart, discuss your answers with your trainer. As you proceed with the rest of the learning activities, you can refer back to the chart and add examples of how teachers can promote social development.

II. Promoting Children's Play

In this activity you will learn:

- to observe how preschool children learn and develop through play; and

- to provide guidance as children play in order to promote their social development.

Young children spend a good deal of their time playing. Through play, children have fun, try new things, make friends, pretend, and learn about the world. Play is a child's work. It helps children grow in all areas. Through play, children develop physically, learn how to think and solve problems, find ways to express themselves in acceptable ways, and develop self-esteem. Play is also one of the most important ways in which children develop social skills. They learn to take turns, share favorite things, understand how a friend feels, and express their feelings. In addition, play helps children try out grown-up roles and overcome their fears.

Children begin playing when they are infants. An infant may discover his or her toes and find that playing with them is a lot of fun. Or a teacher may play with an infant, rolling a ball back and forth. Older infants are keen observers and enjoy imitating adults and pretending. By the time a child is about 18 months old, he or she has learned to pretend in more complex ways. A toddler may take a doll and pretend to feed it or put it to bed, just like a real baby.

Toddlers spend a lot of time doing the same things over and over again. This is how they learn to master a skill. A toddler may play alone with toys that are different from those used by others in the group. Although other children may be nearby, a toddler may not talk to them or move toward them. This kind of play is called solitary play. As children get older, they begin playing alongside each other using the same kinds of toys. This is called parallel play. It may involve some talking between toddlers. Two children sitting at opposite ends of a sand box, both using shovels, and chatting with one another, are involved in parallel play. They are enjoying each other's company but are not yet ready to dig a hole in the sand together.

How Preschool Children Play in Groups

Most preschool children play in groups cooperatively. The children organize their own play, assign roles, make up rules, give out specific tasks, and often work toward a common goal. For example, a group of children may decide to build a town in the block corner. Through discussion and negotiation, they decide who will build roads, who will build houses, and who will build big buildings. They resolve any conflicts that come up by finding a compromise that everyone agrees on. The result, a complete town and the process of working on it together, is more rewarding for the children than building independently. Children at this level of play really enjoy working and playing together. Liking to be with other people is an important part of their social development.

Dramatic Play of Preschool Children

Preschool children enjoy dramatic play, when they pretend to be real or make-believe characters and make up stories and situations to act out. Dramatic play occurs in many areas of the environment: out on the playground, in the house corner, in the block corner, at the woodworking bench, or on the bus on the way to a field trip. Through dramatic play, children develop and practice social skills. They learn to share, listen to each other, take turns, compromise, and see somebody else's point of view. They can learn to control how they express their own feelings and emotions. They can try out being mean and nasty because it doesn't really count; it's only pretend. They can also overcome fears, such as the fear of going to the dentist or doctor or of moving to a new house.

What children do during dramatic play differs according to their age and stage of development. When three-year-olds become characters, they may not really understand that they are consciously deciding to pretend. They may spend a lot of time expressing fear, running away from monsters or another child who is pretending to be a scary creature. At this age children do a lot of collecting and gathering, packing suitcases, filling purses, planning trips. Sometimes the planning is all that they have time for.

Four-year-olds may also run away from scary monsters or ghosts. They often create a safe place to hide out where the monster can't get them. They run and jump a lot, enjoy dress-up clothes and other props, and develop more roles than they did when they were younger. Now they can tell the difference between fantasy and reality. They understand that they have *decided* to pretend to be someone or do something.

The dramatic play of five-year-old children is more involved. They develop complex sets of characters and situations and may pretend to be real people or fantasy figures from stories or television. Children this age may use dramatic play to practice doing something they are afraid of, such as getting a shot at the doctor or going on an airplane trip. They also may use dramatic play to work through anxieties about situations in their lives, such as a new baby at home or a parent about to go on a business trip.

Dramatic play is an important way for preschool children to learn how to get along with their peers. Playing with each other, they share information, offer suggestions, and sometimes tell each other how to behave. Children who are naturally shy may find that it is easier to be a part of a group when they can pretend to be someone else. The social skills developed through dramatic play are used in almost all the other situations a child encounters. The child who learns to follow the rules established by the group will be able to use this skill when he or she gets older and plays organized games that involve rules.

How Teachers Can Help Preschool Children Play

Teachers play an important role in helping preschool children play. They observe closely and then gently and indirectly guide children. By observing, you can see which children get along with one another and what problems or anxieties different children are experiencing. You then can use this kind of information to plan for children's individual needs. Observation also lets you know what is going on in the play situation and when your guidance is needed. You can provide a suitable prop that may help a child get involved in the play. "Kia, here is some money to give the storekeeper. I think he has run out of change." When it's almost time for lunch and the play can't go on any longer, you can use reminders within the context of the play setting. "The baby needs to finish her bottle now so Daddy can have his lunch."

Here are some other ways in which teachers can provide guidance.

- Let the children know that you think their play is important by providing, in an organized environment, enough time, space, and materials for the play.

- Refer to children in their role names. "Doctor, could you move your patient over here? Your examining table is in the way of the construction crew."

- Help children think about something they did in the past. "Do you remember last week when you went on the trip to the beach? You all had a lot of fun."

- Model playful behaviors yourself. "I could smell your bread baking from way over by the easels."

- Help children get started playing, but learn when to step back. "I really enjoyed my dinner, but I have to run to get my bus."

- When you do have to interrupt to remind children about a rule, try to offer guidance within the context of the play. "I think this grocery store can only hold four customers. Susan, can you and Tony take a walk around the block until these customers are finished with their shopping?"

- Reinforce positive social behaviors when you observe them. "I liked the way the two campers took turns wearing the backpack."

The following two articles, "Make-Believe Play: Why Bother?" and "Teaching Play Techniques," provide more information on how teachers can promote children's play.

Make-Believe Play: Why Bother?[1]

Marc has an old towel pinned around his shoulders. He and his friend Rachel crouch near the sand pile where they are stirring mud and gravel with a stick.

Marc says, "Goosh it up. Way up. Now add more soup."

"Pretend this water is soup," he whispers to Rachel.

"These are for the carrots and pepper and salt," Rachel trickles a handful of gravel into the goosh.

Three other children go by on trikes.

"Pretend they're robbers coming to take our soup."

"No, just kids."

"Robbers."

"I don't want robbers."

"Yes, robbers."

"NO!"

"Kid-robbers?"

"Okay."

It is easy to believe that when children play running and climbing games, they practice basic physical skills. If Rachel and Marc were playing with containers and liquids at a water table, we might claim they

---

[1]Reprinted with permission from Dennie Palmer Wolf, "Make-Believe Play: Why Bother?" *Beginnings* (Redmond, WA: Exchange Press, Inc., Spring 1984), pp. 4-6.

were learning simple science. But over-hearing them talk about soup and rob-bers, when they are stirring sand near some other children, prompts lots of adults to ask, "If they are only pretend-ing, what can they be getting out of it?"

So What Are They Learning?

Since the turn of the century, parents, teachers and researchers have recog-nized the emotional importance of pre-tending. By watching children, we have seen that make-believe offers children enjoyment, a *vacation* from real life issues, a chance to try out different feel-ings and roles. Without contradicting those old ideas, researchers are now suggesting that when children pretend, they may be practicing an even wider range of basic skills.

Invention: As they play Rachel and Marc invent new ways of seeing gravel and water. That kind of insight is impor-tant in everyday life: without it, no one would ever have come up with using a coat hanger to rescue keys locked inside a car door, substitutions in reci-pes, or ways to drive around traffic jams. In adults that kind of flexibility in thinking is behind both common sense solutions to practical problems and even new ideas in science or technology.

Jeffrey Dansky, conducting both class-room and laboratory research, suggests that children who are good *inventors* in play, are likely to be flexible thinkers in general. Possibly then, sandboxes and playhouses may provide situations in which to encourage flexible think-ing. In place of the standard boxes and cans, you might stock the shelves of the classroom store with a few blocks or objects made from wood scraps by chil-dren. If children are puzzled, challenge them to see what they can turn these novel items into.

Imagining "what if ...": Marc and Rachel have *skipped out* of the sand-box. For the moment they are some-where quite different—in some cave or witch's kitchen. When children leave the *here and now*, they are exploring the idea of "what if" things were not the way they are. This ability to think—"what if things were different?"—is an important skill. Without it, none of us would be able to think (imagine) what it would be like in some other time, place, or in someone else's shoes.

As young as two, children begin to play "what if ..." Work by Jackie Sachs at the University of Connecticut and Christine Chaille at the University of Oregon has shown that children can grow increasingly skilled at pretending they are someone or somewhere else. This raises the question of what might be done to encourage these skills. A key strategy is to let children know you value their "what if ..." play. For instance:

—Talk to or compliment children about an episode of make-believe play that you observed. Don't interrupt the play, but mention what you saw and liked over snack or while you are help-ing them get ready to go outside.

—As you pass by children who are mak-ing-believe, offer a comment or an object that extends their play. Passing by Marc and Rachel you might say, "Hmmm, I smell soup cooking." Or, you might hand them a pine cone, peb-ble, or whatever, and say something as simple as, "Here are some spices for your cooking."

Independence: The two children making *soup* have taken responsibility for structuring their time, choosing their materials, and making up the rules of their game. Rather than depending on a schedule or the already-fixed rules of a game, this pair manages to plan and choose for themselves. In order for chil-dren to take charge and practice their planning skills, they need uninter-rupted play time (at least on occasion). This means allowing play to spin out, even if it conflicts with another activity. It also means protecting a good play session from intrusions. Play materials should not be ones for which there is hot competition. There should be shel-tered areas where small groups of chil-dren can play uninterrupted. Re-searchers like A.F. Gramza have found that large crates or cardboard barrels provide just the kind of privacy that children enjoy when they are pre-tending.

Language-development: Someday, not too far off, Rachel and Marc will be faced with learning to read and write. Researchers at The Early Symbolization Project, at the Harvard Graduate School of Education, point out that in this kind of play children put sentences together in a way that is similar to the way that the sentences in books build on each other. For as long as they con-tinue to make soup, Rachel and Marc are practicing two basic skills they will need in reading and writing: 1) relating new ideas to a topic and 2) telling events in order.

As an adult, you can help children sus-tain and organize their play episodes in several ways:

—Make boxes which contain props for different kinds of episodes. A trip box might include hats, scarves, purses, keys, tickets and a picture of a car or train to remind children they can incor-porate trikes or wagons into their trip. A birthday box might contain bowls, spoons, candles, boxes wrapped (or painted) to look like presents. Label these boxes with pictures which sug-gest an episode. Occasionally add new items to the boxes or change the boxes.

—If you have to interrupt the play for any reason (putting away items, helping another child to join in, etc.), try not to break into the play. If children are play-ing bakery, and you have to replace some blocks nearby, you might say, "Just delivering the bread for today."

What If Play Turns "Bad"?

Both Catherine Garvey of the Univer-sity of Maine and Ned Mueller at Boston University point out that sharing, turn-taking, listening, and negotiation are all a part of pretend play among children. Group pretending is not always smooth—Rachel and Marc argue and they may even fight about what can happen. But because their play interests them, children will confront each other, argue, and politic to keep it going. Throughout this process, chil-dren work hard at understanding other people and the social situation.

It is not *bad* if children argue or even if the play falls apart. Arguments can lead to figuring out a solution (like *kid-rob-bers*). When trouble occurs don't leap to intervene. Leave children the chance to think through the situation. Instead, keep your eyes and ears open for situa-tions that repeatedly lead to trouble. When those situations arise, offer chil-dren strategies before trouble brews. If superhero play always leads to someone crying, you might tell Batman and Robin to try saving someone rather than capturing people. Or you might see that the child who is often picked to be the victim is safely involved in another activity.

In fact, a number of educators, researchers, and clinicians point out that play isn't all wonderful. The stakes are high in play—children fight over who gets to be the Mother or the only Batman. Less popular children can be cruelly excluded—because they *talk funny* or their noses run. Children push and shove because they all want the biggest bicycle in order to turn it into the fastest car or rocketship. When they play Masters of the Universe, it's a boy's game, no girls allowed.

But precisely because children care so intensely about their make-believe, these activities provide a kind of theatre for noticing problems and issues. The writings of Rosalind Gould, George Scarlett, Marilyn Segal and Charles Wolfgang all suggest that classroom observations of play provide some of the clearest insights into individual children's skills and problems. Passive or isolated children hover around the edges of play, not brave or skilled enough to ask for a role. Aggressive children butt into episodes they were not a part of planning, mow down the scenes set up by other children, and end up more feared and likely to be left out than ever.

However, these same authors also point out that play provides one of the best situations for working on or *healing* problems. Scarlett suggests that teachers spend time as co-players with isolated or aggressive children. As a co-player an adult establishes a trusting, intimate relationship in which she follows and supports the child's play ideas. In this one-to-one setting, the adult shows the child how capable she is of being an equal (rather than weaker or meaner) player. Segal points out that certain props, settings, and groups of children can also be used to make play a problem-solving medium. For example, substitute wagons for bicycles—the wagons insist on cooperative play. Or ask a socially skilled child to work with an isolated child in setting up the housekeeping corner in a new way.

Do Adults Belong in Children's Play?

If play is so valuable, should we make certain that all children pretend for a half-hour every day, just as we schedule reading time or large-scale physical activity? Probably not. Play is a powerful context for learning because children go to it spontaneously. Because they are interested and motivated, Rachel and Marc get around what might, under ordinary circumstances, be obstacles: the fact that they have no real soup or that they can't agree about whether robbers belong in the play. Also, play teaches precisely because it is *unscheduled* and full of surprises. Because Rachel and Marc were *just pretending* (not doing a group activity in pretending) they had the freedom to ignore or notice the children on trikes.

Finally, play is an excellent example of what might be called the *natural exercise* of skills. In play, there are no outside cues telling Marc and Rachel, "Now use your imagination—work on your social understanding ... " Instead, the children recognize for themselves when to reach for and apply different skills. As they continue their soup and robbers play, Marc and Rachel move back and forth between stretching their imaginations and buckling down to solve some very real social problems.

Does this mean teachers should retire to the sidelines? Hardly. If we look again at Marc and Rachel, it is easy to see the enormous contribution that thoughtful adults can make to children's play.

One of the trike-riding children (Nina) gets off and comes over to Marc and Rachel, leans down, and starts stirring in the soup with a stick of her own. "Where'd you get this mud?"

Rachel says, "It's our soup."

"I wanna play with it," Nina complains.

"We made it, it's ours." says Marc.

Nina bits at the mud with her stick.

"Don't!" Rachel and Marc shout. Rachel pushes Nina away.

A teacher, who has been observing out

of the corner of her eye, comes over.

"Nina, they are already making soup. Why don't you make the cake?"

Nina bangs back, kicking at the soup with the toe of her sneaker.

The teacher squats down and starts digging a hole. "Well, here's the oven."

She notices the other two trike-riders watching. "Why don't you park your bikes where other kids can have a turn?" She talks to one of them: "If you can find a jump rope, you could make a phone between the two kitchens." She turns to the second child, "Let's go find some good sticks so you can cook, too."

What's in Play for Adults?

The following quote, from John Holt's book **Freedom and Beyond** was sent to **Beginnings** by Patricia Clark, Director of Westmoreland Children's Center. What Holt suggests is that playing is as important for parents and teachers as it is for children. He raises the question of what we might do for our own spirits and knowledge if we engaged in, rather than supervised, play.

... what makes our truly inventive and creative thinkers whether political, artistic, or scientific, what sets them apart from the great run of us, is above all that they can still play with their minds. They have not forgotten how to do it nor grown ashamed nor afraid of it. They like it and do it every chance they have; it is as natural to them as breathing. The ordinary, "serious," nonplayful man cannot escape things as they are: though he is always talking about "facing reality," he is as trapped by his notion of reality as any rat in a cage. For him, whatever is, is all there can be. The playful man is always saying, and cannot help saying, "But suppose things weren't this way. Let's just for the moment imagine what would happen if this were different. Just for the fun of it." Now we know from experience that out of such play may come, and often does come, ideas that may change the whole shape of human life and thought.

Teaching Play Techniques

Teachers can take on roles and participate in the children's dramatic play through this role. Plan to be in the house corner for a while and have someone else handle the rest of the room. A teacher might sit at the house corner kitchen table chatting with the children as they come and go or pretending to talk on the telephone. This can be a very effective technique for involving children and for verbalizing what the children are doing, and it can serve as an excuse to go on sitting there and yet be somewhat removed from the action. The teacher can continually pick up on what each child is doing, to give the child information, to include the child more deeply in a play theme, or to help the child with ideas about what to do next. Here are some examples.

- To a boy holding a toy coffee pot, the teacher could say,

     "Please put the coffee on the stove to get hot. I don't want any cold coffee."

  This involves the child in the play theme, tells him that the stove is for heating food and that coffee is served hot, and suggests an action for him.

- When a boy starts to leave the house corner, the teacher might say,

     "Where's David going?"

  This may stop the child from just wandering away. It would make him feel included again. The child might respond: "I'm going to the store." Picking up on this, the teacher could give David a few ideas.

     "David, have you got your money?"

     "Hey, bring me some milk, will you?"

  The child is thus free to go but also has a good reason for coming back.

- Pretending to talk to a friend on the phone can be a very useful technique. The teacher can explain what the children are doing.

     "Yes, we're pretty busy here. Raymond is cooking. Hey, Raymond, Minnie wants to know what you are cooking."

  At the beginning of this level of play, the child's actions at the stove may not have been purposeful. By verbalizing, the teacher helps the child to focus on what he is doing and makes him think in order to answer her question.

- Teachers can encourage children to use props to make them a part of the play episode. For example, to a girl holding a doll, the teacher might say,

     "Oh, is your baby sick?"

     "Did you call the doctor? Here, let's get the doctor on the phone."

  In this way the child is involved in the role of parent and in a play episode.

- If the teacher always treats the dolls as if they are babies, she can teach children how real babies must be handled.

  "Take the baby off the table. He might fall and hurt himself."

  "Be careful feeding the baby. Be sure she doesn't choke."

  "Would you put the baby to bed? Be sure to put the blanket on so she won't catch cold."

  By assuming that the children aren't just children holding dolls but are role-playing parents with babies, the teacher is helping the children get into socio-dramatic roles.

In this learning activity, you will observe the dramatic play of a group of children in your room for at least a half-hour during free play or during an outdoor play period. Write a short description of the dramatic play that occurs: what children and make-believe characters were involved, the setting, and what activities took place. Also record examples of what social skills children were developing or using during their play. Then, after reviewing your notes, develop a plan for what you can do to extend the children's play. This might include a way to involve a child who was excluded, props you can add, or words you can use to comment on the play. Finally, implement your plan and record what happens.

Begin by reading the example that follows. It is a shortened version of a complete half-hour observation. Then complete your own observations using the blank forms provided.

Promoting Children's Play
(Example)

Setting: _House Corner_   **Children:** _Tanya, George, Danny, and Carrie_

Dramatic Play Theme: _Camping out_

Props used:

Tent (made out of sheets), two flashlights, one backpack, thermos and cooler, plastic plates and utensils, three sleeping bags, tablecloth, books about the outdoors.

What happened:

Tanya and George were already in the house corner when Danny joined them. They decided to play camping out. George said he would be the daddy and Tanya should be the mommy. Tanya said that was okay. Danny said he wanted to be the daddy. George told him he could be the daddy's best friend, and he could have a flashlight to use. Danny agreed. George put on the backpack. Danny picked up the thermos and cooler. Tanya got a bag from the dress-up clothes rack and filled it with the plates, utensils, and tablecloth. When they were all packed Carrie joined them. Tanya said Carrie could be the other mother. George said there could only be one mother. Tanya repeated that Carrie could be the other mother. Danny said she could be his wife. That was okay with George. Danny gave Carrie the thermos to carry. George lined everyone up and they walked around the room and back to the tent. Then George said they should go to sleep. He and Danny put the three sleeping bags in the tent. They all wanted to lie down right away. The girls got in first, then Danny. There wasn't a sleeping bag for George. Tanya said she was hot so George could have hers. She came out of the tent. Carrie came out too. The two girls decided to set up a picnic. They spread out the tablecloth on the floor.

Social skills used or being developed:

There was a lot of give and take as they worked out who would play which role.

Danny shared the thermos with Carrie so she would have something to carry.

Danny acted as a negotiator, suggesting a role for Carrie.

Tanya gave her sleeping bag to George.

They all shared the props.

The girls figured out a way to play so they wouldn't have to do only what George told them to do.

Ways to extend the play:

The children didn't use the books about the outdoors. I could say to them, "I saw a lot of interesting plants out in the woods. I wonder if there are pictures of those plants in these books?"

I could add some more props so the children could have a pretend fire to cook their food on. I will add some logs and some pots and pans.

There really isn't room for another sleeping bag. I can comment on how they worked out their problem. "That was good thinking to take turns sleeping in the tent. That way it doesn't get so hot."

I can read a story about sleeping out of doors. <u>Three Days on a River in a Red Canoe</u> by Vera Williams would be good, or <u>Sleep Out</u> by Carol Currick.

What happened?

The children still aren't interested in the books. I will put the books in the reading corner and use them when we go on a walk.

They used all the cooking props I added. All the children enjoyed them.

They continued to take turns in the tent.

I read the stories. The next day I saw Tanya and Danny pretending to go canoeing in the wagon.

Promoting Children's Play

Setting: _____ Children: _____

Dramatic Play Theme: _____

Props used:

_____

_____

_____

_____

What happened:

_____

_____

_____

_____

_____

_____

_____

_____

_____

_____

_____

_____

Social skills used or being developed:

_____

_____

_____

_____

_____

_____

_____

_____

_____

_____

Now review your observation notes and write some ways you can extend the children's play. Implement your plans and record what happens.

Ways to extend the play:

_____

_____

_____

_____

_____

_____

_____

_____

_____

What happened?

_____

_____

_____

_____

_____

_____

_____

_____

_____

_____

_____

_____

_____

_____

_____

Discuss this activity with your trainer.

III. Creating an Environment That Supports Children's Social Development

In this activity you will learn:

- to set up the environment so that preschool children are comfortable being in a group all day; and

- to plan the environment so that children are encouraged to play with others.

Setting Up the Environment to Make Group Living Comfortable

Depending on how it has been set up, the physical environment of the center can make it easy or hard for preschool children to be part of a group all day. It is important for you, as a teacher, to arrange furniture and display materials in your room in ways that make children feel comfortable interacting. By doing so, you are promoting their social development.

Preschool children in a child development program have to learn to adjust to group living. No matter how homelike the environment, the center is *not* home. A preschool child who comes to your center may have a number of concerns.

- Do I belong here?

- Will the things I make and the things I bring to the center be protected?

- Do I have to share the things I want to play with?

- How will I know when it's my turn?

- How will I know what to do?

- Will I have friends?

If you have completed Module 3, Creating an Environment for Learning, you will probably remember several ways that teachers can arrange the environment to help preschool children with these concerns.

- Provide a cubby for each child, a dishpan to hold belongings, and a place to display artwork.

- Provide duplicates of materials whenever possible so the demands on preschool children to share are not too great.

- Give preschool children a concrete way to know when their turn will come—a sign-up sheet, a clock, or a timer with a bell.

- Display materials neatly on low shelves and put materials together that are used together.

142

- Set some toys out on tables to encourage reluctant children to sit down and use them.

- Offer occasional special projects or activities that may stir the interest of a passive child, such as mural painting or garden planting. Such projects give children a chance to switch roles or change their usual behaviors.

The physical environment can also be organized to offer preschool children a variety of social choices. Sometimes children want to be alone. They need "time out" from group living. You can plan the environment to support this need by providing:

- earphones in the listening area connected to a tape recorder or record player;

- small enclosed spaces—a platform or "lookout" loft, a large cardboard box, a small defined area with pillows; or

- a small table and chair for one child.

Sometimes children want to play with just one or two other children. They need spaces that can contain a limited number of people. When shelves are used as dividers, the room can be organized to create spaces for a few children. Outdoors, a large tire swing can hold two children. Large hollow blocks and planks are ideal for preschoolers who wish to build their own spaces. A tractor-tire sandbox is a cozy place for a small group.

The environment can also be organized to help children who find it hard to enter a group. If you create "lookouts" and "bridges" in your room, you can encourage children to observe and then take part in a small group activity.

Some preschool rooms are arranged so that the art area isn't far from the dramatic play area. Quiet children who enjoy drawing or painting in the art area can observe the noisier, more social play in the dramatic play area and learn about how that play occurs. When they feel comfortable, they will join in, too. Low walls between areas are good "bridges" that help children observe the interaction around them.

Take a few minutes to look around the environment of your classroom and answer the following questions:

What spaces do you have for children who want to be alone?

_____

_____

_____

_____

_____

_____

What "bridges," "lookouts," or other special spaces have you set up?

_____

_____

_____

_____

All children sometimes need to step away from the group and spend time in a place that allows them to be onlookers. In addition to the places you identified above, what other changes can you make in your room to meet this need?

_____

_____

_____

_____

Planning the Environment to Encourage Children to Play with Others

There are many ways in which the physical environment can encourage children to play with others. The play materials themselves can invite social interaction. Some materials, such as sand, water, playdough, and finger paint, are inviting and soothing. Preschoolers are drawn to them and feel relaxed when they play with these materials. As they play, they are likely to begin to share and talk to each other. When additional props are added, preschool children often begin to pretend and make up play episodes with each other. Adding rolling pins, cookie cutters, plastic knives, and cups and saucers to the playdough table can lead to lots of dramatic play about cooking, baking, and serving.

Small group projects also draw children into cooperative play. The group might even plan such a project together, collect the materials needed, and then carry out the project. Examples of special projects include:

- a cooking experience;
- painting a group mural of something the children have experienced;
- planting and caring for a garden; and
- planning a party.

Pretend play often occurs spontaneously. For example, two children playing side by side at the water table may begin pouring "coffee" into cups and serving each other. Pretend play can also be more organized and planned. Children playing in the house corner may decide to take a plane trip. They talk about who will play which roles and what will happen. Then they act out what they have imagined. They have to cooperate to achieve a shared goal.

Dramatic play tends to take place most often in the house corner, where the scene is set and ready to go. It also occurs in the block area and outdoors, where it's likely to be active. Young children need time to explore with blocks before they can create a setting for dramatic play. Props such as wooden and rubber animals, people, and cars encourage children to use blocks to create settings for dramatic play.

The more interesting and varied the environment, the more children will be drawn into play. If they see the same things day after day, preschool children will be bored and lose interest. But if the environment changes regularly, they will be eager to try out new ideas. Changes to an area, such as the house corner, can be quite small and still make a difference.

Encouraging Play through the Use of Prop Boxes

Children's social development is further encouraged when the materials that teachers put out encourage them to play different roles. Children's interests should be considered in selecting materials. Because you know that young children still are very tied to home, you provide props that encourage them to play family roles. As they get older and more experienced in play, you will want to expand their interests. The props you put out may relate to an experience the group has shared, such as a field trip to a bakery, the shipyard, or a construction site. After the trip, help preschoolers recall what they have seen and use the props to recreate their experiences. Props may also relate to something important that has happened in the children's lives—a child in the class going to the hospital, or a fire in the neighborhood that the children witnessed.

One way to be prepared to extend play through the use of new props is to start creating prop boxes. Any sturdy box will do for storage of the props. Decide on the theme—for example, a hospital prop box or one for a shoe store. Think of what children would need to engage in dramatic play around those themes. Then collect the materials you will need. These should be stored in the prop box until you are ready to bring them out.

In this learning activity you will create a prop box that would be interesting to the children in your room. In the following reading, you will learn many ideas for creating prop boxes. Your imagination, what you know about the community, and what you know about the children's interests will help you think of other ideas. Use the space on the chart to list the items you collect.

Dramatic Play Kits or Prop Boxes[2]

The suggestions listed below are possibilities for the contents of dramatic play kits or prop boxes. You may want to use a few or many of the suggested items. Some of the suggestions below are situations that can be set up by gathering together materials that may be around the room in different places rather than stored in a specific box. Add your own ideas to this list.

Related books and pictures should be used with these collections. You can introduce just a few items or a set at a time and add others as needed. You may want to set items out and wait for circle time, and then make them available for the children's use. The amount of time a specific set of props is left out for the children's play will depend upon their interest. It may vary from a few days to several weeks. Props relating to experiences that are familiar to children are usually the most beneficial. A variety of props should be presented over a period of time so that the interests of all children are included.

Open-Ended Props

Have on hand a collection of props that can be used in many interest centers and can be used by the children in their dramatic play in a number of ways. Examples include swatches of fabric, shells, stones, string, wire, cardboard cylinders, colored cubes, brown paper bags, staplers, tape, construction paper, magic markers, pipe cleaners, and paper plates.

Dress-Ups

Shoes, big boots, handbags, coats, sweaters, capes, dresses, lingerie, skirts, shirts, aprons, scarves, helmets or hats (nurse, firefighter, police officer, cowboy, astronaut, construction worker, fancy and frilly, washable sun and rain hats), wigs, neckties, raincoats, umbrellas, galoshes, old graduation gowns, wedding clothes, fake fur pieces, jewelry, watches, sunglasses, eyeglass frames.

Baby Things

Diaper bag, diapers of suitable size, baby clothes, baby blanket, empty baby powder containers, baby bathtub or basin, cotton balls, Q-tips, towels, baby food, spoons, bottles, rattles.

Cooking/Bakery

Pots, pans, muffin tins, pie tins, rolling pins, cake pans, mixing bowls, cookie sheets, spatula, eggbeaters, spoons, pitchers, salt and flour shakers, medicine bottles with colored water, tablecloths, aprons, hats, flour, salt, and water for making playdough, ingredients for actual cooking.

---

[2]Cheryl Foster, "Dramatic Play Kits or Prop Boxes," in *Competency-Based Training Module No. 24: Dramatic Play* (Suppl. No. 5) (Coolidge, AZ: Institute of Human Development, Central Arizona College, 1982), pp. 41-46. Reprinted with permission from the CDA Training Program at the Institute.

Cleaning/Laundry

Small brooms, mops, dust cloths, feather dusters, cake of soap, sponges, towels, plastic spray bottle, plastic basin, clothesline, clothespins, doll clothes to wash, laundry machines made from cardboard boxes, aprons, clothes basket.

Vehicles

Set of cars, airplanes, boats, trucks, and other miniature vehicles to use, as needed, with blocks, in sandbox, or wherever else dramatic play is going on. Store on open shelves. A steering wheel prop and wheel toys can be another type of vehicle play.

Human Figures

Collections of various types of "people" to use as needed for dramatic play activities. These could include a variety of sizes, materials, expressions, and roles. Some can be miniature plastic figures that you can buy by the hundreds. Some can be wooden cutouts that stand up. Some can be miniature dolls. Some should represent various ethnic groups. Some should be children, others adults.

Doctor

Tongue depressors, real stethoscope, bandaids, cloth for bandages, gauze, red finger paint for blood, cotton balls, discarded plastic hypo syringes without needles (available from clinics and should be boiled), eye droppers, play thermometer, stop watch, scale, height-weight chart, beds and dolls, paper and pencils, prescription pads, telephone, small suitcase or shelves for medical supplies, table, doctor and nurse dress-ups or uniforms, hospital gown, stretcher or cot.

Veterinarian

Stuffed animals, empty (boiled) hypo syringes, scale, dog/cat boxes, leash, cat/dog food dishes, other items from doctor list above.

Post Office/Mail Carrier

Index card file, stamp pads, rubber stamps, crayons, pencils, old Christmas seals, gummed labels, envelopes, money, mailbox(es) made from cardboard box(es) painted to resemble real mailbox (arch piece of cardboard over a carton with slot cut in carton), mailbags (large paper bags with "shoulder strap" attached or old shoulder-strap purses), rubber bands, writing pads, small postal scale, mail carrier hat, mail center badge, counter or table, collection of junk mail.

Supermarket

Cash register, play money, paper pads, pencils or crayons, paper sacks, empty food cartons, wax food, cans with smooth edges, grocery boxes.

Juice Stand

Cups, pitcher, hand juicer, cordless electric juicer (if available), spoon, hats, table, cash register, aprons, some form of play money.

Bookstore

Shelves constructed from hollow blocks or regular book shelves, large selection of children's books, cash register, sales slips, money, store counter or table, paper boxes.

Library

Table with rubber stamp, ink pad, books, shelves, pencils, paper.

Jewelry Store

Old jewelry, jewelry boxes, sales slips, pencils, bags, money, cash register.

Clothing Store

Clothing table for folded clothing, hangers and clothes rack for displaying clothing hung on hangers, boxes, bags, pencils, sales slips, money, cash register, store counter.

Shoe Store

Shoes in shoe boxes, foot measurer, bags, pencils, sales slips, money, table or shelves for shoes, chairs arranged along one side with smaller chair or stool facing them for salesperson.

Office

Table and chair for desk, old typewriter, old adding machine, pencils, pencil holder, paper, waste basket, rubber stamp and ink pad, telephone, assortment of junk mail, discarded business forms of many types.

Theater

Chairs, stage made from hollow blocks, large pieces of white paper for screen (scene can be drawn on screen), colored paper for tickets or roll of expired movie tickets, money, empty popcorn boxes. To offer stage performance plays rather than movies, provide costumes for dancers and actors.

TV Show

Large refrigerator carton with "window" and painted knobs, animal and family puppets.

Puppet Show

Puppet stage (box with curtain, "storefront" with curtain, or covered-over stacked hollow blocks or a table), a variety of puppets.

Train/Plane/Bus

Table for selling tickets, tickets (a roll of expired theater tickets or remaining sections of used plane tickets), paper punch, rubber stamp and ink pad, small chairs lined up to resemble mode of transportation, old small suitcases.

Restaurant

Table, chairs, tablecloths, napkins, dishes, silverware, trays, sales slips, pencils, menus (paste food pictures on pieces of paper), pictures of food or play food to serve to patrons, waiter/waitress uniforms.

Picnic

Blanket, picnic basket, dishes, food (food pictures, empty cans or boxes).

Beach

Blankets or beach towels, sunglasses, empty suntan oil bottles, beach bags, umbrellas.

Fishing

Large tub filled with water, rocking boats, old boat on playground, long twigs with strings attached as poles, magnets on end of poles and "fish" with metal attachments that attract the magnet, to add realistic element.

Beauty Shop/Hairdresser

Mirror, rollers or curlers, hairpins, hairnets, hair dryer and curling iron without cords, aprons or large bibs, towels, empty shampoo bottles (plastic), plastic basin, easy-to-wash brushes, clean wide-toothed combs, small hand mirrors, bobby pins and hair clips, scarves, headbands, barrettes, wigs mounted on wig stands, manicure set, emery boards, magazines, pencil, paper, money.

Barber Shop

Old-fashioned shaving soap in a jar, shaving brush, toy plastic razor or real razor without a blade, stand-up mirror, paper towels, plastic "barber clothes" to place around shoulders while "shaving."

Birthday Party

Hat box as cake, small boxes wrapped with paper and ribbon as gifts, birthday candles, table, chairs, dishes, birthday hats, party rollers, party horns.

Firefighter

Hats, raincoats, boots, short lengths of garden hose.

Farmer/Gardener

Shovel, rake, hoe, seeds, gardening gloves and hat.

Painter

Buckets, paint brushes and rollers to be used with water on various surfaces, painters' caps.

Plumber

Wrench, tool kit, all lengths, widths and shapes of piping to fit together (also 1/2" pipe fittings of different types, pipe nipples, and short pipes), spigots, plungers, hose and nozzles, old shirt, cap, hardware supply catalogues, measuring devices.

Gas Station Attendant

Shirt, hat, tire pump, boxes for cars, short lengths of garden hose.

Automobile Repair

Used (and washed) motor parts (spark plugs, filters, carburetors, cable sets, gears, etc.), hammers, pliers, screw drivers, oil funnel, empty oil cans, flashlights, wiring, air pump, windshield wipers, key carrier and keys, rags, old shirts, gloves, auto supply catalogues.

Telephone Repair

Pliers, wires, two toy telephones, assorted parts from broken toy telephones, plastic electrical tape, small scissors to cut tape, miscellaneous tools.

Furniture Repair

Assorted screwdrivers, screws, nuts, bolts, and a few pieces of wood with holes to put the screws or nuts and bolts into.

Radio and Record Player Repair

Assorted screwdrivers and pliers and other tools to use with old radios and record players.

Forest Ranger/Camper/Cowboy/Cowgirl

Canteen, flashlight, rope, mosquito netting, canvas for tent, knapsack, food supplies, nature books, compasses, small logs, grill, binoculars, old saddle, hats, vests, and boots.

Astronaut/Space Play

Rocket or space capsule, robots, space helmets made from empty ice cream containers, broken computer for space panel, homemade telescope, boots, headphones, camera, walkie-talkie, plastic tubing, silver garden gloves.

Creating and Using Prop Boxes

Prop box: _____

Items collected:

_____

_____

_____

_____

After preparing your prop box, decide how you want to introduce the new theme and the prop box you have prepared. Try it out for a few days and note the results. Would you do anything differently next time?

How you introduced the prop box:

_____

_____

_____

_____

Results:

_____

_____

_____

_____

What (if anything) would you do differently next time?

_____

_____

_____

_____

Share your experiences with your trainer and discuss what other prop boxes you might make. Parents can be a big help in collecting props. Develop a plan with your trainer to start collecting items for two other prop boxes. You can use the form on the next page to help you plan.

Plan for Prop Boxes

Theme: _____

Items to collect: _____

_____

_____

_____

_____

_____

_____

_____

_____

_____

Theme: _____

Items to collect: _____

_____

_____

_____

_____

_____

_____

_____

_____

_____

IV. Helping Children Learn Caring Behaviors

In this activity you will learn:

- to recognize caring behaviors in preschool children; and

- to help preschool children develop caring behaviors.

Children develop caring behaviors, like other forms of behavior, over a long period of time. Some infants demonstrate caring behaviors very early in life. They get upset and cry when they hear another infant crying. Between the ages of one and two, children begin to show real concern for others. When this concern is recognized and reinforced by parents and teachers, children continue to develop caring behaviors. And between the ages of two and six, children begin to develop skills in responding appropriately to the needs and feelings of others.

As they learn to get along with others in their group, young children are also learning caring behaviors. The most direct way in which children learn such behaviors is watching the adults who care for them. As a teacher, you help a child find a lost mitten, applaud a child who finishes a difficult puzzle, and throughout the day let each child know how much he or she is valued. In so doing, you are helping children learn to demonstrate positive feelings toward others. Dependable, responsive teaching helps children feel secure. In turn, this security allows children to show concern for others and to be a cooperative member of the group.

Caring behaviors are sometimes called "prosocial" behaviors. They include certain social skills such as sharing and taking turns, as well as behaviors such as the following:[3]

- **Showing empathy**

  - Feeling and acting concerned when another person is upset or hurt.
  - Sharing another person's happiness or excitement.

- **Showing generosity**

  - Giving a toy or other possession to another person.
  - Sharing a snack or toy with another person.

- **Helping**

  - Helping another person do a job.
  - Helping when another person needs assistance.

One can think of caring behaviors as examples of the "golden rule." People who use caring behaviors behave toward others as they would like others to behave toward them. Teachers model these kinds of behaviors in their relationships with children and with their colleagues.

---

[3]Based on Janice J. Beaty, *Observing Development of the Young Child* (Columbus, OH: Charles E. Merrill Publishing Co., 1986), p. 111.

They also help children learn caring behaviors by letting children know that prosocial behaviors are valued by society. It is natural for young children to put their own needs first. When these needs are met, they will gradually learn to think about the needs of others. Some techniques to encourage prosocial behaviors in preschool children follow.[4]

- Plan group activities that involve thoughtfulness and emphasize a sense of community. For example, make cards for a child who is sick.

- Use each child's name often. Label the children's paintings and cubbies. Sing songs with children's names in them and use other techniques to help everyone learn everyone else's names.

- Help children express prosocial feelings. "You can tell Carlos you were sad because he wasn't here yesterday."

- Give small groups of children cooperative play ideas. Provide activities that call for cooperation, such as moving a large box, folding a large blanket, or creating a collage.

- When guiding children's behavior, pay attention to the child who is hurt so everyone knows that aggressive behavior is not acceptable.

- Read books with themes of helpfulness and friendship. Ask open-ended questions about the stories. Let the children know that you value these kinds of behaviors.

- Talk about exciting things that have happened to the children and teachers. When a child has had a happy experience, share that pleasure by giving out hugs or handshakes. "Tim, I know you are happy to have your mommy back from her trip. Can I give you a hug?"

- Help children learn how to talk about their feelings. "When you hit Juana, she doesn't know what you want. Use your words to tell her what you want."

Prosocial behavior doesn't happen quickly; teachers need to be patient as children take their time in learning the skills of negotiation, sharing, and cooperation. Children with little experience in group living may need to be reassured often that their own wants will be satisfied.

In this learning activity you will learn about the prosocial behaviors of preschool children. Over the next three days, observe the activities in the room for five-minute periods, several times a day. Then review your notes and list examples of children learning caring behaviors. First, read the example that follows. Then use the blank form that follows to record your examples.

---

[4]Adapted from *Teaching Techniques to Encourage Friendly (Prosocial) Behavior in Young Children* (Ames, IA: Iowa State University).

Children's Caring Behaviors
(Example)

CARING BEHAVIORS[5]	CHILDREN'S BEHAVIOR
Showing concern for someone in distress	*Bonita fell down outside. Susan put her arm around her and helped her get up. Then Susan got a teacher to come help.*
Showing delight when someone experiences pleasure	*When Ms. Frilles hung up Tamila's picture, Tamila was very excited. Bonita came over to look at it.*
Sharing something with another	*David gave Shawn part of his muffin at lunch time.*
Giving a possession to another	*Dean found a shiny rock outside and gave it to Maddie.*
Taking turns with toys or activities	*Billy and Lamont took turns putting blocks on their tower until it fell over.*
Helping another to do a task	*Maddie helped Felipe wipe up a spill.*
Helping another in need	*Carlos saw David trying to get a tricycle out of the shed and went over to help him.*

[5]Adapted from Janice J. Beaty, *Observing Development of the Young Child* (Columbus, OH: Charles E. Merrill Publishing Co., 1986), p. 30.

Children's Caring Behaviors

CARING BEHAVIORS	CHILDREN'S BEHAVIOR
Showing concern for someone in distress	
Showing delight when someone experiences pleasure	
Sharing something with another	
Giving a possession to another	
Taking turns with toys or activities	
Helping another to do a task	
Helping another in need	

Discuss this activity with your trainer and with a teacher who also cares for these children.

V. Helping Children Relate Positively to Others

In this activity you will learn:

- to tell when a child needs your help to make friends; and
- to help individual children develop friendship-making skills.

It is very important for teachers to work with individual children to help them learn how to make friends. Every young child eventually needs to have at least one friend to talk to, play with, disagree with, make up with, and care for. Some children seem to develop and use their social skills with ease. They are naturally outgoing and seem to know instinctively how to make friends and find their place in their group. They get a lot of pleasure from being with other children. Other children may take longer to get used to the group, but once they feel comfortable, they are able to join in and make friends.

Children who are not able to make friends and who continue to feel rejected are likely to have serious problems later in life. Such children often have low self-esteem and lack the social skills they need to develop friendships. They feel unloved. Because they aren't accepted by their peers, they have fewer chances to develop social skills. They cannot break the cycle of rejection.

Most preschool children who have trouble making friends fall into one of three categories. (These are very broad categories and should not be used to label children.) They are shy or withdrawn, overly aggressive, or unappealing and therefore unaccepted by the group. If you have children like this in your group, you can make a big difference in that child's life by helping him or her to break the cycle of rejection.

Helping Shy Children Make Friends

Almost every group of children includes one or two children who are very shy. Teachers may feel empathy for these children and want to help them become a part of the group. Before offering assistance, however, teachers need to observe to see if such a child is just moving at a slower pace than others in the group. The child may need to have some successes with solitary play—for example, completing a difficult puzzle—before progressing to group play. A shy child may also need to sit back and observe other children at play to learn how to become part of the group. The child may begin by entering a small group. Then, after becoming more skilled, he or she will move on to playing with a larger group of children.

There are some shy children, however, who need the teacher's intervention and help. Teachers should offer this help in indirect ways, without making it obvious to anyone else that the help is being offered. Saying things such as "be nice to Billy" or "can you let Mary play too?" are not helpful. These tend to make the shy child feel self-conscious or embarrassed. The other children may go along with the teacher's suggestions for a time, but the shy child will not develop the social skills to cope when the teacher isn't there to intervene directly. The following are some techniques that teachers can use to help shy children develop socially.[6]

- **Observe, observe, observe.** Watch what the child does and says, who the child talks to, and who the child watches. When the child is playing alone with Legos, is he or she building with concentrated attention or also watching the fire fighters in the house corner? Observe to find out what the child likes to do, where his or her favorite places are, whether the child behaves differently outside, and what skills the child has.

- **Establish a connection with the child.** Use your observations to comment on whom the child is watching. "I see that you are watching John and Pam at the water table." If the child responds positively, you can ask a question to extend the conversation. "Do you think John's cup will hold more water than Pam's? Perhaps you can play at the water table tomorrow and figure out the answer." You might also comment on what the child is doing. "I see you are building with Legos." Such comments help the child feel more secure because he or she knows that the teacher is paying attention.

- **Be playful with the child.** Encourage the child to express his or her ideas and feelings. "Jason, you seemed to really enjoy that story. What do you like to do on a snowy day?"

- **Use what you know about the child's interests to create special situations.** For example, if you know that Holly really likes to cook, plan a cooking activity that involves several children working together. Include Holly when you conduct the activity and ask her lots of open-ended questions to get her involved.

- **Help children find good friends.** Just as there are several shy children in your room, there are also several children who are very competent and sensitive socially. Try asking one of these children and the shy child to help you do a task. "Dean, could you please help Tommy and me carry the toys outside?" Or let both children know about an activity that you know both would be interested in. "Dean and Tommy, I know you both like the woodworking bench. Ms. Johnson is getting the tools out now. I think there's room for two more carpenters."

- **Help the shy child understand his or her feelings of shyness.** "It's okay to want to play alone when you don't know the other children too well. After a while you'll feel more comfortable and be ready to play with Carlos, Maddie, and some of the other children."

---

[6]Adapted from Dennie Palmer Wolf, ed., *Connecting: Friendship in the Lives of Young Children and Their Teachers* (Redmond, WA: Exchange Press, Inc., 1986), pp. 58-62.

Helping Aggressive Children Make Friends

In any group of preschool children there may be one or two who are not able to control their behaviors. They use aggression as a means to express their unhappiness or to get their own way. These children do not know how to take turns, negotiate, or cooperate with others. They have not learned how to meet their own needs and those of the group. Because they are overly aggressive, other children do not want to include them in their play.

Teachers also may have trouble relating to overly aggressive children. It is natural to want to avoid a child who frequently hurts other children or uses force to make others let him or her into the group. But because teachers are professionals, they must learn to overcome their negative feelings about an aggressive child. It may help to remember that the children who hit or bully other children are troubled or in pain, emotionally. They feel unhappy or insecure, and they need their teachers' help to learn positive ways of relating to other children. These children must feel safe and cared for before they can develop self-esteem and the social skills to make friends and play with other children. The following are some techniques that teachers can use to help aggressive children.

- **Help the child understand the consequences of his or her actions.** "I think you want to play with Crystal and Susan. But when you knock their tower down it makes them angry. It doesn't make them want to play with you."

- **Try to redirect a child's angry energy.** "Shawn, I know you are angry, but you may not hit Bonita. Use your hands to throw this ball at the wall."

- **Identify a challenging physical activity that the child really enjoys.** Set it up so several children can participate. "Denise, you are a great jumper. Use this chalk to mark how far you and Lloyd can jump. You can take turns jumping."

- **Spend time alone with the child, but not immediately after the child has been aggressive.** "David, let's read a story together in the reading corner. There's a couple of new books that Ms. Johnson brought in."

- **Sit with the child and observe the other children at play.** Interpret what they are doing so the child can begin to understand how others use social skills. "Carlos just came over to the sandbox where Tamila and Renee are being mothers baking cakes. I think he wants to play with them. Carlos is making a cake to share with them. He's pretending to be a neighbor."

- **Help the child develop ways to achieve his or her goals without using aggression.** "I know you want to be the doctor, but Emily is being the doctor now. What can you say to Emily to let her know how you feel?"

- **Use the child's positive characteristics to help him or her be accepted by the group.** "Chaundra collected some beautiful leaves on our walk. Let's put them on the table where everyone can see them."

Helping Unappealing Children Make Friends

There are children in every group who are neither aggressive nor shy yet are still excluded from play. These children, who may be loud, clumsy, or bossy, do not know how to get involved with their peers. They may play in the block area for a while, get up and move to the easel, try to join in with the house corner family, and then go back to the blocks. They seem to be unaware of the effects of their behavior. They seem to want to play with others, but because they are not able to understand what a group of the children are playing, they don't know how to get involved. You may hear a lot of complaints about these unappealing children. "She's always butting in." "He talks too loud." "He knocked our buildings over."

Many of the techniques for helping shy or aggressive children are also effective for helping the unappealing child. Often these children have some social skills but may not know how to use them. Observe these children to find out who in the group does accept them. Then find ways to include them together in small group projects. Some other suggestions follow:[7]

- **Teach the child how to ask questions to find out what a group of children are playing.** "What are you playing?" "Who are you pretending to be?" "What are you building?"

- **Suggest that the child watch and listen to find out what the other children are playing before trying to play with them.** "Delores, if you sit here and watch Bonita and Tim play, I'll bet you can guess what they're doing. Which one do you think is the firefighter?"

- **Encourage the child to discuss his or her feelings about being rejected.** "You look sad, Cynthia. Can you tell me what happened?" Telling what happened may help the child understand why she was rejected by the others.

- **Coach the child on how to join and have fun doing what the other children are doing.** To a child who takes too long going down the slide (which annoys the other children), a teacher could say, "Felipe, when it's your turn, slide down quickly. Then the others can have their turns. Very soon it will be your turn again. Everyone will have fun."

- **Help the child state rules or the accepted behaviors of the group as a way to justify attempts to be included.** "I'd like to play, too. There are only three people in the sandbox and four children can play there."

In this learning activity you will assist a child in your room who needs help learning to make friends. Think of a child who needs your help in making friends. Observe this child for five minutes at several different times of the day. Review your notes and summarize your thoughts about the child. Use this new information and the suggestions in this learning activity to plan ways to help the child play with others. Implement your plan over the next two weeks and record what happens. Begin by reading the example on the next page.

---

[7]Adapted from Dwight L. Rogers and Dorene Doerre Ross, "Encouraging Positive Social Interaction Among Young Children," *Young Children* (Washington, DC: National Association for the Education of Young Children, March 1986), pp. 15-16.

Helping Individual Children Relate to Others
(Example)

Child: _Alex_   Age: _4 years 3 months_   Date: _January 15_

OBSERVATION NOTES	SUMMARY
Time: _5:35 p.m._ *Alex is with a small group of children who are listening to Ms. Williams read a story. He is sitting at the edge of the group. When the door opens he turns around to look. The child next to him leaves when her mother comes. Alex follows her when she gets her coat and some things from her cubby. Some of the other children say good-bye to her. Alex walks back to the group. He says, "I don't like this story."*	*Alex seems to want his parents to come. He is easily distracted. Perhaps he wants to go. He doesn't notice that the other children want to hear the story.*
Time: _7:20 a.m._ *Alex comes in with his father. He smiles. His father says, "Say hello to Ms. Williams, Alex." Alex says hello in a loud voice. The other children turn and look at him. Ms. Williams asks Alex what he would like to do. "Blocks," he says. Some other children are playing too, building a big tower. Alex builds beside them. Shawn says, "Hey, we need all the blocks." Alex knocks his own building down. He gets up and goes to the puzzle table.*	*If Alex knew how to join in with the block building group, he might have enjoyed it.*

OBSERVATION NOTES	SUMMARY
Time: _10:45 a.m._ *Alex is helping serve a snack. He is carrying a tray of cut-up fruit to the table. He puts the tray down, then stands behind the table. He is smiling. When all the children have their fruit, Alex takes his. He sits down next to Maddie. She says, "I don't like bananas. Do you want mine?" Alex smiles and takes them. He says, "I like bananas but I don't like grapes." Maddie says, "Can I have them?" Alex says yes and lets her reach over and take them.*	*Alex seems to like Maddie. He let her have his grapes. He seemed to feel good about helping, too.*

Plan:

> *I will tell Alex that I know it's hard to wait for his parents at the end of the day. I will ask him if there is something he would like to do instead of listening to the story. I will explain that the other children do want to hear the story.*

> *When I see Alex watching the block builders, I'll point out to him how the children are working and playing together—for example, "Tony just gave Crystal that block because she needed one that size for her part of the road."*

> *I'll try to set up some times when Alex and Maddie can play together or help me with something. They both like it when we paint outside. I'll ask them to help carry the double easel outside one day next week.*

Results (after two weeks):

> *Alex helps me clean up at the end of the day. It helps keep him busy so he doesn't watch the door as often.*

> *Alex joined a small group at the water play table today. He held the funnel while Tony poured.*

> *Alex and Maddie painted outside. She is very talkative so she kept the conversation going. Later in the week I saw them riding tricycles together.*

Helping Individual Children Relate to Others

OBSERVATION NOTES	SUMMARY
Time: _____	
Time: _____	

OBSERVATION NOTES	SUMMARY
Time: _____	
Time: _____	

Review your observation notes and summaries as well as the suggestions you have read. Develop a plan for helping this child. Implement your plan over the next two weeks and then record the results.

Plan:

_____
_____
_____
_____
_____
_____
_____
_____
_____
_____

Results (after two weeks):

_____
_____
_____
_____
_____
_____
_____
_____
_____
_____

Talk to your trainer about how you helped this child.

Summarizing Your Progress

You have now completed all of the learning activities for this module. Whether you are an experienced teacher or a new one, this module probably has helped you develop new skills for promoting social development. Before you go on, take a few minutes to summarize what you've learned.

- Turn back to Learning Activity I, Using Your Knowledge of Child Development to Promote Social Development, and add to the chart specific examples of what you learned about promoting social development while you were working on this module. Compare your ideas to those in the completed chart at the end of the module.

- Next, review your responses to the pre-training assessment for this module. Write a summary of what you learned and list the skills you developed or improved.

If there are topics you would like to know more about, you will find recommended readings listed in the orientation, which can be found in Volume I.

Your final step in this module is to complete the knowledge and competency assessments. Let your trainer know when you are ready to schedule the assessments. After you have successfully completed these assessments, you will be ready to start a new module. Congratulations on your progress so far, and good luck with your next module.

Answer Sheets

Promoting Social Development

Helping Children Learn to Get Along with Other Members of the Group

1. **How did Ms. Frilles help the girls learn to get along with each other?**

   a. She gave them an indirect suggestion when she told them about a restaurant that had two waitresses.

   b. She stepped back to let them use their social skills to make their own decision.

2. **How did Ms. Frilles help the girls feel good about solving their problem?**

   a. She praised them for solving their problem.

   b. She left them alone so they could continue playing.

Helping Children Understand and Express Their Feelings and Respect Those of Others

1. **How did Ms. Kim let the children know that she understood and respected their feelings?**

   a. She told the children what she thought they might be feeling.

   b. She told the children that she couldn't let them push each other.

2. **How did Ms. Kim help the children express their feelings?**

   a. She told the children to use their words.

   b. She stepped back so the children could work things out for themselves.

Providing an Environment and Experiences That Help Children Develop Social Skills

1. **How did Mr. Lopez turn the daily routine of getting ready to go outside into an experience that helped the children develop social skills?**

   a. He asked two children to help another child find her missing shoe.

   b. He said the bag of balls was so big that he needed help to carry it.

   c. He said he likes it when children work together.

SOCIAL

2. **What social skills did the children learn as they prepared to go outside?**

   a. They learned to work together and help each other.

   b. They learned to feel good about themselves because Mr. Lopez thinks all the children are important and he will wait until everyone is ready before going outside.

Using Your Knowledge of Child Development
to Promote Social Development

WHAT PRESCHOOL CHILDREN ARE LIKE	HOW TEACHERS CAN USE THIS INFORMATION TO PROMOTE SOCIAL DEVELOPMENT
They can understand some rules and limits.	Provide opportunities for children to learn to make rules and play simple games that stress cooperation rather than competition.
They are learning to share and take turns.	Set up a system (a timer or a place to put one's name) for taking turns. Praise children when they do share.
They like to imitate adult activities.	Provide a variety of props for dramatic play, both indoors and outdoors, so children can pretend to be grown-ups doing grown-up things.
They carry on conversations with other children, in pairs or in groups.	Observe and listen to these conversations. You can learn a lot about how the children are getting along, whose ideas are listened to, who needs help learning to get others to listen, and what their interests are. Use this information for planning to meet individual needs.
They may exclude other children from their play.	Observe to see how often a child is excluded. Help the child learn how to become a part of the group by giving him or her a special prop to share or suggesting a role to play.
They are moving from parallel to cooperative play.	Observe often to see what kind of play a child is involved in. Help children move to the next level of play when they are ready. For example, provide two phones or four firefighter hats so children will play together.
They continue to need opportunities for solitary play.	Observe often to learn when a child is playing alone by choice. Provide materials to be used by a child working alone. For example, provide puzzles, beads and string, books, paints, tricycles, and so on.

WHAT PRESCHOOL CHILDREN ARE LIKE	HOW TEACHERS CAN USE THIS INFORMATION TO PROMOTE SOCIAL DEVELOPMENT
They ask a lot of questions.	Use questions to extend children's thinking. Children use their thinking skills when they play in groups.
They begin to develop friendships.	Give children many chances to be with their friends. Allow lots of time for free play so children can choose their own playmates.
They can learn to adapt to a variety of different settings and enjoy visiting new places.	Prepare children for field trips. Discuss the rules they will be expected to follow so they know the accepted behaviors in advance.
They are gaining an awareness of the larger community.	Arrange for visits to the firehouse, parents' jobs, and so forth, or ask visitors to come to the center to discuss what they do in the community.
They want adults to like them.	Give children lots of affection and praise. Let them know they are liked and that you know they are learning about living in a group.

Glossary

Cooperative play	The most common type of play in the preschool years. Children play together in a group that they organize and control. The group has a specific purpose, such as making something, playing a game, or acting out a real-life or fantasy situation.
Parallel play	Play that happens when two- to three-year-old children progress from solitary play to playing alone with other children nearby. Children use the same or similar kinds of toys or materials.
Peer	A friend or companion who is the same age or at the same developmental level.
Social development	The gradual process through which children learn to live as members of a group.
Prosocial skills	Accepted behaviors, such as sharing or taking turns, which children learn and use to get along in society.
Solitary play	The first stage of play, when infants and young toddlers play alone, independent of other children. They use toys or materials that are the same as or different from those of other children in the group.

Module 10
Guidance

What Is Guidance and Why Is It Important?

Children need adults to guide them—to help them learn what is acceptable and what is not, to help them learn to live cooperatively with others. How you as an adult offer this guidance depends on your goals for the children you teach. What kind of people do you want these children to become? Do you want them to behave out of fear or because they have learned what is acceptable and what is not?

There is a reason for all behavior. Children misbehave for many different reasons. They may be at a developmental state where they need to test the limits of their own control. They may be forced into a schedule that conflicts with their natural rhythm. Their parents may have different rules and expectations than those at the center, or there may be a family situation that is upsetting. Sometimes children behave inappropriately simply because they are bored, tired, curious, or frustrated.

To help children learn self-discipline, teachers need to think about the reasons for children's behavior. For example, you may remove a child from the sandbox because he or she won't stop throwing sand. Later you need also to think about why the child was throwing sand. When you identify the need that the child is expressing, you can then try to meet that need. When a teacher has to take something away (the opportunity to play in the sandbox), he or she must later replace it with what the child needs (perhaps some extra one-to-one attention).

Because adults are powerful, they can make children behave certain ways. But children who are punished or forced to behave learn the following lessons:

- I am a bad person.

- I need to watch out for adults.

- I had better not get caught.

These children are likely to behave only when someone is watching, because they don't want to be punished. They do not learn to value acceptable behavior for itself, and they do not learn self-discipline.

Self-discipline is the ability to control one's own behavior. People who are self-disciplined make independent choices based on what they believe is right. They are able to balance their own needs with those of others. They can accept the results of their actions.

Adults who want children to learn to make their own decisions, to know the difference between right and wrong, to solve problems, and to correct their own mistakes have to provide positive guidance to help children develop self-discipline. This module is about guiding children's behavior in ways that assist them in developing self-discipline. Teachers can help children gain self-discipline in many ways. Some actions, such as setting up safe places for running, can prevent certain behaviors. Others, such as redirecting children to climb on the climber rather than the table, are responses to children's behavior.

If you have developed a caring relationship with the children in your room, you are already doing a lot to help them achieve the goal of self-discipline. Children depend on you and want your approval. They look to you to help them learn what is acceptable and what is not. If you set limits that fit their development and individual needs, children will learn the limits easily. If you are consistent in applying rules, children will try to follow them. If you set up an environment that supports self-control, children will find it easier to achieve this goal. And if you learn some techniques and words to use to guide children, you will help them develop self-discipline.

Guiding children's behavior involves:

- providing an environment that encourages children's self-discipline;

- using positive methods to guide individual children; and

- helping children understand and express their feelings in acceptable ways.

Listed below are examples of how teachers demonstrate their competence in guiding children's behavior.

Providing an Environment That Encourages Children's Self-Discipline

Here are some examples of what teachers can do.

- Make sure there are no safety hazards. "Mr. Lopez, that was a good idea to replace the indoor climber. It was just too small for the children in this group."

- Store toys and equipment on low shelves. "Sammy, please put the big blocks back on their shelf now. You can take them down again tomorrow."

- Give children chances to make up rules. "We need some rules for taking care of our new guinea pig. Tell me what you think they should be, and I'll write them down."

- Prepare children for changes in advance. "In five minutes, it will be time to clean up and get ready for lunch. I'll set the timer so you'll know when the five minutes are over."

- Arrange the materials and furniture to encourage appropriate behavior. "When Sandy wants to be alone, she likes to sit in the reading nook."

- Plan child-initiated activities for most of the day. "Good morning, Randy. What would you like to do today?"

Using Positive Methods to Guide Individual Children

Here are some examples of what teachers can do.

- Allow children to learn from their experiences. "I'm sorry your shirt got wet, Andrew. Let's get a dry one to put on. What could you do differently next time, so you'll stay dry at the water table?"

- Use logical consequences to help children be responsible for their actions. "Carla, there's a sponge by the sink you can use to clean up your spilled juice."

- Redirect children to acceptable activities. "Susan's reading that book, Bobby. Pick another book to look at."

- Securely hold a child who is screaming or thrashing. "Laura, I'm going to hold you close, so you won't hurt yourself or anyone else. I will let you go when you are calm and ready."

- Use simple, positive reminders to restate rules. "Use the crayons on the paper, Jerry, not on the table."

- Know when ignoring inappropriate behavior is constructive. "Ms. Williams, I found one of the best ways to get children to stop using bathroom words is to just ignore them. If you don't react to the words, children soon stop using them."

Helping Children Understand and Express Their Feelings in Acceptable Ways

Here are some examples of what teachers can do.

- Make it easier to wait for a turn. "I know you feel angry because you think Marty has been riding the tricycle for too long. After he goes around the track one more time, it will be your turn."

- Redirect an angry child to a soothing activity. "Jane, I can't let you hurt other people or things. I think you might have fun at the water table. We have some new turkey basters you can use."

- Tell a child that you accept his or her feelings. "Tricia, I know you feel angry when Debby calls you names. Tell Debby you don't like it when she does that."

- Use firm words and tones to help children understand how someone else feels. "When you pull my hair it hurts me. You can comb the doll's hair instead."

- Model acceptable ways to express negative feelings. "Barbara, I've asked you three times to please use your inside voice. Your loud voice really hurts my ears."

Guiding Children's Behavior

In the following situations, teachers are providing guidance to help preschool children develop self-discipline. As you read each one, think about what the teachers are doing and why. Then answer each one of the questions that follow.

Providing an Environment That Encourages Children's Self-Discipline

"I wish it were Friday," sighs Ms. Kim. "This has been a terrible week. It seems like the children are constantly fighting over the toys and just about destroying everything we have. I don't know what's the matter with them. And getting them to clean up is like pulling teeth." Ms. Richards nods her head in agreement. "I know what you mean," she says. "Suppose we tried making sharing less of a burden. We could switch some of our toys with Ms. Williams's class so we can have duplicates of the popular items for a while. Then we wouldn't have to spend so much of our time getting the children to share. And I think I have an idea that might help with our clean-up problem. If we make picture labels for all our toys and materials and tape them to the shelves and containers to show that everything has a specific place, then clean- up will be more fun and challenging." Ms. Kim agrees. "Let's try both of your ideas. Maybe we can control our behavior problems by changing the environment. That way we won't have to keep nagging the children."

1. What behaviors did Ms. Kim find frustrating in her group of three-year-olds?

_____

_____

_____

2. What suggestions did Ms. Richards have for dealing with the behavior problems?

_____

_____

_____

3. How might her approach help?

_____

_____

_____

Using Positive Methods to Guide Individual Children

Ms. Williams and the group of four-year-olds are outside in the play yard. Travis, a very active child, has collected some pine cones and is throwing them at other children. Ms. Williams walks over to him. She bends down, looks at him, and says, "Travis, you are learning to be a good thrower. But if you hit someone with a pine cone, they might be hurt or angry. Where can you practice your throwing safely?" Travis looks around and answers,

"Over on the grass." Ms. Williams nods and says, "Yes, that's a good place. There aren't any children over there." Travis picks up his pine cones and walks over to the grass. Ms. Williams watches for a few minutes and then goes over to the sandbox to play with other children.

1. **What did Ms. Williams know about Travis?**

_____

_____

_____

2. **How did Ms. Williams let Travis know that she respected him?**

_____

_____

_____

Helping Children Understand and Express Their Feelings in Acceptable Ways

"No!" screams Billy. His arm extended, he leans over ready to hit Sam, who has just grabbed a piece of orange from Billy's plate. "Billy," says Mr. Lopez, extending his hand between Billy's hand and Sam's arm. Billy looks up at Mr. Lopez. "That was good stopping," Mr. Lopez says. "I know you don't like it when someone takes your things. Tell Sam not to take your orange. You can talk to people when you are angry, but I can't let you hit them." Billy looks at Sam and says, "I don't want you to take my orange." Sam puts the piece of orange down and goes back to eating his lunch.

1. **How do you think Billy felt when Sam grabbed his piece of orange?**

_____

_____

_____

2. **How did Mr. Lopez help Billy learn to express his feelings in acceptable ways?**

_____

_____

_____

Compare your answers with those on the answer sheet at the end of this module. If your answers are different, discuss them with your trainer. There can be more than one good answer.

Your Own Self-Discipline

Often your behavior is automatic. You don't stop to think about what you should do; you just do it. When you put money in a parking meter, come to work on time, or thank a store clerk, you are probably acting without thinking about what you are doing. You have learned and accepted certain rules of behavior and, because you have self-discipline, don't need to be reminded of them.

Your self-discipline guides your behavior at work in many ways.

- You let the center director know when you're sick so a substitute can be called.

- You let a colleague know you are angry with her by telling her what you feel.

- You volunteer to help a colleague who's having difficulty understanding the needs of a child.

- You don't make long-distance calls on the center phone.

List a few other examples of how self-discipline guides your behavior at work:

_____

_____

_____

_____

_____

Self-discipline also guides your behavior at home.

- You remember to water the plants because you know they'll die if you don't.

- You clean the frying pan so it will be ready to use in the morning.

- You say no to a second piece of cake because you shouldn't have so much sugar.

List several other examples of how self-discipline guides your behavior at home:

_____

_____

_____

_____

_____

Think of a time when you did not show self-discipline. What affected your loss of control?

_____

_____

_____

_____

_____

What does this tell you about what children need to gain self-discipline?

_____

_____

_____

_____

_____

Some adults have problems making their own decisions about how to behave. They are most comfortable when they have rules and guidelines to follow. They may respond only to promises of rewards or threats of punishment. Perhaps they come to work on time only because they're afraid of being fired or having their pay docked.

When these adults were children, they probably didn't have many opportunities to make their own decisions. They weren't able to develop inner controls.

Being in control of your own behavior usually results in higher self-esteem. Having good feelings about yourself will make you a more effective and skilled teacher. Your self-discipline is a good model for the children. They will learn a lot from being cared for by a responsible and competent person.

When you have finished this overview section, you should complete the pre-training assessment. Refer to the glossary at the end of this module if you need definitions for the terms that are used.

Pre-Training Assessment

Listed below are the skills that teachers use to guide children's behavior. Think about whether you do these things regularly, sometimes, or not enough. Place a check in one of the columns on the right for each skill listed. Then discuss your answers with your trainer.

SKILL	I DO THIS REGULARLY	I DO THIS SOMETIMES	I DON'T DO THIS ENOUGH
PROVIDING AN ENVIRONMENT THAT ENCOURAGES CHILDREN'S SELF-DISCIPLINE 1. Providing a balanced daily schedule with time for both active and quiet play, indoors and outside.			
2. Providing a variety of materials and activities to meet children's needs and interests.			
3. Providing sufficient materials for the number of children in the group, including duplicates of popular items.			
4. Involving children in setting limits and making rules for the group.			
5. Providing timers or lists of names to show children when it will be their turn.			
6. Making a place for everything and using picture labels to show where things go.			
7. Keeping materials and toys on low shelves so children can help themselves.			

SKILL	I DO THIS REGULARLY	I DO THIS SOMETIMES	I DON'T DO THIS ENOUGH
USING POSITIVE METHODS TO GUIDE INDIVIDUAL CHILDREN 8. Trying to understand why a child is misbehaving.			
9. Helping children use their problem-solving skills to develop resolutions to conflicts.			
10. Focusing on the child's behavior, not on the child.			
11. Stating directions and reminding children of rules in a positive way (e.g., "walk in the room").			
12. Reinforcing children's positive behavior with genuine praise.			
HELPING CHILDREN UNDERSTAND AND EXPRESS THEIR FEELINGS IN ACCEPTABLE WAYS 13. Modeling appropriate ways to express negative feelings.			
14. Providing soothing activities, such as water play or playdough, and redirecting frustrated children to these activities.			

SKILL	I DO THIS REGULARLY	I DO THIS SOMETIMES	I DON'T DO THIS ENOUGH
15. Reminding children to use words to tell others how they feel.			
16. Working with parents and other staff to help a child with a problem (such as hitting) express his or her feelings in acceptable ways.			

Review your responses, then list three to five skills you would like to improve or topics you would like to learn more about. When you finish this module, you will list examples of your new or improved knowledge and skills.

Now begin the learning activities for Module 10, Guidance.

I. Using Your Knowledge of Child Development to Guide Children's Behavior

In this activity you will learn:

* to recognize some typical behaviors of preschool children; and

* to use what you know about child development to help children develop self-discipline.

Understanding children's behavior is the first step in providing guidance and promoting self-discipline. By learning more about what children can and can't do at each stage of development, you are more likely to have appropriate expectations for them.

Most preschool children understand the difference between right and wrong. Because of this, they can be helped to develop self-discipline. They can use words to express their feelings and to work out problems. Of course, they don't always do this. Although preschool children are less likely than toddlers to have all-out tantrums, they sometimes lose control and express their feelings by hitting, kicking, or screaming. Conflicts and disagreements are to be expected. Preschool children need understanding adults to help them use their words, not their hands or feet, to express their anger or frustration.

Most preschool children are not yet able to understand the long-term consequences of their behavior. Teachers can help children learn the immediate, natural consequences of their actions. For example, if a child breaks a toy, the teacher can help the child understand that he or she cannot play with the toy until it is fixed.

Preschool children feel more comfortable when they can follow established routines. Order and consistency in the day help these children develop a sense of security and self-control. When a child can say, "I know what we do after snack, we go outside!" he or she is feeling in control of the day.

The chart on the next page lists some typical behaviors of preschool children. Included are behaviors relevant to guiding children's behavior. The right column asks you to identify ways that teachers can use this information about child development to help children develop self-discipline. Try to think of as many examples as you can. As you work through the module you will learn new strategies for guiding children's behavior, and you can add them to the child development chart. You are not expected to think of all the examples at one time. If you need help getting started, turn to the completed chart at the end of the module. By the time you complete all the learning activities, you will find that you have learned many ways to guide children's behavior.

Using Your Knowledge of Child Development
to Guide Children's Behavior

WHAT PRESCHOOL CHILDREN ARE LIKE	HOW TEACHERS CAN USE THIS INFORMATION TO GUIDE CHILDREN'S BEHAVIOR
They are eager to please adults.	
They want to make decisions for themselves.	
They often like to try new things and take risks.	
They can take turns and share but don't always want to.	
They sometimes lose control and start kicking and screaming.	
They have lots of energy. They run fast, climb high, jump, gallop, and hop.	

WHAT PRESCHOOL CHILDREN ARE LIKE	HOW TEACHERS CAN USE THIS INFORMATION TO GUIDE CHILDREN'S BEHAVIOR
They may use bathroom words and swear words to get attention.	
They like to feel powerful and important. They can sometimes be very bossy.	
They like to get attention and will act out if they feel ignored.	
They sometimes strike out in anger at other children or even at adults.	
They are beginning to understand the consequences of their actions.	

When you have completed as much as you can do on the chart, discuss your answers with your trainer. As you proceed with the rest of the learning activities, you can refer back to the chart and add more examples of how teachers guide children's behavior.

II. Guiding Children's Behavior

In this activity you will learn:

• to use positive approaches to guide children's behavior; and

• to use strategies tailored to an individual child's needs.

Often the words discipline and punishment are used to mean the same thing, but they are actually very different. Discipline means guiding and directing children toward acceptable behavior. The most important goal of discipline is to help children gain inner controls. Teachers discipline children to help them learn the consequences of their actions.

Punishment means controlling children's behavior through fear. Punishment makes children behave because they are afraid of what might happen to them if they don't. Punishment may stop children's negative behavior temporarily, but it doesn't help children develop self-discipline. Instead, it may reinforce their bad feelings about themselves.

Children need choices and need to make decisions knowing what the logical consequences will be. Teachers must clearly state in advance the choices and the consequences. For example, a teacher might say, "Shawn, if you keep knocking David's blocks down, you will have to leave the block area. Do you want to leave David's tower alone, or leave the block area?" This type of guidance helps a child develop self-discipline. It results in less anger and fewer power struggles than does punishment.

Teachers can use a variety of approaches to guide children's behavior. No single approach works for every child or every situation. The approach used should relate to the child and to the problem. Positive guidance approaches include the following:

• Helping children use their problem-solving skills to develop solutions. "I can see it is hard for you to share your bear, Carlos. Where can you put it until you go home?"

• Avoiding problem behaviors by anticipating and planning for them. "Let's talk about what will happen on our trip tomorrow. First, how will we get to the fire house?"

• Trying to understand why a child is misbehaving. Discuss the situation with a colleague or your supervisor. "Bonita's mother is going out of town next week. Maybe Bonita is afraid she won't come back."

• Take time to see and hear yourself and your environment through a child's eyes and ears. "Was my voice perhaps too loud just then? I'll speak more softly to Joey."

• Focusing on the child's behavior, not on the child. "I like the way you cleared your dishes, Marguerite" (rather than "you're a good girl for clearing your dishes").

- Helping children understand the consequences of their actions. "Tim, your tower fell down on top of you because it was taller than the limit we all agreed on."

- Making sure logical consequences follow children's actions. "Felipe and Kim, the doll broke when you were both pulling its arms. You will have to wait until it's fixed before you can play with it again."

- Explaining to children what their choices are. "If you want to drive your truck, Susan, you must drive on the rug, not in the house corner."

- Assuming the role of the authority only when necessary—but doing so firmly, so children learn to obey automatically at certain points. "Don't move, Chaundra! A car is coming."

- Treating children with politeness at all times. "Could you please help me by holding my bag for a minute? Thank you."

- Helping children take small problems or mistakes lightly so that they learn to move on. "You tipped over your paint cup? Was it your silly elbow that did it? Let's go find a sponge to clean up!"

- Watching for restlessness in younger preschool children and giving them room to release their energies and frustrations physically. "Susan, you seem fidgety this afternoon. Why don't you and Tamila try out the climber for a little while? I'll watch you climb."

The chart on the next page shows some typical behaviors of preschool children and some positive guidance approaches that can be used to guide children's behavior.

TYPICAL BEHAVIOR	POSITIVE GUIDANCE APPROACH
Two children fight over a funnel at the water table.	Find a way for them to take turns. Give the second child something else to use in the meantime.
A child writes on the table.	Direct the child to a logical consequence— wiping the table.
A child who used to have trouble taking turns offers another child the helicopter in the block corner.	Reinforce this behavior in a private moment. "Dean, it was nice of you to give Shawn the helicopter today."
A child is very restless at circle time.	One teacher can sit nearby to calm the child or can take the child aside to draw a picture or read a book.
The whole group is restless at circle time.	Cut the activity short and move on to a more active activity.
Two children fight over a favorite hat.	Encourage them to use their problem-solving skills to work out a way to take turns using the hat.
A child who used to forget hangs up her coat three days in a row.	Reinforce the behavior using genuine praise. "I really like the way you hung up your coat, Crystal."

In this learning activity, you will observe a child's behavior over a five-day period. Take notes on what you see the child doing. After reviewing your notes, plan ways to use the information to help the child develop self-discipline. Begin by reviewing the example on the next page.

Guiding Children's Behavior

Child: _Shawn_   **Age:** _4 years 3 months_   **Dates:** _February 6-10_

WHAT DOES THIS CHILD DO WHEN:	HOW YOU CAN USE THIS INFORMATION TO PROVIDE POSITIVE GUIDANCE
A task is too challenging? _He couldn't put the attribute blocks in the tray. He started banging the pieces and tried to put them in the wrong slots._	_Ask, "How can you get them in without banging?" Then he and I could study each piece and talk about which slot looks like it is the same size._
He has to wait for a turn? _He wanted the police officer's hat in the house corner and took it from Felipe. Felipe yelled._	_Tell him that our rule is to ask to use something that someone else has. Ask, "How can you let Felipe know that you want to wear the hat? What can we do when several children want to share one hat?"_
His parents leave in the morning? _He usually handles this well. If he's sad or not feeling well, he starts to cry as his mother leaves and asks her to stay._	_Tell him that it's okay to feel sad when you miss someone. Remind him that his mother returns after we've spent our day together._
It's time to change activities? _He's okay in most areas except the house corner. He gets very involved and some-times has trouble stopping to clean up. Sometimes he refuses to take off his dress-up clothes._	_Give him several direct warnings that clean-up is in 10 minutes, 5 minutes, and 2 minutes. Help him clean up and move to the next activity._

WHAT DOES THIS CHILD DO WHEN:	HOW YOU CAN USE THIS INFORMATION TO PROVIDE POSITIVE GUIDANCE
He has trouble getting involved in an activity? *This is not a problem in the house corner, art, and block areas. He has trouble sticking with one thing in the table toy area—sometimes he takes toys that are too difficult.*	*Help him select toys that are at his level. Remind him to finish playing with one before taking another toy.*
He's not ready to sleep at nap time? *He is not a sleeper. He often says he's not tired and gets off his cot when I'm not nearby.*	*Tell him that it's okay to not sleep, but he must rest. Offer him choices of quiet things to do on his cot during nap time (like books or puzzles).*
He doesn't like the food at mealtime? *He likes most foods. If he can't figure out what's in a stew, he won't eat it.*	*Encourage him to taste all foods. Help him to name the "mystery foods" in stews and soups.*
He's not ready to go home at the end of the day? *Often this is a problem. During the late afternoon free play time he gets very involved in dramatic play or easel painting.*	*Give him several warnings about cleaning up before going home. Remind him that he'll be back soon. Ask him what he wants to do the next day, write it down, and hang the note in that area so we'll remember.*

Guiding Children's Behavior

Child: _____ Age: _____ Date: _____

WHAT DOES THIS CHILD DO WHEN:	HOW YOU CAN USE THIS INFORMATION TO PROVIDE POSITIVE GUIDANCE

WHAT DOES THIS CHILD DO WHEN:	HOW YOU CAN USE THIS INFORMATION TO PROVIDE POSITIVE GUIDANCE

Discuss your observations with your trainer.

III. Arranging the Room to Promote Self-Discipline

In this activity you will learn:

- to observe children's behavior for clues to problems in the environment; and

- to use the room arrangement and display of materials to help preschool children develop self-discipline.

There are times when everything seems to go wrong, no matter how hard you try. The children seem restless. They may run a lot in the classroom, fight over toys, and wander around unable to choose things to do. They might be easily distracted and have trouble sticking with tasks, or they use materials roughly and resist cleaning up.

There are many possible reasons for these behaviors. Most young children act in these ways sometimes. But if you see many of these behaviors day after day, it's a good idea to check your room arrangement. How you arrange the furniture and select and display materials can be working against you. The environment can encourage the very behaviors you want to discourage.

In this activity you will consider how room arrangement affects children's behavior. You will look at two common behavior problems and how the environment can be the cause—or the solution. On the next page there are two examples. Then you will plan ways to change the environment so that the room arrangement helps you address three other common behavior problems.

Arranging the Room to Promote Self-Discipline
(Example)

CHILDREN'S BEHAVIOR	POSSIBLE PROBLEMS IN THE ENVIRONMENT	HOW YOU MIGHT CHANGE THE ENVIRONMENT
Running in the classroom.	*There is too much open space. The room is not divided into smaller areas.*	*Use shelves and furniture to divide the space better.*
Fighting over toys.	*There is only one of each toy. Children are asked to share too often. You can use a ringing timer, a sand timer, or a list of the children waiting for their turn.*	*It's better to have duplicates of toys. Show children when it will be their turn.*

Arranging the Room to Promote Self-Discipline

CHILDREN'S BEHAVIOR	POSSIBLE PROBLEMS IN THE ENVIRONMENT	HOW YOU MIGHT CHANGE THE ENVIRONMENT
Wandering around. Unable to choose something to do.		
Easily distracted. Has trouble staying with and completing a task.		
Using materials roughly and resisting clean-up.		

Check your answers with the answer sheet at the end of the module. There can be more than one right answer.

Think about the children in your group. Do you see any of the same problem behaviors? If so, which ones?

_____

_____

_____

Look at your room arrangement. Are there any changes you could make to improve the arrangement? Use the space below to note the changes you wish to make.

_____

_____

_____

Discuss your ideas with your trainer and colleagues before trying them out.

IV. Using Words to Provide Positive Guidance

In this activity you will learn:

- to use words to guide children's behavior; and

- to use words to remind children of rules and limits.

By the time children are in preschool, they can use words to express their feelings. They also listen to and understand what you say to them. The words you use and your tone of voice are very powerful positive guidance tools. Angry, insensitive words can make children feel sad, ashamed, or angry. Teacher who use words in a positive way, however, help promote children's self-discipline. Your words can help children understand their own feelings and those of others.

Adults often talk to children with a loud "discipline voice." It is better to talk to children in a natural though firm tone of voice all the time. When children hear a quiet, firm tone, they feel safe and cared for. Try to get close enough to a child to speak at a normal level. When an adult shouts, children may be so startled that they don't really hear the words. Getting close to a child by crouching or kneeling allows you to have a private discussion. Look into the child's eyes, touch an arm or shoulder, and give him or her your full attention. (Note: Some children are taught that it is disrespectful to look an adult in the eye. Be sensitive to cultural differences.)

If you're not sure how your voice sounds when you're talking to children, try tape-recording a part of the day. Play it back for yourself and ask, "Would I like to listen to this person all day?"

The words you use also are very important. Sometimes, an adult who is angry with a child lets out a flood of words. This may make the adult feel better, but the child probably does not hear the message. Try to use simple statements, spoken once, so the child can focus on the real issue. These statements should be very clear and should include brief descriptions of the following:

What happened:	"Theresa, you have torn Joey's pictures two times this morning."
What behavior is acceptable:	"You can do your own work."
What isn't acceptable:	"I can't let you tear Joey's picture. It's his work."
Suggested solution:	"Let's get some tape and fix Joey's picture. He feels bad that you tore it. Then you can tear some magazines for a collage, or you can read a story with me."

This example includes offering the child two choices. Both of these are acceptable to the teacher. Be careful to offer choices only when you mean them. When you ask a child "would you like to clean up now?" it sounds as if the child has a choice. The child could easily say "no." Probably you really mean "it's time to pick up now."

Teachers can use words to give directions in a positive way. Instead of saying "no running" or "don't leave your coat on the floor," you can say "walk" or "hang your coat on the hook." Children respond well to positive directions.

You can use words to show respect for children's feelings and help children feel good about themselves. Avoid comparing one child to another. Instead of saying "Susan is nice and quiet at story time—can you be quiet like Susan?" you could say, "Please be quiet now so we can begin the story." Phrases such as "four-year-olds don't suck their thumbs" should also be avoided. They make children feel bad, and they do not change behaviors.

The chart below provides more examples of words you can use to provide positive guidance.

SITUATION	YOU MIGHT SAY
Emilio and Tim both want to sit next to the teacher as she reads to them in the book corner.	"There's enough space for each of you to sit right next to me. Emilio, you sit on my right side. Tim, you sit on my left side. Now we can share this big pillow and the book."
Maddie and Vanessa both want all the cylinder blocks.	"There are many shapes of blocks on the shelves for you both to use. There are only six cylinder-shaped blocks, so see if you can each use some of them."
Dean wants to play in the house corner with two children who don't want him to join them.	"Dean, it's hard when your friends say they don't want to play with you. They still like you, and you're okay. This time they want to play with each other. There is room at the work bench. Would you like to go there, or would you like to start a game of your own and invite some other friends to join you?"
Lloyd and Chaundra both want to play in the same areas.	"There is space for both of you to play in the truck area. You need to share the space. Each of you has the trucks that you want to use. Let's talk about who can drive near the gas station and who can go in the direction of the school. Maybe later you'll decide to change places."

Using words to guide children's behavior takes some practice. It may be a while before new ways of talking to preschool children feel natural to you. You will be rewarded when the children you care for let you know how much better they feel because of your understanding and caring.

In this learning activity you will practice using words to guide children's behavior and help them learn self-discipline. First read the examples. Then write down words that you can use in typical classroom situations.

Words You Use to Provide Positive Guidance
(Example)

When a child pushes another child:

"George, you want to have the doll carriage but you may not push Debby out of the way. She was already wheeling the carriage. Ask Debby if you can have a turn. If she says yes, you can have the carriage. If she says no, you must wait for your turn."

When a child takes playdough from another child:

"You may have some of your own playdough. You may not take Tamila's playdough from her. Ask Tamila to share her playdough, or ask me for some."

When a child paints on another child's picture:

"You may paint a picture of your own. I can't let you paint on Lamont's paper. You can have your own piece of paper, and Lamont can have another piece too. Or, you can ask Lamont if he wants to paint a picture with you."

When a child is having a hard time waiting for a turn:

"Marguerite, you've waited a long time for the trike. You're getting tired of waiting so you are calling Renee stupid. You may not call her stupid. She is not stupid and neither are you. You can tell Renee that you have waited a long time and want your turn now."

When a child screams because there aren't enough of one kind of toy:

It's okay to want to have your own shovel like the other children. But screaming doesn't help you get a shovel. You need to use your words. Ask if anyone is ready to give you their shovel. Or let's see what else you can use to dig with."

When a child is upset because a friend won't play:

"It's okay to want to play with Kenny. You feel a little sad when he says no. It's not okay to hit him when he wants to play alone. You can play by yourself on the jungle gym, or ask someone else to play with you."

Words You Use to Provide Positive Guidance

When a child calls another child "stupid":

_____

_____

_____

_____

_____

_____

_____

When a child refuses to clean up:

_____

_____

_____

_____

_____

_____

_____

When a child pushes another child away from the water play table:

_____

_____

_____

_____

_____

_____

_____

When a child talks very loudly:

_____

_____

_____

_____

_____

_____

_____

When a child tears another child's painting:

_____

_____

_____

_____

_____

_____

_____

When a child is upset because it's too rainy to go outside:

_____

_____

_____

_____

_____

_____

_____

_____

When _____ **(add your own example here):**

_____

_____

_____

_____

_____

_____

_____

Now share your words with your trainer. You could also write these words on a chart and hang it in your room to help you get used to using them.

V. Setting Rules and Limits

In this activity you will learn:

- to set clear, simple rules and limits and to communicate them to children; and

- to enforce rules consistently.

Rules and limits help both children and teachers understand what behaviors are acceptable. Young children need simple rules that are stated clearly and positively. For example, "walk in the room so you don't hurt yourself" rather than "don't run in the room" tells children what they can do and why. Children feel safer when they know that adults have set limits. These feelings of security tend to make children feel freer to explore and experiment.

Young children often act on impulses. Teachers can help children understand the consequences of their actions. "Screaming won't make Vanessa give you the book, Tim. When she has finished reading it, you can have a turn." Teachers also help children learn that limiting what they are doing now may mean they can do something else later. "If we stop playing a little early and clean up now, we can go for a walk before lunch."

It's important to have just enough rules to keep the room functioning smoothly. When there are too many rules, children can't remember what to do. Too few rules might mean that the children aren't safe and that the environment is disorderly.

Rules should reflect what children are like at each stage of development. For example, most preschool children can't easily sit and listen for very long. It would be unfair to ask them to sit at the table with nothing to do for ten minutes while you brought out the materials for an activity.

Children respect rules when they understand the reasons behind them. They also are more likely to follow rules if they help create them. Talk to children about the consequences of actions. "What might happen if we squirt water on the floor?" Children could come up with answers and also think of a rule. "Keep the water in the water table. When the water spills, the floor gets slippery. Someone might fall and get hurt."

Some rules and limits are set by the way the room is arranged. Activity areas can be labeled to show how many children can play there at a time. (How the environment affects children's behavior is discussed in Learning Activity III, Arranging the Room to Promote Self-Discipline.)

Teachers in the room need to be sure to apply the rules and limits consistently, so children learn what to expect from their environment. "Ms. Williams, we should remind the children not to run near the water table—Kim slipped today."

There are many times during the day when teachers must remind children of the rules and limits. Children are more likely to internalize the rules when the teachers' reminders are worded positively and delivered in a brief and firm manner. Some examples follow:

SAY OR DO THIS	INSTEAD OF THIS
"Use quiet voices inside; you can talk loudly outside."	"Will you stop screaming?!" or "Sit over there and shut up!"
"If you feel like hitting, go hit the punching bag."	"Haven't I told you not to hit other children?"
"Use the shovel to dig with; if you want to throw something, you can throw the ball."	"If you don't put that shovel down right now, I'm going to take it away."
"Keep your feet on the floor. Climb only on the climber."	"Get down off that table this minute!"
"It's dangerous to push people on the slide. They may get hurt."	"If you don't stop pushing children on the slide, I'm going to push you."
"Careful drivers put on their brakes or or sound their horns."	"Stop running those trucks into the walls!"
"Throw the stick over the fence so no one will get hurt."	"Put that stick down. Don't you know you might get hurt?"
"Keep the puzzle on the table so the pieces don't get lost."	"Did you dump the puzzle pieces on the floor again? I told you not to do that."
"Sit down on the rug, so the others can see."	"Get out of the way! The other children can't see."
"Wipe your brush on the jar, so it won't drip."	"You're dripping paint all over the floor!"

As children grow and mature, they can handle more freedom, more activities, and more responsibility. Teachers need to be careful observers to see when individual children or the whole group can handle greater freedom. There is a fine line between keeping children safe and keeping them from having chances to grow and be independent. The limits set for four-year-olds in September may need to be adjusted in a few months' time.

In this activity you will use positive phrases to list the rules you have in your room. Then you will answer some questions about one of the rules in your room. First read the example below and then complete the blank forms that follow.

Rules for the Preschool Room
(Example)

Staying healthy and safe:

Climb on the climber, not on the furniture.

Blocks are for building, not for throwing.

Wash your hands before eating snacks or lunch.

Respecting the rights of others:

Stay out of other people's cubbies.

Your turn on the tricycle is three rides around the track.

When you want to be alone, you can go to the quiet area.

Not hurting yourself or others:

Use your words to tell others how you feel.

If you feel like hitting, you may hit the punching bag.

Go down the slide one at a time.

Caring for our equipment and materials:

Everyone helps at clean-up time.

Turn the pages carefully.

Keep the puzzle on the table.

Now select one of the rules or limits you listed and answer the following questions.

(Example)

Rule: *Everyone helps at clean-up time*

Why do you have this rule?

Our room is set up so that children can get toys themselves and put them back when they are finished. They feel good about doing things for themselves and learn self-discipline.

How do you fit this rule to each child's development, strengths, and needs?

Most of the children are able to clean up by themselves. For the children who need help, we break down the tasks into smaller ones.

How do you see that all adults apply the rule in the same way?

We both work with the children at clean-up time. If there are problems with consistency, we talk about them at nap time.

How do you follow through and support your words with actions?

If a child doesn't respond to the reminder, I walk over to the child. Then I kneel or crouch and repeat the reminder: "Peter, pick-up time." If reminders don't work, I might lift a child off the climber, take a brush out of a hand, help put the puzzle pieces back, and so on.

Give an example of a simple statement that is clear and states the rule positively.

"It's clean-up time. Let's put the toys away so we can go outside."

What might you say to respect and acknowledge a child's feelings?

"Juana, I know you are having fun now. It's hard to stop playing when it's so much fun. You can play some more after nap time."

How do you act with authority and show confidence?

I always give children a ten-minute warning, then a five-minute warning. I never apologize when I announce that it's clean-up time. When a child is slow to stop playing, I walk over and re-state that it is clean-up time. I don't ask the child to clean up. I just say, "It's clean-up time."

Rules for the Preschool Room

Staying healthy and safe:

_____
_____
_____
_____
_____

Respecting the rights of others:

_____
_____
_____
_____
_____

Not hurting yourself or others:

_____
_____
_____
_____
_____

Caring for our equipment and materials:

_____
_____
_____
_____
_____

Discuss these rules with a teacher who also works in your room.

Now select one of the rules or limits you listed and answer the following questions.

Rule: _____

Why do you have this rule?

_____

_____

_____

How do you fit this rule to each child's development, strengths, and needs?

_____

_____

_____

How do you see that all adults apply the rule in the same way?

_____

_____

_____

How do you follow through and support your words with actions?

_____

_____

_____

Give an example of a simple statement that is clear and states the rule positively.

_____

_____

_____

What might you say to respect and acknowledge a child's feelings?

_____

_____

_____

How do you act with authority and show confidence?

_____

_____

_____

Discuss your answers with your trainer.

VI. Responding to Challenging Behaviors

In this activity you will learn:

- to look for the reasons behind a child's challenging behavior; and

- to develop a plan for responding to challenging behavior.

Often, young children cannot say how they feel. Even after they begin talking, they may still find it hard to express their feelings with words. When children kick, cry, bite, or have temper tantrums, teachers need to think about what the behavior means. Teachers can then respond in ways that help children control their behavior. Children's behaviors may be telling you many different things.

- "I feel lonely. That's why I'm crying."

- "I am angry. That's why I hit Shawn."

- "I am afraid. That's why I won't let go of your hand."

- "I want to be good at something. That's why I keep ripping up my pictures."

- "I need some limits. That's why I'm running around the room."

- "I can't do what you asked me to do. That's why I threw my sneaker at the wall."

It's important for teachers to accept children's negative feelings. We all have days when we feel bad or don't want to do certain tasks. Teachers can help children learn to recognize when they aren't feeling good. Teachers can also provide ways for children to express their negative feelings without hurting themselves, other people, or the things in the room. When you see that children are feeling frustrated, you can redirect them to make something with playdough, play at the water table, or begin finger painting. These are soothing activities that help many children feel better. When children feel very angry, throwing bean bags or hammering may help release their feelings.

Some inappropriate behaviors are accidental or careless more than deliberate. A child may accidentally spill paint and then laugh when asked to clean up, for example. Such behaviors should be responded to firmly but quietly; they don't need to be dwelt upon, as they aren't part of a pattern of challenging or limit-testing behaviors.

Challenging behaviors, such as biting or temper tantrums, are likely to occur again and again. This often means that something in the child's life is disturbing. The child doesn't know how to express his or her feelings with words, so he or she acts out.

In such cases, all the adults who care for the child need to discuss the possible causes of the problem. Perhaps a situation at home is causing the child to be upset or frustrated. Or the environment at the center may be causing the child's behavior. The schedule, activities, or room arrangement may not meet this child's needs.

You can reassure the child's parents that there are times when some preschool children behave this way, but the behavior cannot be allowed at the center. You can then agree on a plan for consistent responses to the behavior. It is very important to let the child know that he or she is still loved and cared for, even if he or she has a problem behavior.

The following reading, "But Problems Are Sure to Occur," includes many suggestions for responding to challenging behaviors.

But Problems Are Sure to Occur[1]

But Problems Are Sure to Occur

Not all adults react in the same way to children's problems, and what is a crisis to one adult may be easily handled by another adult. Children who talk and move around or act sad or cry or speak loudly are easily accepted by adults who know what it is like to be a child. There are situations, though, that almost always cause adults (no matter how skilled they are) to ask, "What do you do when . . . ?"

What do you do when children run around the room, knocking into people and things? First, you try to understand why the children are behaving this way as you settle them down. Understanding does not have to be a long, slow process; it can happen at lightning speed. Children may act wild and restless because they are hungry or scared or excited by what they see in the room or because they are just feeling high. Adults who respond with anger and loud voices may excite children and speed them up just when the aim is to get them to stop and focus on something.

It works well for adults to greet overexcited children with a firm hand as they come into the room. You can speak to them kindly, with authority, and with some direction about what they should do first. You might ask whether they would like to start the day building with blocks or working at the water table. Or you can simply take a galloping child by the hand or put an arm around the child and say, "No more running for now. I want you to play over here for a little while." You can lead the child there, sit down together, and create as much interest in the activity for the child as you can. In this way, one adult can usually redirect two or three restless children at once.

You will often find that the rough, runabout child calms down gradually and proceeds to work independently. Sometimes, though, a restless child must be guided in this manner through an entire day. If you have more than one such child, you may need extra

Adults who respond with anger and loud voices may excite children and speed the children up just when the aim is to get them to stop and focus on something.

---

[1] Reprinted with permission from Jeannette Galambos Stone, *A Guide to Discipline* (Washington, DC: National Association for the Education of Young Children, 1978), pp. 18-22.

adults to assist you. Many teachers find volunteer help for assistance.

It may sound unfair for one or two children to get a lot of attention, but it is not unfair, because *all* children learn from what goes on between one adult and one child. If you settle down one restless child, or befriend a shy one, all those present will learn that you take good care of children. The children will feel that you are in charge and that they are safe with you. They will learn some ways of handling problems, too. Of course, if you use sarcasm or physical force, they learn something else—that you are someone to tease or fear. But if you keep calm, fair, loving, and strong, they learn to trust you and cooperate with you.

What do you do when children just stand around and refuse to join in? What is happening inside these children? Can we play our hunches, quickly? Such children might not be feeling well; have been scolded or punished at home; have seen or heard something scary; or feel inferior. Whatever it is, they do not gain courage when people point at or embarrass them or try too hard to coax them. They probably feel better able to respond to adults who simply accept them the way they are, who move about with an air of gentle control, who make it clear they will help if the children want help, and who do not press but do not neglect them. The child will usually respond when you say, "If you want to watch for awhile, that's OK . . . and if you need help or want to talk, I'll be right here." In other words, good teachers move with the grain not against it.

What do you do when a child spits? No time to guess about causes until later, because spitting often builds up fast to outbursts of wild aggression. The quickest, fairest, calmest way to deal with this is to stop the child (without hurting) and announce, "I will not let you spit on anybody. If you have to spit, do it in the sink (or in this dish or over here in this corner of the yard)." No scolding is necessary; it probably will not be effective anyhow. Tell children firmly *where* they can spit, but that they cannot spit at people.

What do you do about hitting, kicking, scratching, attacking? Again the adult must state the rules. "I cannot let you hit people. If you have to hit, then bang on the floor (or punching bag or lump of clay). I know how you feel, but I cannot let you hurt people, and I cannot let them hurt you." That's that. You can kneel down and talk to the child directly while looking into his or her eyes, holding the child if necessary.

Some children may have to be held or carried or allowed to thrash around away from the other children (who will need to be reassured by another adult).

These storms pass, though, and skilled adults do not waste their breath talking, scolding, or explaining when children cannot really listen. You can stay nearby, do not panic, do not rage back at the child, but simply remain firm in your stand: No hurting is allowed. When the child has quieted down—and it may take a long time—you can put an arm around and reassure the child that it will be all right. You can tell the child you are willing to listen. You may say that you keep children safe and that is why you had to stop the hitting. You may add that people have hard times but that you think the child now feels better and will have a better time for the rest of the day.

Biting is considered, by some, to be the worst thing a child can do. Biting is dangerous, and it frightens both the biter and the bitten person. The adult first separates the two children. You can comfort the bitten child and make sure that he or she is all right, receiving first aid if necessary. You may need another adult to help, because you will want to stay with the biter, making it clear immediately and firmly that you will not allow biting of people. "I will not permit biting. It is dangerous. I want children to be safe here." You can assure the biter that you will not let harm come to anyone. A soothing activity like water play or a favorite puzzle can be given to the child. The hurt child must also be comforted and then interested in something else.

It does no good to encourage other children to bite back to show how it feels. Biting is wrong because it is powerfully destructive and dangerous. Since it is wrong, it is wrong for everyone at all times.

Do you ever punish a child? We are adults talking about teaching children. Spanking or isolation or shaking or angry shouting at children have no place in teaching anything. When adults hit children to get them to mind, too much has already gone wrong, and discipline has broken down. The best teachers in the world get so angry or frustrated at times, though, that they reach an emotional breaking point. Afterwards, they wonder just where the situation got out of hand and how to live with themselves.

Most adults do not like themselves after they hit a child. They may make excuses by saying that it was the only way to make the child stop misbehaving. And they feel relieved because children *can* make us angry enough to hit. At the same time, they feel deep within that a big person should not hit a small person. Adults set the example for good behavior, and we know that children cannot follow our good example if we are setting a bad one!

Therefore, you do not hit children when you want them to stop hitting. You do not yell at children to get

them to stop yelling, or spit at children to indicate they should not spit. Of course, you want children to know how to sympathize with others and to know how it feels, but you have to show them *how to act,* not how *not* to act. If you were to teach only by copying children's bad behavior to show them how it feels, you would knock down their block buildings, tear up easel paintings, cry when they cry, and so on. If you did these things, you would become a child when what children need most is an adult. They need an adult who is trustworthy, who is in charge of them, and who has self-control.

There are effective and decent ways to conduct yourself during a child's explosive outburst, without becoming childish. Use your hands and arms and body to hold the child in your arms or in a small room with you. The child will benefit by your control and by your understanding, will finish with the outbreak, and be all right. The child will remember, next time angry feelings come up, that you are not an enemy and that

you have ways to help establish self-control. And you will not have hit the child.

The difference between stopping children by hitting or by holding is tremendous. When adults hit, they take very unfair advantage of children. But when you hold, you are protecting as well as controlling the child. These are two very different methods, even though the holding may have a fairly physical look to it. Occasionally, you may find it necessary to hold children's arms if they try to strike you, or grasp their chins if they try to bite you, or place your ankle over their legs if they try to kick you. If you do this only to control children's actions, because you believe that it would be wrong to strike them, they are safe and you are safe. Both of you will come out of the crisis able to work together and with respect for each other.

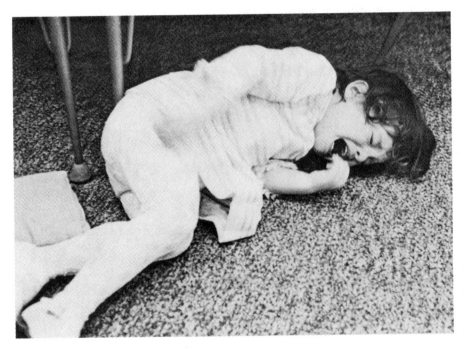

Spanking or isolation or shaking or angry shouting at children have no place in teaching anything. There are effective and decent ways to conduct yourself during a child's explosive outburst, without becoming childish.

In this activity you will first think of a child in your room who has a challenging behavior. You will describe the behavior and your response. Next you will talk with the other adults who care for the child about the child's behavior. Together, you will develop a plan for responding to the behavior. Review the example below, then complete the blank form that follows.

Responding to Challenging Behaviors
(Example)

Child: _Renee_   **Age:** _3 years, 3 months_   **Date:** _April 16_

What behavior is challenging?

Renee hits other children, usually on their arms.

How often does this occur?   **How long has it been going on?**

Two or three times a week.   *Two weeks.*

When does it happen?

When Renee wants a turn with a toy. Sometimes when she's outside on the playground and wants to swing or slide and other children get in line first.

How do you respond now?

One teacher comforts the child who was hit and gets the child ice, if necessary. The other takes Renee aside and tells her she cannot hit people. Then she has to sit on the grass until we all go inside.

How does the child respond?

She cries and screams. Then she sometimes pulls up the grass or sucks her thumb.

Did something happen at home that might have upset the child?

Renee has a new baby brother, who shares her room. She does not seem very interested in him. Renee doesn't hit at home.

Did something happen at the center that might have upset the child?

We can't think of anything that has changed.

Conclusion:

Renee may feel jealous of her new brother. We need to look at the ways we are responding now to see how we could improve. We think separating Renee is making her feel very bad about herself. We need to help her use her words to express her feelings about the new baby.

Plans for responding to this behavior at home and at the center:

Renee's parents will help her express her feelings about her baby brother. They will try to set up a special place at home that is just for Renee.

At the center, we will also provide ways for Renee to talk about her brother. We will read <u>A Baby Sister for Francis</u>, by Russell Hoban, at circle time. We can ask the other children who have baby brothers or sisters at home to tell us what it's like.

When Renee hits, one teacher will still comfort the hurt child. The other teacher will respond to Renee. This teacher will bend down, hold her firmly, look in her eyes and say, "It hurts people when you hit them. I won't let anyone hit you. I won't let you hit anyone." Then the teacher will try to get her involved in a calming activity, such as playing with playdough, water, or sand. We know Renee hits when she wants a turn on the swing or wants something another child has. We agreed that we will not let her have the turn or the toy if she hits.

Responding to Challenging Behaviors

Child: _____ Age: _____ Date: _____

What behavior is challenging?

_____

_____

_____

How often does this occur?   **How long has it been going on?**

_____   _____

_____   _____

_____   _____

_____   _____

When does it happen?

_____

_____

_____

How do you respond now?

_____

_____

_____

How does the child respond?

_____

_____

_____

Did something happen at home that might have upset the child?

_____

_____

_____

Did something happen at the center that might have upset the child?

_____

_____

_____

_____

Conclusion:

_____

_____

_____

_____

Plans for responding to this behavior at home and at the center:

_____

_____

_____

_____

_____

_____

_____

_____

What happened at home and at the center when you tried out your plans? Has the challenging behavior changed or gone away?

_____

_____

_____

_____

_____

_____

Discuss this activity with your trainer.

Summarizing Your Progress

You have now completed all of the learning activities for this module. Whether you are an experienced teacher or a new one, this module has probably helped you develop new skills for guiding preschool children's behavior. Before you go on, take a few minutes to summarize what you've learned.

- Turn back to Learning Activity I, Using Your Knowledge of Child Development to Guide Children's Behavior, and add to the chart specific examples of what you learned about helping children develop self-discipline while you were working on this module. Compare your ideas to those in the completed chart at the end of the module.

- Next, review your responses to the pre-training assessment for this module. Write a summary of what you learned and list the skills you developed or improved.

_____

_____

_____

_____

_____

_____

_____

_____

_____

_____

_____

_____

_____

_____

_____

If there are topics you would like to know more about, you will find recommended readings listed in the orientation, which can be found in Volume I.

Your final step in this module is to complete the knowledge and competency assessments. Let your trainer know when you are ready to schedule the assessments. After you have successfully completed these assessments, you will be ready to start a new module. Congratulations on your progress so far, and good luck with your next module.

Answer Sheets

Guiding Children's Behavior

Providing an Environment That Encourages Children's Self-Discipline

1. **What behavior did Ms. Kim find frustrating?**

    a. The children are constantly fighting over toys.

    b. They are rough with the toys and destroying them.

    c. They resist cleaning up.

2. **What suggestions did Ms. Richards have for dealing with the behavior problems?**

    a. To switch some toys with another group so they could have duplicates of popular toys.

    b. To reduce the need to share.

    c. To make picture labels to show that there is a place for everything.

3. **How might her approach help?**

    a. Children won't have to share as often, and sharing is difficult for three-year-olds.

    b. An orderly room with labels for all materials teaches children that the toys and materials are important and should be cared for.

    c. Clean-up will be a matching game, and children may find it more interesting and challenging.

    d. Teachers won't have to give negative messages to the children about their behavior.

Using Positive Methods to Guide Individual Children

1. **What did Ms. Williams know about Travis?**

    a. Travis could help find his own solutions to problems.

    b. Travis liked to throw things.

    c. Travis responded well when his behavior was redirected.

    d. Travis was very active.

2. How did Ms. Williams let Travis know that she respected him?

a. She walked over to him and bent down to talk to him.

b. She told him he was learning to be a good thrower.

c. She asked him to think of a safe place where he could throw pine cones without hurting anyone.

Helping Children Understand and Express Their Feelings in Acceptable Ways

1. How do you think Billy felt when Sam grabbed his piece of orange?

a. Angry

b. Frustrated

2. How did Mr. Lopez help Billy learn to express his feelings in acceptable ways?

a. He told Billy it was okay to be angry.

b. He helped Billy stop hitting.

c. He told Billy not to hit Sam but instead to tell him to leave the piece of orange alone.

Using Your Knowledge of Child Development
to Guide Children's Behavior

WHAT PRESCHOOL CHILDREN ARE LIKE	HOW TEACHERS CAN USE THIS INFORMATION TO GUIDE CHILDREN'S BEHAVIOR
They are eager to please adults.	Reinforce positive behavior. Let children know you are pleased when they do a good job cleaning up, helping friends, or completing games so they feel good about themselves.
They want to make decisions for themselves.	Offer children choices about what they want to play with, what books they would like to read, and so on.
They often like to try new things and take risks.	Make sure children are not in danger. Help them judge what risks are safe and what risks are not. Encourage them to think before they act so they learn to develop good judgment and self-discipline.
They can take turns and share but don't always want to.	Set up a system (a sign-up sheet, a timer, or cards) for taking turns with popular toys or activities. If children can see when they will have a turn, they find it easier to wait.
They sometimes lose control and start kicking and screaming.	Be there to hold the child until he or she gains control again. Stay with the child until he or she has calmed down and can listen to your words. This is the start of self-discipline.
They have lots of energy. They run fast, climb high, jump, gallop, and hop.	Give them time and space to be active and to use their energy in acceptable ways. Don't expect them to sit for long periods.
They may use bathroom words and swear words to get attention.	Try ignoring this so you aren't giving them attention. If they don't stop soon, say "we don't use those words here" and go on to something else.

WHAT PRESCHOOL CHILDREN ARE LIKE	HOW TEACHERS CAN USE THIS INFORMATION TO GUIDE CHILDREN'S BEHAVIOR
They like to feel powerful and important. They can sometimes be very bossy.	Avoid power struggles. Set clear limits and be consistent. Invite children to help you so they can feel useful and competent.
They like to get attention and will act out if they feel ignored.	Give children attention for positive reasons, not when they act out. Let them know what they do well so they learn the right things to do.
They sometimes strike out in anger at other children or even at adults.	Stop the hitting immediately—do not ignore it. Calmly but firmly say, "Hitting hurts. It's not okay to hit. Use your words to tell her how you feel."
They are beginning to understand the consequences of their actions.	Help children see the connection between their actions and what happens afterward. For instance, provide short-handled brooms and sponges so children can clean up their own spills.

Arranging the Room
to Promote Self-Discipline

CHILDREN'S BEHAVIOR	POSSIBLE PROBLEMS IN THE ENVIRONMENT	HOW YOU MIGHT CHANGE THE ENVIRONMENT
Wandering around. Unable to choose something to do.	The room is too cluttered. The choices are not clear. There aren't enough materials to choose from. Nothing appeals to the child and so the child is bored.	Get rid of the clutter. Make the room simpler. Take out materials you've had in storage. Make new games, puzzles, or prop boxes. Put out some different art materials.
Easily distracted. Trouble staying with and completing a task.	Areas are too open so children can see everything going on in the room.	Use shelves to define areas so children are not distracted by other activities.
Using materials roughly and resisting clean-up.	Materials on the shelves are messy. There is no order to the display of materials.	Make a place for everything. Use picture labels to show where materials go.

Glossary

Challenging behavior   Behavior such as biting or temper tantrums that is often difficult to handle.

Consequence   The natural or logical result of a behavior.

Discipline   The actions that adults take to guide and direct children toward acceptable behavior.

Limits and rules   Guidelines set by teachers and children as to what is acceptable behavior.

Positive guidance   Methods that teachers use to help children learn to behave in acceptable ways. These methods help children develop self-discipline.

Punishment   Control of children's behavior by use of fear.

Self-discipline   The ability to control one's own behavior.

Module 11
Families

Why Is Working with Families Important?

Recent studies have shown that the most effective child development programs are those which actively promote and encourage the involvement of families. Good working relationships with families enable teachers to be more responsive to each child's needs. When parents and teachers work as a team, they can share information and discuss ways to provide consistent care at home and at the center.

No matter how much time children spend at the center each day, their parents are the most important people in their lives. Teachers can acknowledge parents' roles as the first and primary educators of their children by reinforcing family ties and by doing whatever they can to increase parents' pleasure in their children. Parents can teach you a lot about their children—what they like to do, what they don't enjoy, things they do well, skills they are developing. Teachers can share similar information with parents on a regular basis. In this way, parents can feel connected to their children's lives at the center. They can also feel good about the quality of care their children are receiving.

Some parents may not show any interest in becoming involved at the center. They may need to feel more comfortable with you and the other staff, or they may be too busy. You may find ways to involve these families; however, there are always some families who prefer to keep their involvement to a minimum.

Working with families can be a very rewarding part of your job. Most parents are concerned about their children and want to do what's best for them. Let them know that you share their concern and that you want to provide high-quality child care. Make sure they know that you enjoy caring for their child and that you share their excitement when their child helps make breakfast or makes up a song.

Teachers work with families in a variety of ways. Daily conversations with parents are opportunities to get to know each other and to exchange information about a child's activities at home and at the center. Teachers also encourage parents to become involved with their child's life at the center. Parents should always be welcome at the center. For those who cannot visit during the day, you can provide a variety of other ways for them to participate. Often parents have questions about their child's development. They may ask you about child development or how to respond to their child's behavior. You can respond to these requests by drawing on your own experience, or you can refer parents to books or other resources on child development.

Working with families involves:

- communicating with family members often to exchange information about their child at home and at the center;

- providing a variety of ways for family members to participate in their child's life at the center; and

- providing support to families.

Listed below are examples of how teachers demonstrate their competence in working with families.

Communicating with Family Members Often to Exchange Information About Their Child at Home and at the Center

Here are some examples of what teachers can do.

- Encourage parents to drop in at the center at any time. "Mr. Jackson, we're looking forward to your visit at lunch today."

- Share some good news with parents every day. "Connie tried a new vegetable today. She really feels good about tasting the beets."

- Use information about children's interests that was provided by parents. "Look, Teresa, this puppy has spots just like the ones on your puppy, Trixie."

- Give parents information about their child's routines and activities. "Mary wasn't very hungry at lunch time. She ate only half her fruit."

- Suggest ways parents can extend learning at home. "Mark really enjoys water play at the center. When he takes a bath, you could give him some plastic cups and bottles so he can practice pouring."

- Learn each parent's name and something about them as a way to build trust. "I thought of you last night, Mr. Parker, when I watched the television special on Houston. That's where your family lives, isn't it?"

Providing a Variety of Ways for Family Members to Participate in Their Child's Life at the Center

Here are some examples of what teachers can do.

- Give parents opportunities to make decisions about their child's activities. "Deena seems ready to use puzzles with more pieces. What do you think?"

- Ask parents to help you include their culture in your activities. "Would you share your recipe for stir-fried vegetables with us? The children have been learning about good nutrition. I'm sure they would enjoy cooking something healthy."

- Set up workshops on topics in which parents have expressed interest. "Many of the parents wanted to know more about how to help young children understand and express their feelings when their parents have to travel for work, so we're having a workshop next month."

- Sponsor a weekend fix-up day when parents and teachers work together to spruce up the center. "Mrs. Hanes, the children are having a great time jumping on the old tires you set up."

- Find innovative ways for working parents to help when they can't come to the center during the day. "Thanks so much for typing this month's newsletter for us, Mrs. Peterson."

Providing Support to Families

Here are some examples of what teachers can do.

- Support families under stress. "It's often hard to adjust when one parent is away. We'll help Sherrie as much as we can at the center."

- Respond to a parent's request for suggestions on how to deal with a behavior. "Many children go through a phase where they use bathroom words a lot. Our first response is to ignore them. Usually the phase passes very quickly."

- Help parents understand the effects of "rushing" their children's development. "When Jessica builds in the block corner, she is learning a lot about math concepts. Young children learn best when they can play with real objects. When she's older she'll learn to add and subtract."

- Use familiar terms instead of jargon when you talk to parents. "When Sammy plays with the pegboard and beads, that helps the small muscles in his hands and fingers develop. This is important for writing later on."

- Interpret children's behavior to their parents. "Loren is happy that her Grandma's coming to visit. I heard her telling her doll about the things she will do when Grandma comes."

Working with Families

In the following situations, teachers are working with families. As you read each one, think about what the teachers are doing and why. Then answer the questions that follow.

Communicating with Family Members Often to Exchange Information About Their Child at Home and at the Center

Yesterday was an exciting day for Janet. For the first time she climbed to the top of the ladder and went down the slide by herself. Ms. Kim watched her go down the slide and gave her a big hug when she reached the bottom. Over the last few weeks, Ms. Kim and Janet's parents, the Carters, have been sharing information about Janet's progress. First she watched the other children use the slide, then she climbed up the ladder holding Ms. Kim's hand, and recently she climbed up and down the ladder by herself. Ms. Kim knew that Janet's family was very pleased that she was learning to conquer her fears. She decided not to say anything about Janet's accomplishment so they could see it for themselves. Today Janet and her mother arrived a little early. "Guess what," Mrs. Carter says. "Janet went down the slide by herself." Ms. Kim smiles and says, "You must be very excited. Janet is going to really explore the world in different ways, now that she has learned to take a risk. We'll have to be very careful to make sure she can explore safely."

1. Why did Ms. Kim decide not to share the news about Janet's accomplishment?

_____

_____

_____

2. What kinds of information will Ms. Kim and the Carters need to share, now that Janet is learning to take risks?

_____

_____

_____

Providing a Variety of Ways for Family Members to Participate in Their Child's Life at the Center

At the beginning-of-the-year orientation for parents, Mr. Bradley comes up to Ms. Williams to discuss how he can be involved in the center's program. "I don't know much about young children and I'm not very good at talking to them. I want to be a part of Jerry's life at the center, but I'm not sure what I can do." Ms. Williams asks Mr. Bradley several questions about his work and other interests. Then she says, "Often the children really enjoy learning about something an adult is interested in. Your excitement makes them excited too. I can tell from your tone of voice when you mentioned cooking that you really enjoy it. That's something the children like to do, too. We could plan a cooking activity together, and you could do it when you come to visit our room." Mr. Bradley thought for a minute, then said, "Well, if you can give me some tips on how to cook with preschoolers, I'd like to try it. I'll look at my work schedule to see when I can get time off." A few weeks later Mr. Bradley brings Jerry to the center and stays all morning. He helps several small groups of children make "healthy bars" and talks to them about all the nutritious ingredients they are mixing together. All the children eat "healthy bars" for a snack. As he is leaving, Mr. Bradley turns to Ms. Williams and says, "Thank you for showing me a way to be involved. I'll be glad to come back again. This was a lot of fun, and it was great to see Jerry with all his friends."

1. **How did Ms. Williams help Mr. Bradley think of something he could do with Jerry's group at the center?**

    _____

    _____

    _____

2. **How did Ms. Williams help Mr. Bradley feel more comfortable about working with preschoolers?**

    _____

    _____

    _____

Providing Support to Families

"I just don't know what to do," says Mrs. Thomas when she drops three-year-old Marita off one morning. "Marita's been coming to the center for almost a month now, and she still cries and clings to me when I leave. I have to go to work, I can't stay with her all the time. Do you have any suggestions?" Mr. Lopez says, "Marita usually stops crying a few minutes after you leave. It takes some children a while to get used to being separated from their parents. We'll keep working with her to help her feel secure. What can we do to help you? Would you like to make an appointment to talk about separation? I could tell you more about what Marita does at the center. When you know more about her day, you can help Marita adjust to the center." Mrs. Thomas says, "You may be right. Let's talk tomorrow afternoon." Mr. Lopez says he will make the necessary arrangements for a parent conference. "Remember, this is a partnership. We'll work together to help Marita deal with separation." Mr. Lopez takes Marita over to the reading corner to read about what mommies and daddies do at work. Mrs. Thomas leaves for work looking a lot less worried.

1. **What did Mr. Lopez do to help Mrs. Thomas understand Marita's behavior?**

    _____

    _____

    _____

2. How did Mr. Lopez help Marita and her mother cope with separation?

_____

_____

_____

Compare your answers with those on the answer sheet at the end of this module. If your answers are different, discuss them with your trainer. There can be more than one good answer.

Your Own Family Experiences

Early childhood teachers bring many firsthand experiences to their role in working with families. Most of us grew up in a family. Some of us are now raising families of our own or have grown children. Our own experiences influence how we view families, what we think a family should look like, and how parents should raise their children.

Think for a moment about what the word "family" means to you. Do you think of a mother and father and one or more children living together? Do you think of different kinds of family relationships?

The families of the children you work with may resemble your own experiences or they may look very different. Children may be growing up with a single mother or father or with step-parents. Some children are being raised by grandparents or by a teenage mother living at home with her own parents. The traditional view of a family is not always true today. Additionally, the stresses families experience can make parenting a very difficult job.

It is not uncommon for teachers to blame parents when their children are having problems. This is especially true when teachers see parents who behave very differently toward their children. It may help to remember that all parents want the best for their children, and they are probably trying as hard as they can to be good parents. They too are guided by their own experiences growing up in a family.

Before you begin the learning activities in this module, spend a few minutes thinking of how your own views and experiences may affect the way you work with families. Consider the following questions:

Whom do you consider to be part of the family you grew up in?

_____

_____

_____

_____

_____

How are families of the children in your group different from your own family?

_____

_____

_____

_____

_____

What pressures do parents have today that your parents didn't experience?

_____

_____

_____

_____

_____

What pressures are the same?

_____

_____

_____

_____

How do you think your views and experiences affect your work with families?

_____

_____

_____

_____

_____

_____

_____

_____

_____

Discuss your responses with your trainer and a group of other staff members. When you have finished this overview section, you should complete the pre-training assessment and then go on to the learning activities in this module.

Pre-Training Assessment

Listed below are the skills that teachers use to work with families. Think about whether you do these things regularly, sometimes, or not enough. Place a check in one of the columns on the right for each skill listed. Then discuss your answers with your trainer.

SKILL	I DO THIS REGULARLY	I DO THIS SOMETIMES	I DON'T DO THIS ENOUGH
COMMUNICATING WITH FAMILY MEMBERS OFTEN TO EXCHANGE INFORMATION ABOUT THEIR CHILD AT HOME AND AT THE CENTER 1. Learning each parent's name and something about them, to build trust.			
2. Providing parents with daily information about their child's routines and activities.			
3. Encouraging parents to come to the center at any time.			
4. Suggesting ways to extend the child's learning at home.			
5. Holding parent-teacher conferences to share information about each child's progress and to make plans for the future.			
PROVIDING A VARIETY OF WAYS FOR FAMILY MEMBERS TO PARTICIPATE IN THEIR CHILD'S LIFE AT THE CENTER 6. Involving parents often in making decisions about their child's care.			
7. Surveying parents' needs and interests and providing appropriate workshops or resources.			

SKILL	I DO THIS REGULARLY	I DO THIS SOMETIMES	I DON'T DO THIS ENOUGH
8. Providing alternative ways for parents to participate when they can't come to the center during the day.			
9. Holding regularly scheduled parent meetings at times that are convenient for most parents.			
PROVIDING SUPPORT TO FAMILIES 10. Helping parents understand the stages of development every child goes through.			
11. Working with parents to come up with strategies for dealing with a behavior.			
12. Using knowledge of child development to help parents understand why their child may be behaving in a certain way.			
13. Providing support to families under stress, such as when a parent must travel for extended periods of time.			
14. Helping parents recognize signs of a child's readiness to learn something new.			

Review your responses, then list three to five skills you would like to improve or topics you would like to learn more about. When you finish this module, you will list examples of your new or improved knowledge and skills.

_____

_____

_____

_____

Now begin the learning activities for Module 11, Families.

I. Developing a Partnership with Parents

In this activity you will learn:

- to recognize and address the need that parents and teachers have to share information about children; and

- to develop and maintain a partnership with parents.

High-quality early childhood programs depend on a strong partnership between teachers and parents. This partnership must be based on respect, trust, and the understanding that the child's development will be enhanced when all the adults who care for the child work together.

Developing a partnership may take a lot of work. Sometimes a child's teacher and parents have different views on child rearing. They may even have different ideas about the child's strengths, interests, and needs. Parents and teachers may not always understand each other's point of view and may disagree about how to solve a problem. What they almost always have in common, though, is genuine concern for the well-being of the child.

Strong partnerships benefit everyone involved. Parents feel reassured about their parenting skills. Teachers also feel confident about their role, and they learn more about how to provide care that is based on their own and the parents' understanding of the child's needs, interests, and strengths. Children feel more secure knowing that both their parents and their teachers are people who can keep them safe and help them learn.

Although both the teacher and the parents know a lot about a particular child, this knowledge and information needs to be combined to create a total picture of the child. Here are some examples of the kinds of information each half of the partnership can provide.

What Parents Know

The child's parents have information about the following areas in the child's life:

- **Health and growth history.** "The information you provided about Ben's health and growth will help us get to know him and meet his needs in the best way possible."

- **Relationships with other family members.** "Carla really enjoys being with her brother. Every morning they eat together and talk about their plans for the day."

- **Ways the child likes to be held or comforted.** "When Yancey is tired he likes to have his back rubbed. It helps him settle down."

- **Which foods the child enjoys.** "Tom tried broccoli for the first time last night. He really enjoyed it."

- **Which foods the child can or cannot eat.** "Donna is allergic to all kinds of berries."

- **How the child reacts to changes in routines.** "Sonia gets very upset if I ask her to dress before breakfast. She likes to eat first, then put her clothes on."

- **What the child likes to do at home.** "Timmy always wants to stay in the bathtub and play. He hates to get out."

- **What the child is afraid of.** "Travis is afraid of clowns. We're not sure why, but he always cries when he sees one."

- **What the child did last night, over the weekend, or on vacation.** "We went to the beach for our vacation. Stacy collected buckets full of shells."

- **Who the child plays with at home.** "Our eight-year-old neighbor likes to play with Roxanne. Roxanne runs around after her."

- **The family's lifestyle.** "We like to get outdoors as much as possible. Peter likes to go hiking with us in the mountains."

- **How the child "used to be" as well as how the child is now.** "When he was three, Nick liked trucks. Now that he's four, he's more interested in playing make-believe with other children."

What Teachers Know

The child's teacher has information about the following areas in the child's life:

- **Favorite play materials.** "When Tanya first comes in the morning, she goes right to the blocks. She really has fun making tall buildings."

- **Which toys are too frustrating.** "Tory isn't ready to do the farm puzzle yet. He's learned to pick out the ones that don't have as many pieces."

- **What challenges the child enjoys.** "Shauna spent a lot of time today taking apart the clock in the science center. She really wants to see what's inside."

- **How the child plays with others.** "Janna likes to watch before she joins in with the other children."

- **How the child reacts to changes in the environment.** "Whenever we put new props in the house corner, Ellen is the first child to use them."

- **How the child tells others what he or she is feeling.** "When Gina is angry with another child she says, 'I don't like you. You're not my friend.'"

- **What the child talks about during the day.** "Today Carlos talked about going to see his cousin, Louis. He's very excited about it."

- **What the child does when his or her parents leave.** "Today I heard Jerry telling Sandy, *'Don't cry, your mom will come back soon!'* I think that's his way of assuring himself that you will always come back."

Establishing the Partnership

Your relationship with a child's parents begins when their child first enters your room. Although the parents probably don't know you, you are the person who will care for their child for most of the day, five days a week. It is natural for them to want to learn as much as they can about you, the program, the other children in the group, and how their child will spend each day. Share this information and tell them something about yourself. Let the parents know what you are like and why you enjoy working with children. Describe the day's activities and what their child will be doing. It may be helpful to give parents a copy of the daily schedule.

Begin to get to know the parents, too. Find out what their interests are, what kind of work they do, and how they feel about leaving their child at the center. Reassure parents that you accept them as their child's first teacher. Let them know how you will work with them to share information about their child and to make decisions about the child's care.

When a child first comes to the center, you and the parents will get to know each other through brief conversations at drop-off and pick-up times. Show that you are interested in the parents by always greeting each by name. Share interesting, positive information about their child's day. Let them know by your attitude and tone of voice that their child is well-cared for. "Susanna had fun today. She played with Carrie in the sand box, she painted, and she sat in my lap at story time." These kinds of daily communications will build trust and acceptance, which will lead to a stronger partnership.

If parents don't respond to your efforts to establish a partnership, try to put yourself in their place. Try to understand their feelings about leaving their child at the center. Often parents are concerned about not spending as much time with their children as they would like. It is helpful to think about your own feelings about the parents and how you may be conveying these through your tone of voice, facial expressions, or the kinds of information you share.

Although you do many things for children that parents also do (such as providing guidance or serving lunch), a teacher's role is not the same as that of the parents. Always remember that parents need your support, but they don't need you to take over their role.

Maintaining a Strong Relationship

Once a trusting relationship has been established, teachers need to continue to involve parents in the care of their children. The partnership is strengthened by continued communication and appreciation for each partner's role in caring for the child. The partnership also grows when both parents and teacher can see how the child benefits from their teamwork. "Janine doesn't cry any more when you leave. I think your idea of making her a book of family pictures to keep at the center really worked."

Some suggestions for maintaining a strong partnership follow.

- **Respond to parents' concerns or questions even though they may seem trivial.** Such concerns are important to the parents and therefore should be acknowledged. "Yes, some of the children can zip their coats, but others, like Sam, aren't ready yet. We will provide more chances for him to use his finger skills."

- **Try parents' suggestions,** unless you think they will hurt the child, even when they differ from what you would do. "We'll be sure to let Jason slice his sandwich in four pieces if you think he likes it better that way."

- **Help parents focus on their child's accomplishments** instead of comparing their child to others the same age. "Denise always has a smile ready. All the teachers feel good when she smiles at them."

- **Help children and parents feel good about belonging to the same family.** "Mr. Bradley, Jerry is so excited when he knows you're coming for lunch. He really likes it when the other kids talk about your visits."

- **Wait until you are asked before offering advice.** When you are asked, make sure you are clear about what is fact and what is opinion. "Child development experts say that children Billy's age are too young for formal reading lessons."

- **Tell parents about the good things that happen each day.** It's not necessary to report every time their child has a fight or loses his or her temper. Share problems when you need to work together to help the child. "Erica hits children when she gets angry. When can we meet to discuss ways to help her?"

- **Acknowledge events and transitions in the families' lives.** "Congratulations on your promotion. Your wife told me the whole family had a party to celebrate."

- **Be sensitive to normal guilt feelings parents may have when they leave their children at the center.** Be careful not to make assumptions about parents or judge them because their lifestyle is different from yours.

- **Help children and parents cope when one parent is away.** Suggest sending art work, letters, or stories to the parent who is away. Remind children that their parents love them even when they are gone.

- **Keep in touch when the child is absent or ill.** "Hello, Mrs. Carson, how is Paula feeling today?"

- **Maintain confidentiality when parents share something private with you.** "I'm glad you told me about this. It will help me work with Brian. Don't worry about me telling someone else. I understand that this is confidential."

The following article, "How Parents and Teachers See Each Other," describes how parents and teachers build strong relationships.

How Parents and Teachers See Each Other[1]

When I was a teacher, I used to sit in on those proverbial teacher room discussions, but I don't think it was until I became a parent that I became aware of the way that teachers talk about parents: "Can you believe the way she dresses that child?" "Why can't that father ever be on time?" I became curious as to why there is so much griping about parents. The way that teachers talk about parents seemed almost comparable to racism, a stereotypism of some sort.

I've been working on this issue off and on for ten years. Most recently, I have been surveying day care teachers to learn about their attitudes about parents. When asked to describe the parents they work with, teachers choose words that are frequently negative—*overwhelmed, anxious, demanding, struggling, busy, tired, ambitious, confused, depressed, angry.* They use some positive terms, too, but the preponderance is negative. Of course, this is not to say that their judgments may not be realistic responses to life in our time.

One of my purposes in my last book, **Between Generations**, was to help teachers understand what was normal about parental growth so that they could view issues through the eyes of parents as well as their own.

In interviewing parents across the country, I found that being a parent, especially of an infant or toddler, was often anxiety provoking. Before they had children they were sure of themselves, now with young children they are less certain. The relationship with the child changes the parent. Parental growth is affected by child growth, but the changes occur on a different level. As the child is figuring out who he or she is (that is as separate from the adult), the parent is figuring out who he or she is as a parent. The child feels dependent; the parent feels dependent.

[1]Reprinted with permission from Ellen Galinsky, "How Parents and Teachers See Each Other," *Beginnings: Parents and Teachers* (Exchange Press, PO Box 2890, Redmond, WA, 98073, Fall 1984), pp. 3-5.

Feelings and Expectations

There are four factors that figure into this caregiver-parent relationship. The first factor is the possessive feelings. Parents may feel that they are the only ones capable of caring for the child. Unexpected feelings of envy or jealousy arise when other people get involved with the child. There are also possessive feelings that parents can feel toward their spouses or even the other children in the family. All of this goes into the formula when you think about the parents' relationship with the caregiver.

Teachers likewise start to get attached to the child. I think that somehow the young child who needs to be cared for, who needs to be protected, engenders these feelings. Yesterday, for example, I talked with teachers at a center who were distressed at the sudden departure of a child who had been in their care for two years. The family left without discussing it with them and they felt distressed. They had a big investment in this child, and they were expressing feelings of a very strong and normal attachment.

The second factor in the caregiver-parent relationship is the parents' expectations of what they should be doing with their child—what kind of child care the child should have, whether or not the mother should be working. These expectations, according to the research, make a critical difference in the impact of child care on children.

The third factor is the normal anxieties people have around the time of separation. When someone leaves or goes to do a new thing, the person leaving always has irrational flashes of danger or disaster—the loss becomes translated into a fear of a more permanent loss. Parents worry that the child is not going to be safe or that the child will come to love the caregiver more than the parent.

Defensive feelings are also involved. Parents and teachers are in a judgmental relationship, and both are not very high on the social hierarchical scale of important jobs in the world. Certainly there are no more important jobs than being a parent or teaching, but in terms of the outside world and

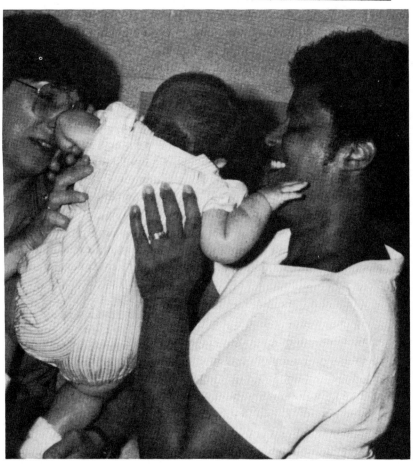

Photograph by Subjects and Predicates

the rewards and deference society gives to people, these jobs are unfortunately low.

In the beginning parents do not differentiate themselves from the children. If something wrong happens to a child, it's like something wrong happens to the parent. Even though every parenting book tells parents that they shouldn't feel this way, they do. When parents leave their child with a teacher, they know that they're going to be judged as parents; and they want to get high marks. It's a tense feeling.

Parents don't realize that the teachers (who look so secure to them) can also feel tense. They can feel that the parent is judging the way they're teaching the child.

Stronger Teacher-Parent Relations

There are several ways for parents and

teachers to establish a healthy partnership. First, both parents and teachers should learn about the normal range of feelings. If a child doesn't want to go to the center, parents have to decide if there is really something wrong or if this is just a phase. When teachers are feeling annoyed or negative toward the parents, they have to determine whether there is a problem or if these are normal feelings of possessiveness.

Also, it's important to understand that these normal feelings are positive. If teachers didn't get attached to children, they wouldn't be very good teachers. When I look at the words the teachers I surveyed used to describe parents, I don't, therefore, think of them as totally negative. They mean that teachers have made the first step—they care about the kids.

If it is clear that no problem exists, a method must be found for overcoming these normal feelings. For staff, it usually is very helpful if they can talk to each other about their feelings. Yesterday I asked teachers what they did when they were feeling mad at a parent. They all laughed and looked at each other—"We talk a lot!"

What happens in really good child care programs (and perhaps should be consciously done) is that one or more people on the staff take on the role of helping people see the world through both the parents' and the teachers' eyes. This person can help broaden people's perspective. For example, in an incident involving parent and staff, this person would ask questions that help the teacher understand how the parent is feeling.

Parents also need people to talk with about their feelings. It can be a network of people who are in the child care program or other parents. If a child is having a hard time, parents need someone they can turn to in order to figure out what's going on—

Photograph by Judy Burr

to help them determine if this is typical or if there is a problem in the program. It's a lot less anxiety producing to raise a child when one feels one has support. So it's important for parents to find people who will give them support, to help them solve problems, and to help them look at the other person's perspective. This makes them feel good. There's great potential for this type of parenting support through the child care center.

It also helps if people can see problems as outside of themselves, as situations to be resolved. If they can view things from a teamwork perspective rather than an adversarial approach, they are more likely to clear up difficulties without undue strain. This approach can be facilitated by establishing open channels of communication between parents and staff. Summit Child Care Center in New Jersey, for example, has a *parent rep* system. Representatives from each group call all the parents each month to ask for positive and negative feedback. When parents

bring up suggestions, there is the instinct to be defensive; but there is also a sense that the problem is there to be worked on together.

There is one final issue for teachers to consider in working with parents. Teachers need to be the kind of expert who facilitates the expertise of others rather than holding onto the expertise and dispensing it from a lofty position. For example, if a parent is having a very difficult time leaving her child, there are temptations to tell the parent what to do or to criticize the parent. But by helping the parent, encouraging the parent to talk, then making non-threatening suggestions, the teacher gives the parent options and lets the parent try to solve the problem. Making the parent feel competent is a particular way of being an expert. It is very constructive and builds in a partnership of people who are different but equal. Teachers are, in general, not trained for this role, yet it's part of being a child care professional (and one of the reasons teachers deserve respect).

When I was a parent in a child care class, one of the teachers began complaining early in the year about the parents. She said that the parents didn't care about the kids; they just wanted to dump their kids and run away. I knew I didn't feel this way and decided to find out how the other parents felt. I happened to be doing a study so I had the opportunity to interview the parents. I discovered that the parents were having a terrible time with the separation. There were as many different reactions as people, and most of them were uncertain about how to respond to their powerful and conflicting feelings. It wasn't that they didn't care. What the teacher interpreted as running away from children was really running away from the pain of leaving children.

It's easy to be critical of parents, to say they don't care, but that's rarely been my experience. There are very few parents who don't care. They may not express their care in a way that is useful, but they do care. It can be hard for teachers to step beyond their own feelings about parents, but when they do so, the rewards are rich—for the teachers, the parents, and, of course, the children.

In this learning activity, you will focus on strengthening the partnership between yourself and the parents of one of the children in your care. Select a child and family with whom you feel comfortable but whom you would like to know better. Let them know you have selected them. Then, for two weeks, record your daily communications with the parents—any information you each shared. At the same time, look for any changes in how you are able to meet this child's needs. Read the shortened example that follows; then begin the activity.

Parent-Teacher Daily Communication Record
(Example)

Child: *Donna*   **Age:** *3-1/2 years*   **Dates:** *June 6-20*

Parents: *Karen and Frank Anderson*

How long child has been coming to the center: *4 months*

Day One

A.M. *Greeted Mrs. Anderson and told her about this activity. She was pleased to hear that I am working on this module. She told me Donna is excited about playing dress-up.*

P.M *Mr. Anderson came to pick up Donna. I told him that Donna played dress-up with her friend Sheila. They put on lots of jewelry. He said she likes to wear her Grandma's jewelry. Mrs. Anderson had told him I was doing this learning activity. He wished me luck.*

Day Two

A.M. *Mr. Anderson brought Donna. I told him we were going to bring the water play table outside today and that Donna really liked to use the turkey baster to fill up cups and bottles. He asked if she could do that at home. I told him she could do it at the sink, in a dishpan, or in the bathtub. He seemed pleased with my ideas.*

P.M *Mrs. Anderson picked up Donna. I told her that Donna helped us carry out the water play toys today and that Donna ate a big lunch and made fruit smoothies this afternoon. She was surprised because Donna doesn't eat much fruit at home. I said that often the children eat more when they help make it. She told me Donna would be late on Friday because she's going to the dentist for the first time. I asked if Donna has expressed any concern about going to the dentist. She said, "Yes, a little." I asked if Donna knew what to expect. She said, "No, I don't think so." I said she could borrow our book, Going to the Dentist. She and Donna could read and discuss the book. It would give Donna an idea of what to expect. Mrs. Anderson thanked me and took the book with her.*

First Weekly Summary

(Example)

Information you shared:

That I'm doing this learning activity.

Donna played dress-up with Sheila.

Donna likes to use the baster.

Ways Donna could play with a turkey baster at home.

Donna helped carry the water play toys.

Donna likes fruit smoothies.

Information parents shared:

Donna is excited about dressing up.

Donna likes to wear her Grandma's jewelry.

Donna doesn't eat much fruit at home.

Donna is going to the dentist and she's a little scared.

How has the partnership helped you meet this child's needs?

I know more about what Donna likes to do.

I can suggest things for her parents to do with her at home.

I suggested a book to help her parents prepare her for going to the dentist.

Parent-Teacher Daily Communication Record

Child: _____ Age: _____ Dates: _____

Parents: _____

How long child has been coming to the center: _____

Day One

    A.M. _____

            _____

            _____

            _____

    P.M. _____

            _____

            _____

            _____

Day Two

    A.M. _____

            _____

            _____

            _____

    P.M. _____

            _____

            _____

            _____

Day Three

    A.M. _____

            _____

            _____

            _____

Day Three (continued)

P.M. _____

_____

_____

_____

Day Four

A.M. _____

_____

_____

_____

P.M. _____

_____

_____

_____

Day Five

A.M. _____

_____

_____

_____

P.M. _____

_____

_____

_____

First Weekly Summary
(Complete after five days)

Information you shared:

_____
_____
_____
_____
_____
_____
_____
_____
_____
_____
_____

Information parents shared:

_____
_____
_____
_____
_____
_____
_____
_____
_____
_____
_____
_____
_____

Day Six

A.M. _____

_____

_____

_____

_____

P.M. _____

_____

_____

_____

Day Seven

A.M. _____

_____

_____

_____

_____

P.M. _____

_____

_____

_____

Day Eight

A.M. _____

_____

_____

_____

_____

P.M. _____

_____

_____

_____

Day Nine

A.M. _____

_____

_____

_____

P.M. _____

_____

_____

_____

Day Ten

A.M. _____

_____

_____

_____

P.M. _____

_____

_____

_____

Second Weekly Summary
(Complete at the end of another five days)

Information you shared:

_____
_____
_____
_____
_____
_____
_____
_____
_____
_____
_____
_____
_____

Information parents shared:

_____
_____
_____
_____
_____
_____
_____
_____
_____
_____
_____
_____
_____

Review all your notes and complete the following.

How has the partnership helped you meet this child's needs?

(Give at least five examples)

_____

_____

_____

_____

_____

_____

_____

_____

_____

_____

Discuss this activity with the child's parents and your trainer.

II. Keeping Parents Informed About the Program

In this activity you will learn:

- to keep parents informed about the program; and

- to improve parent-program communication.

One of a teacher's most important responsibilities is to work with one's supervisor and other staff to keep parents up-to-date on activities at the center. Parents feel more involved in the program when they know specific things that are happening. For example, parents like to know there's a new piece of equipment in the playground, the staff are participating in training, vegetable soup is on today's lunch menu, one of the teachers will be on vacation next week, and this month's workshop for parents is on promoting self-esteem. Some of this information is passed from teachers to parents during the times when children are picked up or dropped off. These times, however, are usually too brief to keep all the parents informed about everything that goes on at the center. The staff need to use ongoing communication techniques to keep all parents up to date on current activities and future plans.

One of the most common ways to keep parents informed is through center newsletters. Newsletters are distributed to all parents and contain general information that affects all families as well as specific information about each room. Often one person is responsible for putting the newsletter together; however, all staff contribute news. Parents also can be involved in gathering information, writing articles, or typing an issue. In addition to news and information about coming events, the newsletter also can include the month's menus, suggested activities for parents and children to do at home, and reviews of children's books or books on parenting. The newsletter also can include space for parents to make suggestions for future issues or provide news, information, or a favorite recipe. This can reinforce the partnership between parents and teachers and lets parents know that the newsletter is one useful result of the partnership.

Another kind of newsletter covers the activities and news of one room. A parent may volunteer to help produce such a newsletter, or the teachers for the room can take the lead. While this type of newsletter may include the same kinds of information just discussed, it can also be more personal, providing details about what takes place in the room.

Here are some other suggestions for keeping parents informed.

- Establish a **message center** where each family has a box or message pocket. These can be used to provide parents with general news and information about their child.

- Provide each family with a **journal** that stays at the center and can be used by both parents and teachers to share information about the child. Notices or flyers can be tucked in the journal so parents will see them.

- Set up a **parent bulletin board** in the lobby or some other area that all parents pass by. Post articles, a calendar of events, reminders of upcoming meetings, the week's menus, and other items of general interest.

- Develop and maintain a **parent handbook**. Issue copies to each parent and provide revisions whenever necessary. The handbook can address the center's policies and procedures and list opportunities for parents to become involved.

In this learning activity you will answer some questions about a communication technique that your center uses to keep parents informed. First review the abbreviated example that follows. Then think about one communication technique used in your center. Suggest ways to improve it, implement your suggestions, and report on the results.

Communicating with Parents
(Example)

Communication technique: *Classroom newsletter*

What information is included?

Upcoming field trips, birthdays, something about each child, new toys or other materials, trips, and activities parents and children can do at home.

How often is the information shared or updated?

Weekly.

What is the role of the center director?

She reads it over before I make copies and includes some of the information in the center newsletter.

What is the role of teachers?

We take turns writing it and making copies.

What is the role of parents?

They read it.

How could parents be more involved?

Parents could help in producing the newsletter. They could provide us with information or articles to include. We could ask parents what they would like to read about.

After trying out your ideas, what were the results?

I sent a parent questionnaire home asking for suggested newsletter items and for help preparing the newsletter. I got lots of suggestions, and two parents offered to help. They worked with me on the latest issue. We included some parent-written articles, including one about a new park that one of the families visited last month. Several parents said they really liked this issue.

Communicating with Parents

Communication technique: _____

What information is included?

_____

_____

_____

How often is the information shared or updated?

_____

_____

_____

What is the role of the center director?

_____

_____

_____

What is the role of teachers?

_____

_____

_____

What is the role of parents?

_____

_____

_____

How could parents be more involved?

_____

_____

_____

After trying out your ideas, what were the results?

_____

_____

_____

Discuss this activity with your trainer.

III. Providing Ways for Parents to Be Involved

In this activity you will learn:

- to use techniques for parent involvement; and

- to plan and implement a parent involvement strategy.

Most parents are interested in becoming involved in their child's life at the center, but they may not know about all the different ways they can become involved. Sometimes parents can arrange their work schedules so they can go on field trips, eat lunch with the children occasionally, or work as a volunteer teacher on a regular basis. It benefits both parent and child when the parent can visit the program during the day; however, many parents are not able to participate in this way. You and other staff need to work together to create a variety of options for parent involvement that match the interests, skills, and schedules of the parents. When parents first register their children at the center, they could complete a brief questionnaire about how they can support the program while playing an active role in their child's development.

In addition to matching parents' interests with several options for involvement, you also need to let parents know how much their participation benefits the program. Parents who come on field trips may enjoy themselves so much that they don't need much encouragement to offer to do it again. The parent who sews new curtains for the children's puppet theater, however, may never see the theater in action. In such a case, be sure to send a note home thanking the parent. You could describe how the children are using the theater or enclose a picture of the theater in action. Similarly, the parent who types the newsletter should be listed in every issue as the one who makes it possible for the news to get out to the other families.

Here are some suggestions for helping parents become more involved in your center.

- Hold an **orientation** for new parents several times a year. Because a certain number of families come and go during the year, you need to provide more than one orientation.

- Keep a **job jar** in your room containing index cards listing center-related jobs you never get around to doing that a parent could do at home. Parents can select a job from the jar, then see you for additional instructions. Jobs could include repairing broken toys, making name tags for future field trips, mending dress-up clothes, or making lotto boards or other materials for the room.

  Organize a **family dinner** when parents can eat dinner at the center on their way home. The food can be prepared by the children or it can be something simple prepared by the staff.

- Provide opportunities for parents to participate in **building or landscaping projects** that can be worked on over a period of time. When a project is completed, hold a celebration party.

- Hold a **family movie night**, planned and hosted by parent volunteers. Parents could sell popcorn and soft drinks to raise funds for extra materials or field trips.

- Schedule a **"fix-it"** night or a Saturday when families can work together to spruce up the center, paint walls, make a tire playground, or prepare a plot of ground for a garden.

- **Open the center for one evening** when the children come to their room as though it were a regular day. Parents come too and play with the children, lead activities, serve snacks, or sit back and observe how their child plays with others. Set this up so small groups of parents take turns being with the children while the rest of the parents are involved in another activity.

- Set up a **parent corner** at the center. Include books, magazines, brochures, and other resources of interest to parents. If possible, provide comfortable chairs and refreshments.

- Ask a parent to organize a **photo album** about the center. You can provide the pictures and the book; the parent can put it together. Display the photo album in the lobby. Include a cover page thanking the parent who organized the album.

- Use parents as **book reviewers**. Parents may read children's books or books on child development or parenting that they'd like to recommend to the center. Provide a book review form that they can complete, listing the title, author, publisher, and price. For children's books, leave space on the form for parents to record what ages the book is appropriate for, what the book is about, and why they and their child liked it. You can use these recommendations to select books for your room.

In this learning activity you will try out a parent involvement strategy. Select from those mentioned earlier, and discuss your selection with your supervisor and the other teachers in your room. Ask for their ideas about implementing this strategy. If your supervisor or colleagues think this strategy is not appropriate for the parents at your center, then select another one. First read the example; then complete the chart that follows it to describe the strategy you chose and how it helped parents become involved.

Parent Involvement Strategy
(Example)

Strategy:

Parent volunteers will tape themselves reading stories. We have a tape player, but most of the story tapes you can buy are too expensive or the stories are for older children.

Plans:

I will send a notice home with the children asking for volunteers. The center will supply blank tapes. The books can come from our room or can be favorites from home. I'll try to make sure we tape a variety of books. The tapes will be used in the quiet corner, where children like to go to be alone for a while.

Results:

Four parents volunteered to make tapes. Each parent made four tapes so now we have a good supply for the quiet corner. The children really enjoy hearing their parent's voices on tape. All four parents said they would be happy to make more tapes whenever we need them.

Follow-up:

I will make this an ongoing parent involvement project. I asked Mrs. Porter, one of the four parents who made tapes, to help me keep track of which books we tape and which parents help. I think the children would like it if all the parents took a turn making story tapes. This could be a good project for parents who don't seem interested in participating at the center.

Parent Involvement Strategy

Strategy:

_____
_____
_____
_____
_____
_____

Plans:

_____
_____
_____
_____
_____
_____

Results:

_____
_____
_____
_____
_____
_____

Follow-up:

_____
_____
_____
_____
_____
_____

Discuss this activity with the other teachers in your room and your trainer.

IV. Planning and Participating in Parent-Teacher Conferences

In this activity you will learn:

- to prepare for a conference by reviewing information about a child's development; and

- to participate in a parent conference.

At least twice a year, parents and their child's teacher need to meet to review how the child is progressing in all areas of development and to set goals for the child's continued growth and learning. Parent-teacher conferences are opportunities to focus on one child and family without any distractions or interruptions. Conferences can help parents understand the program's goals. This meeting can reaffirm your partnership with parents. Although much information about the child is shared daily, conferences are times when you and the parents can discuss the child in depth and reaffirm your trust in each other.

Usually there is no single goal for the conference. Conferences can meet a number of different needs. Here's what other early childhood educators have said about their goals for parent conferences:[2]

> "To make the parents aware of how their child is developing, at what level she/he is functioning, and if she/he is in need of any special help." Janet Rogers, Lycoming Child Day Care, Williamsport, PA.

> "To project the importance of the child as a person and how necessary it is for parents and teachers to work together to develop in the child a good self-image." Louisa Pola, Guantanamo Bay Nursery School, U.S. Naval Station, Guantanamo Bay, Cuba.

> "To get to know the parents enough to feel comfortable with them and them with me; and to better understand the child through the parent." Lois Grigsby, Kendal Lab Child Care, Evanston, IL.

> "To give the parent confidence in the teacher; to establish a social relationship between parent and teacher." Margaret Frederickson, Northedge School, Sudbury, MA.

> "To discuss the child's development; to identify future goals." Shelly Brick, Kensington-Kingstowne Child Care Center, Philadelphia, PA.

---

[2]Reprinted with permission from "Ideas for Effective Parent Conferences," *Child Care Information Exchange* (Exchange Press, PO Box 2890, Redmond, WA, 98073, November 1979), pp. 26-27.

"To foster greater awareness of the importance the environment plays in a child's development—to educate the parents." Jan Lucas, Westend Day Care, Portage la Prairie, Manitoba, Canada.

"To provide support for working parents by supplying any information on child development, available social services, etc." Tracy Neri, The Day Care Center, Norwich, VT.

Parents also have goals for the conference. They may have a specific concern they would like to discuss or a suggestion for how they would like you to work with their child. They may have a concern about the program or a complaint about something you did or didn't do. Often parents want to be reassured that you like their child, that you are competent, and that you think they are doing a good job raising their child.

Planning for Conferences

To make the best use of the time set aside for the conference, it's important to do some planning. Talk to parents before the conference to let them know its purpose. Ask them to think of any questions they might have. Find out if there is any topic they want to cover. Tell them you hope to learn more about the child's life at home so you can better support the child's growth at the center. Ask parents about the best time to hold the conference. Offer several options and provide enough lead time so parents can make plans.

You also need to think about what points you want to cover. Review your observation notes, anecdotal records, and any other written materials that provide objective information about the child. You can also collect samples of the child's art work or other creations. Organize your notes to make sure you have covered all areas of development—physical, cognitive, language, social, and emotional. If you have any concerns about the child's health, these should be documented. Ask the other teachers in your room to provide any information they have about this child.

Parents often want to know what the child is like in a group situation. They would like to know as much as possible about what their child does all day, with whom he or she plays, what makes the child happy or sad, and what the child enjoys doing. Try to collect "stories" to share that will help parents picture and understand how their child spends his or her day.

Sometimes teachers feel a little uneasy before a conference. It may help to role play with your supervisor or a colleague. You can practice sharing your observations and answering the kinds of questions the parents are likely to ask.

Participating in the Conference

At the start of the conference, try to establish a relaxed and comfortable tone. Schedule conferences at times that are convenient for parents and allow enough time so you and the parents don't feel rushed. Anticipate at least five minutes of social conversation before beginning your more serious discussions. Before the conference, decide which of the center staff will take the lead in the conference. This person should begin by telling the parents how the conference will proceed: "I'm so glad you could both come today. Let me tell you how we will proceed. We'll first talk about Karen's development. I'll provide information based on our observations at the center, then you can tell us what you've seen at home. . ."

During the conference, be sure there are many opportunities for parents to provide input and ask questions. After discussing all areas of the child's development, the next step is to set some goals and develop strategies to promote the child's development. These strategies will be implemented at home and at the center. These goals and strategies will serve as the framework for discussions at the next conference.

Here are some other suggestions for conducting successful conferences.

- Begin and end the conference with a positive statement about your relationship with the child. "We really enjoy Timothy's playfulness. He makes us all smile."

- When parents seem reluctant to talk about their concerns, ask them an open-ended question. "Is there anything else about Rebecca or the program that you'd like to discuss?"

- Summarize your discussion at the end of the conference, emphasizing what actions you each have agreed to take. "I will spend more time looking at books with Laura now that I know she likes to do that at home. And you'll bring in her special blanket, so she can have it during naps. That will make her feel more secure."

- When parents ask you for advice about handling a specific situation, offer more than one suggestion. Encourage them to think about what would be best for their child. "Some parents find it helpful to allow their child to select what clothes to wear. Others let their child choose between two items, for example, the red sweater or the blue one."

In this learning activity you will develop a plan for holding a conference with the parents of one of the children in your room. Include information from your own observations and those of other teachers in the room. Conduct the conference, then answer the evaluation questions.

Planning a Conference

Child: _____   Parent: _____

Age: _____   Age at last conference: _____

Date of conference: _____   Date of last conference: _____

What does this child like to do?

_____

_____

_____

_____

What makes this child happy?

_____

_____

_____

_____

What makes this child sad?

_____

_____

_____

_____

What new skills is this child working on?

_____

_____

_____

_____

Whom does this child play with, and in what ways?

_____

_____

_____

_____

Anecdotes to share:

_____

_____

_____

_____

Any concerns:

_____

_____

_____

_____

Summary of Development

Use this form to summarize the child's progress in all areas of development. List the goals set at the last conference (if there has been one). For each area shown on the chart, provide specific examples of what the child does (for example, cuts with scissors, builds tall towers, usually plays with two or three other children).

	GOALS FROM LAST CONFERENCE	WHAT THE CHILD DOES
Physical		
Social		
Emotional		
Cognitive		
Language		

Suggested Goals for the Next Six Months

Use the space below to list some suggested developmental goals for the next six months.

Physical	
Social	
Emotional	
Cognitive	
Language	

Now hold your conference with the child's parents. Ask for their ideas on suggested goals and add them to the list above if you both agree.

Conference Evaluation

After the conference, think about what happened and answer these questions.

How did you establish a relaxed tone?

_____

_____

_____

_____

_____

How did you start the conference?

_____

_____

_____

_____

_____

How did you provide for parent input?

_____

_____

_____

_____

_____

Were you asked for advice?

_____

_____

_____

_____

_____

What stories or anecdotes did you tell about how the child spends the day?

_____

_____

_____

_____

What goals did you and the parents set for the child?

_____

_____

_____

_____

_____

How did you summarize the conference?

_____

_____

_____

_____

_____

How did you end the conference?

_____

_____

_____

_____

_____

What would you do differently next time?

_____

_____

_____

_____

_____

Discuss this learning activity with your trainer.

V. Reaching Out to Families

In this activity you will learn:

- to recognize signs that families are under stress; and

- to provide support to families under stress.

Parents of preschoolers—especially first time parents—are often under stress. Balancing the demands of a job and family, feeling unsure about sharing the care of their child, and not understanding children's behavior can all leave parents feeling in need of support. In your role of teacher, you are in an excellent position to lend a helping hand. Some parents will feel comfortable sharing their worries and seeking advice. Others will not. Regardless of whether parents approach you or you approach them, remember that supporting parents means enhancing their sense of competence by helping parents discover their own answers.

You can support parents by helping them locate resources and giving them information and guidance on the growth and development of preschoolers.

You can reach out to parents by providing help, support, encouragement, and information. You can:

- recognize when parents are under stress;

- help parents locate resources; and

- give parents information and guidance on child growth and development.

Recognizing When Parents Are Under Stress

When a family is under stress, the parents may seem disorganized, frequently forgetting important items such as mittens on a cold day or a child's special blanket. A parent might seem frustrated when a child is slow to get ready to go home, or the parent might state that he or she doesn't know how to handle the child's independent behavior. Parents under stress might be unwilling to accept help, or they might be more interested in talking about their own problems than their child's.

When you see signs of stress, it is important that you do not add to them. You can discuss their child's behavior or tell them about your upcoming vacation on another day. However, you will want to share information about their child's day that will help them get through a difficult evening. For example, letting a parent know that their preschooler has been tired and cranky all day allows you to discuss whether the child might be coming down with the flu. Because the parent knows the reasons for the child's behavior, he or she is less likely to be frustrated or angered by the crankiness and more likely to comfort the child. When parents feel less stress they are more likely to interact positively with their children and are less likely to become angry and lash out at them.

Here are some events that may cause stress:

- lack of sleep;
- serious illness or death of a family member;
- separation and divorce;
- an unplanned or unwanted pregnancy;
- failure to receive a promotion;
- extended travel; and
- geographic or social isolation.

Make an effort to really get to know the parents of the children in your group. Invite parents into the room when they bring their children to the center and pick them up. Place a suggestion box in a prominent place and draw attention to it. Invite parents to visit often, and make them welcome. Remember that you, the center, and the parents are part of a team working for the child's good.

Always notify your director when you think parents may need professional help. Your job is to help parents get the support they need, not to provide it yourself. Never make recommendations to parents without first clearing them with your supervisor.

Helping Parents Locate Resources

Parents often need information on where they can get help for themselves, their child, or the family. Your director can provide you with information about parent education opportunities. Here are some things you can do to help.

- Help parents connect with one another.

- Call parents' attention to resources, newspaper or magazine articles, workshops, and television or radio shows on stages of child development, positive guidance, and family life.

- Post notices of special programs offered by the center and in the community.

- Display books on topics of interest to parents—step-parenting, juggling home and work responsibilities, health and nutrition—and invite parents to borrow these resources.

- Tell them about services provided by the social services organizations in your community.

- Provide names, phone numbers, locations, and hours of operation when you suggest a program or event.

- Offer reluctant parents help in contacting other resources.

Giving Parents Information and Guidance on Child Growth and Development

Parents sometimes know very little about child development. As a result, they may expect too much of a particular child at a particular age. Here are some things you can do to help.

- Observe a child together, asking yourselves "what is he or she experiencing?" to help parents see the world through the eyes of their preschooler.

- Tell parents about workshops on building self-esteem, adjusting to a new baby, independence, and other topics of interest.

- Be sure parents see information on growth and development in the center's newsletters.

- Invite parents to attend staff workshops.

- Lend books or videotapes from the center's library.

- Ask the director to schedule conferences to discuss particular problems.

- Introduce parents who are dealing with similar developmental issues.

Also, during drop-off and pick-up times and in longer visits during the day, without any extra effort or planning, you model for parents various developmentally appropriate ways to meet children's needs. For example, visiting parents might see the following interactions between a teacher and the children in her care:

> Ms. Danforth encourages Gina (3 1/2 years) to help put away the blocks, talks and laughs with Evan (3 years) as she ties his shoes, and asks Bart (4 years) a question about his painting—"Tell me how you made these long, squiggly lines?" These children's parents might comment, "I can't get her to put her things away at home." "He squirms around so much at home that I just want to get the shoes tied as quickly as possible." "All his paintings look the same to me." Ms. Danforth uses these comments to open conversations about ways to promote children's self-help skills, take advantage of routines to communicate with children, and support creativity by asking about children's paintings.

When you demonstrate positive ways of working with children, you do a lot to help parents improve their interactions with their children.

In this activity, you will keep records of times when you reached out to parents in response to their requests or because you noticed that they needed your support. Over the next few weeks, make a note of what you did. Write down the problem, what the parent asked for or what you saw was needed, how you responded, and what the outcome was. Begin by reading the example on the next page.

Reaching Out To Families
(Example)

Child: _Larry_   **Age:** _4 years, 3 months_   **Date:** _October 23_

Problem:

Larry is extremely jealous of his new baby sister. His parents have stated that he hits and pinches her.

What parents asked for or what I saw was needed:

Help in stopping Larry from hitting and pinching her.

My response:

We talked about the problem. I suggested they spend extra time with Larry alone. I also gave them materials they could read to Larry about having a new baby in the family.

The outcome:

The parents say that the suggestions seem to be working. Larry is not as upset, and he really likes story time with his Dad. He said, "Sissy can't read with Daddy, but I can."

Reaching Out to Families

Child: _____   Age: _____   Date: _____

Problem:

_____

_____

_____

_____

What parents asked for or what I saw was needed:

_____

_____

_____

_____

My response:

_____

_____

_____

_____

The outcome:

_____

_____

_____

_____

Reaching Out to Families

Child: _____   Age: _____   Date: _____

Problem

_____

_____

_____

_____

What parents asked for or what I saw was needed:

_____

_____

_____

_____

My response:

_____

_____

_____

_____

The outcome:

_____

_____

_____

_____

Reaching Out To Families

Child: _____ **Age:** _____ **Date:** _____

Problem:

_____

_____

_____

_____

What parents asked for or what I saw was needed:

_____

_____

_____

_____

My response:

_____

_____

_____

_____

The outcome:

_____

_____

_____

_____

Discuss your responses with your trainer.

Summarizing Your Progress

You have now completed all of the learning activities for this module. Whether you are an experienced teacher or a new one, this module has probably helped you develop new skills in working with families. Before you go on, take a few minutes to summarize what you've learned. Review your responses to the pre-training assessment for this module. Write a summary of what you learned and list the skills you developed or improved.

_____

_____

_____

_____

_____

_____

_____

_____

_____

_____

_____

_____

_____

_____

_____

If there are topics you would like to know more about, you will find recommended readings listed in the orientation, which can be found in Volume I.

Your final step in this module is to complete the knowledge and competency assessments. Let your trainer know when you are ready to schedule the assessments. After you have successfully completed these assessments, you will be ready to start a new module. Congratulations on your progress so far, and good luck with your next module.

Answer Sheets

Working with Families

Communicating with Family Members Often to Exchange Information About Their Child at Home and at the Center

1. **Why did Ms. Kim and Janet decide not to share the news about Janet's accomplishments?**

   a. They knew that Janet's parents were very excited and wanted to be there when Janet first went down the slide alone.

   b. Ms. Kim knew Janet would go to the park with her parents and they would enjoy the surprise.

2. **What kinds of information will Ms. Kim and the Carters need to share now that Janet is learning to take risks?**

   a. What other tasks Janet is trying to master.

   b. How they can help her to take safe risks.

Providing a Variety of Ways for Family Members to Participate in Their Child's Life at the Center

1. **How did Ms. Williams help Mr. Bradley think of something he could do with Jerry's group at the center?**

   a. She asked him about his work and interests.

   b. She told him she'd noticed that he was excited about cooking.

2. **How did Ms. Williams help Mr. Bradley feel more comfortable about working with preschoolers?**

   a. She told him that the children liked cooking activities.

   b. She helped him plan a cooking activity for preschoolers.

Providing Support for Families

1. **What did Mr. Lopez do to help Mrs. Thomas understand Marita's behavior?**

   a. He explained that Marita's behavior was typical of three-year-olds.

   b. He explained that Marita was getting used to being separated from her parents.

2. **How did Mr. Lopez help Marita and her mother cope with separation?**

   a. He scheduled a meeting with Mrs. Thomas to tell her more about separation and what Marita did during the day.

   b. He read a book to Marita about what parents do at work.

Module 12
Program Management

What Is Program Management and Why Is It Important?

Teachers play many roles. The primary and most obvious role of teachers is to provide for children's health, safety, and developmental needs. But teaching involves much more. It includes building children's self-esteem. It may include supporting families and helping parents deal with working outside the home. And it certainly includes effective management, as teachers work with other staff to ensure the smooth operation of the center.

We often think of managers in child development programs as the people who direct centers, provide training for adults, develop budgets, hire staff, and make schedules. These people are managers at the center, and their roles are important. But teachers are also managers of a child development program. Their management role includes planning, conducting, and evaluating the program. As they perform these managerial tasks, teachers become more effective in promoting children's self-esteem, guiding children's learning, setting up the environment, and handling other responsibilities.

A systematic approach to managing a child development program can make this job easier. As you observe children's play and record what they do each day, you are gathering useful information. You then use that information to plan a program for each child. As you meet with other teachers to discuss what the children will look for on a neighborhood walk, you are working as a member of a team. And as you complete your time sheets and required reports on time, you do your part to keep the center running smoothly.

Managing an early childhood program involves:

- observing and recording information about each child's growth and development;

- working as a member of a team to plan an individualized program; and

- following administrative policies and procedures.

Listed below are examples of how teachers demonstrate their competence in managing a program.

Observing and Recording Information About Each Child's Growth and Development

Here are some examples of what teachers can do.

- Watch and listen to a child at play and write down what he or she does and says. "Mr. Lopez, can you stay in the art area while I observe how Maria uses the nesting cups?"

- Use systematic observation to record information that is objective and accurate and avoids labeling. "Marita spent the entire outdoor playtime running in circles around other children."

- Work with parents to identify each child's strengths, needs, and interests. "Could you tell me what activities Henry enjoys, Mrs. Lee, so that we can plan ways to extend his interests?"

- Use all opportunities to gather information about children. "You've climbed to the third rung on the jungle gym, Leroy. I don't think you've done that before!"

Working as a Member of a Team to Plan an Individualized Program

Here are some examples of what teachers can do.

- Meet regularly with other teachers to develop plans for the group. "Let's discuss the things we'll ask children to look for at the market next week and get some new props to add to the house corner for a follow-up activity."

- Use information gathered from observing children to plan for each child and the group. "Sam and Travis have been quickly putting together all our puzzles lately. How else can we help them with eye-hand coordination skills?"

- Include parents in planning for their children's growth and development. "Pam tries lots of new foods at the center. Let me tell you about the foods she especially likes in case you want to serve them at home, too."

- Provide substitute teachers with adequate information on the planned activities and needs of individual children. "We keep this weekly plan posted on the closet door. It shows the special activities planned for the week and the names of the children we will encourage to participate."

Following Administrative Policies and Procedures

Here are some examples of what teachers can do.

- Review center policies before starting a new task. "I need to find out how we arrange a trip to the children's museum."

- Complete management tasks according to a schedule. "I'd like to review the parent evaluations, Ms. Snyder, so we can begin to make improvements."

- Use the center's system for recordkeeping. "Can you keep an eye on the children while I fill out the accident report for Paul's skinned knee?"

- Keep informed about teachers' job responsibilities. "I've heard that new child abuse reporting regulations are being developed. Will we have a staff meeting to discuss them?"

Being an Effective Manager

The following situations show teachers managing a child development program. As you read, think about what the teachers are doing and why. Then answer the questions following each episode.

Observing and Recording Information About Each Child's Growth and Development

As Eric rips lettuce leaves in half, Mr. Lopez crouches near the food preparation table, cards in hand. "You're ready to finish your lettuce roll-up, Eric. What do you want to put on the leaf?" "Crunchy peanut butter!" Eric answers. He picks up the knife and holds it with his fist, straight down. Then he dips it into one of the bowls on the table. He holds the leaf in his left hand and spreads peanut butter partly on the leaf and partly in his palm. "Why don't you lay the leaf on the paper towel to do that?" Mr. Lopez asks. "Okay," says Eric. Mr. Lopez helps Eric hold the leaf down on the paper towel. Eric finishes spreading the peanut butter, rolls the leaf, and takes a bite. Mr. Lopez jots down on a note card that Eric chose crunchy peanut butter, how he dipped the knife into the bowl, how he attempted to spread the peanut butter, how he responded to a suggestion, and how he completed the task.

1. **How did Mr. Lopez use a regular activity to gather objective and accurate information about Eric?**

   _____

   _____

   _____

2. **What are three things Mr. Lopez learned about Eric?**

   _____

   _____

   _____

Working as a Member of a Team to Plan an Individualized Program

Ms. Kim asks each teacher in her room to focus on children's outdoor play during the week. "I'd like us to meet on Friday to talk about the kinds of things we currently do in the play yard and develop plans for new activities." She has copies made of weekly planning and evaluation forms to be filled in at the meeting. As she plays with the children outdoors, she thinks about the objectives set for each child and notes skills they are using while they ride tricycles, play in the sand box, and paint the side of the building with water. On Friday the teachers share their observations and develop plans for making a vegetable garden and new props to add to the sand box. Ms. Kim offers to bring some painters hats and other props outside.

1. How did Ms. Kim use a team approach to planning?

_____

_____

_____

2. How did the teachers use observation information for planning?

_____

_____

_____

Following Administrative Policies and Procedures

Ms. Williams reviews the staff handbook as she sits in the break room. "Even though I've been a teacher for a while," she tells Ms. Frilles, "I need to review our policies now and then. I want to find out what the procedure is for scheduling my vacation. I'm sure that's in here. Also, do you know where I'll find information on preparing for a field trip?" Ms. Frilles replies, "It's in the section on program activities. Samples of completed field trip forms are in the appendix. My group recently went to the fire station, and I used the sample forms to help me get the permission forms to the parents and back on time and to request use of the van." Ms. Williams finds the program activities section and locates the sample forms. She later submits a request for annual leave, fills out the field trip request form, and sends permission slips home to the parents.

1. How does Ms. Williams stay informed about administrative policies and procedures?

_____

_____

_____

2. What tasks did Ms. Williams complete according to the center's policies?

_____

_____

_____

Compare your answers with those on the answer sheet at the end of the module. If your answers are different, discuss them with your trainer. There can be more than one good answer.

Managing Your Own Life

Many of the things you do at home contribute to your performance as a manager. You may be responsible for paying bills, buying food and clothing, deciding on major purchases such as a car or furniture, or planning a vacation or weekend outing. The same skills you use in managing the center program are used at home. When you make a grocery list, for example, you consider what foods each member of your family likes, how many people will be eating each meal, and what ingredients you need for each recipe. You can do this because you observe each member of your family, include them in planning balanced meals, and follow recipes, the "policies and procedures" for food preparation.

Just as at the center, the more orderly and efficient you are in managing your home, the easier your life is. You have more time to spend on things other than chores. The more planning you do as a team, the more likely it is that you and your family will enjoy the time you spend together.

Think about times when careful management makes it easier to get chores done efficiently.

- You plan which errands need to be run and do them all at once rather than making several trips.

- You make sure you have all the tools and materials you need before starting a project such as painting the kitchen cupboards or baking a cake.

- You keep records of all bills and file receipts promptly.

- You keep emergency phone numbers posted beside the telephone.

- You talk with your family about what to do in case of fire and develop an evacuation plan.

- You plan outings or vacations that are of interest to everyone.

- You borrow a folding table and extra chairs from a neighbor when you are having a crowd over for a holiday meal.

Organizing your time and your environment to work *for* you rather than *against* you helps you manage more effectively. Use the chart on the following page to identify ways to manage your life more effectively.

FRUSTRATING SITUATIONS IN MY DAILY LIFE	WHAT I COULD DO TO IMPROVE THE SITUATION
I spend time practically every day searching for my keys.	*I will put a hook on the inside wall by the door where I will hang my keys every day when I get home.*

The skills you use in managing your life help you manage your role as a teacher and help you enjoy that role and feel good about your performance.

When you have finished this overview section, you should complete the pre-training assessment. Refer to the glossary at the end of this module if you need definitions of the terms that are used.

Pre-Training Assessment

Listed below are the skills used by teachers who are effective managers. Think about whether you do these things regularly, sometimes, or not enough. Place a check in one of the columns on the right for each skill listed. Then discuss your answers with your trainer.

SKILL	I DO THIS REGULARLY	I DO THIS SOMETIMES	I DON'T DO THIS ENOUGH
OBSERVING AND RECORDING INFORMATION ABOUT EACH CHILD'S GROWTH AND DEVELOPMENT 1. Watching and listening to each child and writing down what he or she does and says.			
2. Recording children's behavior in an objective, accurate way and avoiding the use of labels.			
3. Asking parents for information about things their children do at home and including that information with observations.			
4. Observing children during different periods of the day: arrival, indoor and outdoor play, meal, naps, and departure.			
5. Recording many instances of a child's play before drawing conclusions about that child's abilities, interests, and needs.			
WORKING AS A MEMBER OF A TEAM TO PLAN AN INDIVIDUALIZED PROGRAM 6. Meeting regularly with other teachers to plan developmentally and culturally appropriate activities for the group.			

SKILL	I DO THIS REGULARLY	I DO THIS SOMETIMES	I DON'T DO THIS ENOUGH
7. Using observation information to plan for each child in the group.			
8. Including information from parents when planning activities for children.			
9. Planning for changes in the environment, special activities, and specific experiences for specific children.			
10. Including evaluations of the experiences provided for children as part of planning for future activities.			
11. Working with other center staff to provide input on program issues.			
12. Appreciating (or recognizing) and using the strengths of other team members; other teachers, aides, parents, and volunteers.			
13. Knowing social services, health, and education resources in the community or region and using them as needed.			
FOLLOWING ADMINISTRATIVE POLICIES AND PROCEDURES 14. Knowing and understanding responsibilities as outlined in the staff and parent handbook.			
15. Reviewing center policies before starting a new task.			

SKILL	I DO THIS REGULARLY	I DO THIS SOMETIMES	I DON'T DO THIS ENOUGH
16. Completing management tasks according to a schedule.			
17. Following the center's system for recordkeeping.			
18. Reviewing memorandums and other documents to keep informed about teachers' job responsibilities.			

Review your responses, then list three to five skills you would like to improve or topics you would like to learn more about. When you finish this module, you will list examples of your new or improved knowledge and skills.

_____

_____

_____

_____

_____

_____

_____

_____

_____

_____

Now begin the learning activities for Module 12, Program Management.

12

I. Using a Systematic Approach to Observing and Recording

In this activity you will learn:

- to identify reasons for making observations in a child development program; and

- to develop a system for regularly observing and recording children's behavior.

At some point in their lives, most adults spend time observing children. They watch them play and thrill at hearing their first words, first phrases, and first sentences. They watch them grow and marvel at their first steps, first hops, and first words. Observing children is an ongoing process for people with children in their lives.

Observations of children made by teachers may be different from those made by parents because each observes children for different reasons. Observation in a child development program is used to provide high-quality care for all children. High-quality care is based on knowledge of each child and the use of accurate information to meet each child's needs. When teachers know how each child is growing and developing and plan a program based on this knowledge, the care they provide is more likely to be developmentally appropriate.

Teachers observe children for a variety of reasons.

- They **determine each child's interests, strengths, and needs**. "Bobby likes to organize new items on the science table. He sorts the collections in egg cartons."

- They **plan a program** based on the interests, strengths, and needs of each child. "There's been a lot of interest in dinosaurs lately. Let's talk about using a dinosaur theme in several interest areas next week."

- They **measure each child's progress**. "I've recorded Sarah's new skills in gross motor development."

- They **resolve particular problems** a child might have. "I've been keeping notes, and it seems that Jim hits other children when he doesn't know how to enter a group."

- They **report children's progress** to parents, colleagues, and specialists. "I'd like to set up a meeting with you, Mrs. White, to talk about Jared's progress."

- They **evaluate the effects of the environment** and the activities of the child development program. "Please bring your assessment information to Friday's meeting so we can discuss the accomplishments of this year."

To undertake these and other tasks, teachers must observe children carefully and systematically. This involves watching, listening to, and writing down what children do and say as it happens, according to a particular method. The information written down is called a recording. To determine each child's interests, strengths, and needs, more than one observation and recording are required. Teachers must observe children as they play indoors and outdoors, eat, prepare to sleep and wake up, arrive in the morning, and leave at the end of the day.

A series of brief (five- to ten-minute) observations can provide the information needed to assess a child's level of development. These observations should take place over a period of time. You can make these recordings during your regular activities as you care for and interact with children.

Some teachers feel that making observations and recording them will take away from their time with children. They try to jot down at the end of the day the things that happened. It is impossible, however, to remember accurately everything that happened: what each child did and said, new skills each child attempted, and so on. It is best to record observations throughout the day as you interact with children or as soon as possible after the observation. Here are some examples of teachers completing recordings.

- Mr. Lopez is helping Josh learn to cut with a knife. He talks with Josh as the child tries a variety of ways to hold his knife and praises him when Josh is able to cut his food with the knife. After lunch Mr. Lopez helps his group settle down for their naps. Then he gets his pad and records how Josh tried to use his knife.

- Ms. Williams holds one end of a jump rope and four-year-old Marcia holds the other. Several children take turns jumping. After a few minutes she asks Rocky to take her place. She pulls a few index cards from her jacket pocket and records the names of the "jumpers" and a few notes on each child's skill in the activity.

In addition to using these methods, you might also ask another teacher to cover for you while you step back from an activity to record children's interactions with each other, with the environment, or with an adult. Developing a system can help you and the teachers you work with integrate observing and recording into your day. Here are some suggestions for observing children systematically.[1]

- Write what you see, not what you think is happening.

- Jot notes frequently. Carry a pad or index cards and pencil with you.

- Write in short phrases rather than complete sentences, to save time.

- Try to abbreviate and shorten what a child said—don't try to write all the words, but get the gist of what is said.

- Describe *how* a child is doing or saying something.

---

[1]Adapted from materials developed by the Head Start Resource and Training Center (College Park, MD: University of Maryland, 1975).

- Develop a system of abbreviations or initials for materials and equipment; for instance, for colors of paint, use red-r, blue-b, black-bl, and so on.

- Use arrows to indicate movement.

- Make diagrams of the environment showing the child in relation to the setting, other children in the room, and adults.

- Underline words to indicate a particular intensity (for instance, "said *loudly*").

- Date each note you make on a child.

- Plan time in your daily schedule to observe a child, if only for ten minutes.

- Work out a schedule for the month and year to observe all children in your group.

- Have a reason for observing each child, for example, to find out how this child plays in small groups or how many times and how frequently this child changes activities during free play.

- Use your observations to change activities or to meet a child's needs.

- Share your observations with fellow staff members in a confidential and professional manner.

- Use your observations as you make recommendations to parents about their children's interests, needs, and progress in your program.

To be complete, recordings must include several facts. These are:

- the child's name and age;

- the date of the observation;

- the setting (where the activity is taking place and who is involved—for example, "Debby and Ron sit on the floor in the book area looking at books");

- the observer's name; and

- the behavior (what the child you are observing does and says).

Throughout the year, recordings should be made in all areas of each child's development. You can organize your observations in the following categories:

- fine and gross motor development;
- cognitive development;
- language development;
- creativity;

- self-discipline;
- self-help skills;
- self-esteem;
- social development.

It may be useful to develop a format for observing that includes spaces for the needed information on a notepad or on index cards. Your format may look like the sample below.

SAMPLE OBSERVATION FORM

Child: _____   Age: _____   Date: _____

Setting: _____   Observer: _____

Behavior: _____

_____

_____

_____

_____

_____

A single observation cannot provide a complete picture of a child. Children, like adults, do not behave in the same ways all the time. Illness, reactions to events at home or at the center, and other things affect what a child does and says. Children's abilities, interests, and needs change over time; therefore, observation is an ongoing process. When teachers have collected several recordings on a child, they can make comments such as the following:

- "Tara has a special interest in books about dinosaurs."

- "Sarah can build a tower with the large cardboard blocks."

- "Leo can match primary and secondary colors. He can name red and black."

To draw conclusions like those just given, teachers must be sure that their recordings are both objective and accurate. Objective and accurate recordings include only the full facts about what is seen and heard. They do not include labels or judgments. Compare the following excerpts from an observation of a child at the water play table.

Example 1
Objective and Accurate

Behavior: *Tony moved the water back and forth with the funnel. The water splashed inside and outside the basin. Some fell on other children's shoes. Tony began to giggle.*

Example 1 is an objective recording. It includes only the facts of what Tony did ("moved the water back and forth"), what happened ("the water splashed inside and outside the basin"), and his reaction ("Tony began to giggle"). Accurate recordings include *all* the facts about what a child does and says in the order they happen. Information is not omitted or recorded out of order. Read the following two examples about the same observation.

Example 2
Not Objective

Behavior: *Tony was bad today. He angrily splashed the water on the floor and on other children at the water basin. Then he laughed at them.*

Example 2 is not an objective recording. A label ("bad") is used and judgments are made ("he angrily splashed the water," "he laughed at them"). Given what the teacher saw, he or she could not know what Tony was laughing at or whether he acted in anger. A recording that he was "bad" does not tell anything useful about his behavior, since "bad" is a word that means different things to different people.

Example 3
Not Accurate

Behavior: *Tony stood at the water basin looking to see if a teacher was watching him. He giggled and began to splash water on other children.*

In Example 3 a fact is added that has not been observed ("looking to see if a teacher was watching him"). A fact is omitted ("Tony moved the water back and forth with the funnel"). And a fact is written out of order ("He giggled and began to splash water...").

Making an objective and accurate recording such as Example 1 requires practice. This skill can be developed during regular child care activities. As a teacher plays with a child in the sandbox, the teacher gains valuable information. A skilled teacher takes the time to step back from his or her interactions to record that information. Opportunities for taking brief notes are present throughout the day. With practice, teachers can complete recordings as they play with, care for, and eat with young children. Here are some examples.

Examples

Child: _Alexis_   **Age:** _4 1/2 years_   **Date:** _Oct 6_

Setting: *Housekeeping area, Alexis and Sophie are playing mommy and daddy.*

Behavior: *Alexis knocks loudly on the side of the wooden refrigerator at the entrance to the housekeeping area. "I'm home. It's cold outside," he announces to his "wife" Sophie. Alexis tosses his heavy man's jacket on the chair. He is wearing men's boots. Alexis puts a split log in the play stove. "It's cold in here too. How's the baby?" Alexis says to Sophie.*

Child: _Natalia_   **Age:** _3 years, 3 months_   **Date:** _Feb 4_

Setting: *Near the entrance, in cubby area, at morning arrival time.*

Behavior: *Natalia enters, holding her grandfather's hand. Grandfather pulls her parka off over her head. Natalia smiles at her grandfather as he pats her hair down. Natalia sits on the floor and silently lifts her foot up. Grandfather kneels down and takes her boots off. Then grandfather leaves and Natalia stands by her cubby, looking around the room.*

Child: _Anthony_   **Age:** _4 years, 4 months_   **Date:** _Aug 30_

Setting: *Outdoors, Anthony is kneeling by the 18" high slice of tree stump that was added to the carpentry area 2 days ago when a neighborhood tree was cut down.*

Behavior: *Anthony rubs the palm of his right hand back and forth across the surface of the tree stump. He traces a tree ring with his right index finger. He picks up the hammer in his right hand and a large-topped roofing nail in his left hand. Holding the nail between his left index finger and thumb, he begins to pound the nail into the tree stump. He looks up at the volunteer who is approaching him and says to her, "My dad is building new steps on our house."*

Child: _Luke_   **Age:** _3 years, 10 months_   **Date:** _March 16_

Setting: _Table, Luke sits with four children and Mr. Lopez lunchtime_

Behavior: _Mr. Lopez passes the plate of meatloaf and beans to Luke. Luke looks at him. "What's for lunch?" "It's meatloaf and beans. Help yourself. Take a piece of bread, Luke." Luke takes bread from plate. "Apple, too." Mr. Lopez passes bowl. Luke takes two slices. Puts one slice in mouth, holds other in left hand. Puts slice down, picks up fork with left hand. Holds fork upside down, stabs several times at meat. Moves meat around plate._

Child: _Julie_   **Age:** _5 years_   **Date:** _Feb 14_

Setting: _Table toys area, Julie at table with parquetry blocks and patterns_

Behavior: _Julie dumps blocks out of basket. Takes pattern card. Looks at card, lays it down on table. Moves blocks, picks up red diamond, places it on matching shape on card. Selects each block to complete pattern, moving from upper left to lower right of pattern card._

Child: _Mike_   **Age:** _4 years, 2 months_   **Date:** _Nov 21_

Setting: _Outdoors, Mike in the fort with Julie and Chris_

Behavior: _Mike climbs ladder into fort, hand over hand. Stands on platform._

"I'm fort leader. Everybody, let's go." He slides down ramp, Julie and Chris follow. "Up the ladder again," he yells. All climb up ladder. "Let's stay here now and be lookouts for dinosaurs." All sit.

After making several recordings about a child engaged in a variety of activities, you will learn a lot about that child. For example, you might learn about the child's:

- ability to choose an activity;

- interest in "messy" play;

- eye-hand coordination;

- temperament;

- ability to manipulate an object; and

- understanding of limits.

In addition to recording in an objective and accurate way, teachers must be sure that they are seeing and hearing what others are seeing and hearing. People often perceive the same situation differently. Eyewitness accounts of an accident demonstrate how several people, seeing the same event, have different stories to tell. This may happen to teachers as well.

One teacher may see Linda feeding her baby doll dirt and Julie snatch it away and try to drown it. Another, watching the same children, may observe Linda smearing mud on a doll and Julie taking it away to give it a bath. Knowledge of what a child has done in the past, your feelings about a certain type of behavior, tone of voice, and many other factors influence what you observe and record.

It is useful to compare your recordings about a child with another teacher's observation information. If they are similar, an accurate record of a child's growth and development is being maintained. If they are very different, the information collected may not be useful. Two teachers with different perceptions of a child's behavior should observe the child together over a short period of time. After each observation they can compare their recordings and discuss what they have seen. This method helps ensure accurate recordings. If the recordings still differ greatly, the center director can assist them in solving the problem.

In this learning activity you will practice observing and recording. Select a child to observe for a two-week period. Observe the child for five to ten minutes, once per day. Ask your center director, co-teacher, or trainer to observe the same child at the same time as you are observing, on at least four occasions. Compare your recordings after each co-observation and at the end of the two-week period.

Make several copies of this form before recording your observations.

Observation Form

Child: _____   Age: _____   Date: _____

Setting: _____   Observer: _____

Behavior: _____

_____

_____

_____

_____

_____

_____

_____

_____

_____

_____

_____

If your recordings are objective, accurate, and similar to those of your co-observer, begin the next learning activity. If your recordings differ and are not objective and accurate, select another child to observe, and repeat this learning activity. Ask your trainer to observe with you again and record information about the same child. Then discuss your recordings with your trainer and begin the next learning activity.

You may also want to review other types of observation and ways to record them. These can be found in the books included in the additional readings listed in the bibliography that appears in the orientation.

II. Individualizing Your Program

In this activity you will learn:

- to use observation information to better understand each child's interests, strengths, and needs; and

- to plan appropriate activities for each child in your group.

In your role as manager, you have very important responsibilities to meet for each child in your group. It is up to you to build upon a child's sense of trust in the world and self that begins at home. As a "home base" in a child development program, it is up to you to help children feel safe and secure so they will be free to explore and take advantage of the rich experiences your program has to offer. To meet these responsibilities, you must individualize your program.

Creating an individualized program requires knowing children as individuals. As you spend each day with children, you learn a lot about their skills, interests, and needs, and the way they deal with the world. In an individualized program, teachers know which children like to put together puzzles with many pieces. The table toy area includes a table for quiet, individual play and a collection of puzzles. Teachers know which children like to show their finished product to an adult, and teachers are ready to look at and praise the children's work. Teachers also know which children like to play together in the house corner or re-enact a trip to the firehouse or a visit to the clinic or doctor's office. They make sure that dress-up clothes are hung where the children can reach them, and they prepare prop boxes to support children's dramatic play.

Systematically observing and recording can help you confirm your impressions and fill in your pictures of each child. You can also learn about children by talking with their parents. As discussed in Module 11, parents know their children best of all. By developing a partnership with parents, you will have their help in getting to know their child.

Individualizing involves setting up the environment and interacting with children in ways that help them grow and develop. You provide experiences to match each child's interests. You also provide toys and activities that allow children to practice their newly acquired skills. And you offer them challenges to move to the next step. The preschool child who can eat with a spoon and fork may be ready to use a knife to butter her bread or slice fruit for snack; and the child who can play a game involving classification by color may be ready to classify by color and shape. You give each of these children opportunities to try new things.

In this activity you have the opportunity to practice your observation skills again. You will observe two children in your group over a period of two weeks. First decide how you will record your observations. You can use a notepad, index cards, or copies of the observation form in Learning Activity I. Your recordings should include at least the information asked for on the observation form in Learning Activity I.

Then select two children to observe. Observe each child for a five- to ten-minute period at least once each day. After you have collected all your observations, re-read them to see what you have learned about these children.

On the next page you will find an example of an "Individualization Summary Form." It shows you how one teacher summarized what she learned from her observations of two children. After you have read this example, you will be ready to complete the blank "Individualization Summary Form" provided for you, using your own recently collected observations.

Individualization Summary Form
(Example)

	Child: _Peggy_ Age: _3 years_	Child: _Gary_ Age: _4 1/2 years_
How does this child usually play (alone, with one or two friends, in a group)?	*Usually with two children —Sue and Roy, or Sue and Larry.*	*Likes to look at books by himself. Plays with 3-4 children outdoors. Likes circle time songs and dances with small groups.*
What kinds of play does this child like (favorite toys and activities, quiet or active play)?	*A lot of time spent in sand play using shovels and toy boats. Also dances with friends. Sometimes sings.*	*Some free play time in book area. Most often he builds with table toys and large hollow blocks.*
What kinds of play does this child start, join in, or invite others to join in?	*Usually joins in with friends, especially if they are singing. She sometimes goes off by herself to the sand table or asks Sue to play with her there.*	*Likes to be by himself in book area. Often starts games outside or builds with table toys. Waits to be invited into the circle but enjoys songs a lot.*
What skills has this child acquired?	*Can play near others and with some children. Can use objects to move other objects. Can play make-believe games.*	*Can turn pages of book without tearing. Can name some words. Can lift heavy objects and build towers. Can balance small and large objects.*
What new experiences can you provide for this child to build on these skills?	*Provide new songs to sing and records to play. Talk with her at sand table, asking open-ended questions.*	*Read with him and point to words as I read them. Put Unifix cubes in bookcases in table toys area.*

	Child: _____ Age: _____	Child: _____ Age: _____
Individualization Summary Form		
How does this child usually play (alone, with one or two friends, in a group)?		
What kinds of play does this child like (favorite toys and activities, quiet or active play)?		
What kinds of play does this child start, join in, or invite others to join in?		
What skills has this child acquired?		
What new experiences can you provide for this child to build on these skills?		

Discuss your observation recordings and your plans for these two children with your trainer. If you found it difficult to complete your recordings, talk with your trainer about why that was so, and try to find ways to make it possible to record observations on a regular basis.

Provide new experiences for the children you observed in this learning activity. Observe them again for several days to assess any changes in their interests or strengths. Plan to observe all the children in your group on a regular basis to provide an individualized program.

III. Working as a Team to Plan the Program

In this activity you will learn:

- to recognize planning as an effective management tool; and

- to develop weekly plans.

Planning forces you to think about what you want to do and how you will do it. It means taking time to think through what activities you will offer each week, what materials you will need, and which children you want to focus on. It also means that each teacher must assume responsibility for carrying out the plans.

Teachers who plan for each week are better prepared. They have materials ready for the children and are less likely to make children wait. Therefore, their daily program runs more smoothly. The children are involved and engaged in activities suited to their needs and interests.

It is very important that all members of the teaching team, teachers, aides, and parents and community volunteers be aware of daily plans. The more involved in planning you are, the more likely you are to realize the important role you play in carrying out the plans.

As the teacher, you are the team leader. As an aide or volunteer you are an important team member. In the planning process, there is a place for each team member's particular strengths, interests, and talents. Each member may have valuable observations, ideas, or concerns to contribute. An attitude of trust and respect toward other team members enables each one of you to communicate problems and to recognize and appreciate successes.

What Kind of Planning Is Needed?

Two types of planning are useful for teachers: long-range planning and weekly planning. Long-range planning involves thinking ahead, perhaps a month or more, to what you want to make available to the children in your care. For example, if you know that you want to convert the house corner into a grocery store the following month, you need to think ahead. You may want to prepare a prop box with items you will be using, such as a cash register, play money, and shopping bags. You will need to begin collecting empty food containers and cans for the store. By planning ahead, you will be ready with the materials and props you need. Long-range planning also is necessary if you want to arrange a special event such as a trip or a party. Thinking ahead and planning ahead ensure that special events will really happen.

Weekly plans are more detailed than long-range plans. Programs often design their own formats for weekly planning. What works well for one teaching team may not work for another. A good place to start is to ask yourself, "What do I need to plan that will help me be a better manager?"

Many teachers find it useful to plan in the following categories.

- **Changes in the environment**—the addition of new props or materials, or changes in the arrangement of indoor or outdoor space. For example, new transportation props might be introduced in the block area along with a collection of keys to sort and classify in the table toy area, or the easels might be moved to the outdoor area on warm days.

- **Special activity**—an activity planned for a small group of children or the whole group. Teachers might plan a visit to a grocery store or a tie-dying activity.

- **Target children**—those children who may have special needs or interests that teachers want to address during a given week. Target children may include a child whose mother is about to have a baby. This child may need extra time with the teacher, or books about new babies and older brothers or sisters.

- **Special focus**—a theme or topic emphasized during a given week. The theme or focus for the week guides planning of materials and activities. For example, if the theme is "going to the doctor," new props may be added to the house corner; books on doctors and going to the hospital may be included in the book area; and a visit to a clinic might be arranged.

- **Teacher responsibilities**—the assignment of specific tasks to each teacher to ensure that they get done. For example, if the plan is to have children prepare a snack of lettuce roll-ups, someone must be responsible for getting lettuce and peanut butter for the day the activity is planned.

What Guides the Planning Process?

Teachers have many tools and strategies they can use to help them plan. First, they know what children can and should be doing at a given age and stage of development. The child development charts at the beginning of Modules 1 through 10 in this training program define the skills and abilities of children at each stage of development.

Second, teachers have specific knowledge about each child. Information gathered through observations and recordings, and from home visits with parents, is invaluable in the planning process. Knowing, for example, that one child is going on a trip may lead teachers to add suitcases and books about trips to the play area. Teachers sometimes find it helpful to identify specific children who have a particular interest or strength, special need, or skill they are struggling to master. By targeting these children during the planning process, teachers can design activities and materials to meet their needs.

Teachers use yet another strategy that guides the planning process: they carefully observe how children are using the environment each day. Daily observations give teachers important clues as to what changes are needed in the environment. For example, if the same toys have been on a low shelf in the room for several weeks, teachers may note that there is little interest in the area. Putting some toys away, adding new ones, or even changing the location of some toys can gain children's interest. Daily observations also let teachers know when something planned is not working. For example, if children are unable to complete the puzzles and often leave them out unfinished, the puzzles may be too difficult for them. This tells teachers that they should try puzzles with fewer pieces and less complex shapes.

Finally, teachers consider what special activities they want to offer in a given week. Special activities are usually planned on the basis of the children's interests. For example, if a group particularly likes wearing capes and playing superhero, teachers might help children plan and perform a play about superheroes. Special activities may coincide with the time of year—in the fall, a walk to collect seeds or dried grasses—or they may simply be activities that teachers think the children will enjoy—making applesauce or planting a garden. The special interests or talents of the teaching team are valuable here. An adult's enthusiasm for music or weaving is quickly communicated to the children and can extend the children's interests.

What About Flexibility?

Anyone who has worked with young children knows that even the best plans don't always work out as intended. Preschool children have so many new skills and interests that planning for them is particularly important. With this age group, teachers must be flexible. A trip to a special playground may turn out to be a trip to a construction site that captures the children's interest.

How Is Planning Done?

Weekly planning does not need to be a lengthy process. Finding time for planning can be difficult; however, in many centers, teachers conduct planning meetings before children arrive, after they leave, or during rest time. Teachers who work together should plan together. In many centers, parents are regularly invited to participate in both the planning and the doing of activities.

A planning form can be very helpful. In your center there may be a planning form that everyone uses. You can also use the form provided in this module. Whatever format you use for planning, it should include the categories discussed:

- changes in the environment;
- special activities;
- target children;
- special focus or theme; and
- teacher responsibilities.

What About Evaluation?

Evaluation of the experiences you provide for children is an integral part of the planning process. After you have prepared for and conducted activities, it is helpful to think about the following:

- **What happened during each day?** What types of activities did children engage in? What did teachers do to respond to children's actions? What activities did teachers initiate?

- **How was each child's learning and development facilitated?** What worked well? What did not work well? Did each child have many opportunities to explore, experiment, and learn by doing?

- **In light of each day's experiences, what changes should be made in the environment?** Should furniture and equipment be rearranged? Should new toys or props be added to the room? Should a different style of interaction be tried with certain children? What activities should be repeated?

It is important for teaching teams to go through an evaluation such as this one during each planning meeting.

What About Program Planning?

Because of their knowledge of children's strengths, interests, and needs as well as their awareness of what is appropriate for child development programs, teachers are often called upon to provide input on program issues. Teachers should take the opportunity to talk with other center staff about ways to improve the child development program as a whole. Suggestions on staffing patterns, enrollment policies, and other practices and procedures will be welcomed by administrators whose goal is to provide a high-quality program that meets the needs of children, parents, and staff.

In this learning activity you will review a sample planning form that includes all the categories discussed. Begin by reviewing the sample weekly planning form for your age group. Then agree on a time to meet with a colleague to plan together. Develop a weekly plan using the blank form provided after the examples on the following pages. Finally, implement the plan and evaluate how it worked.

Weekly Plan
(Example)

Week: _November 4-8_   Special Focus (if any): _Our Bodies_

DAY	CHANGES IN ENVIRONMENT	SPECIAL ACTIVITIES	TARGET CHILDREN
Monday	House corner—add small suitcases. Blocks—add wooden people. Art—add orange and brown paint.	Face painting in front of long horizontal mirrors. Shaving cream to trace reflection of own body on vertical mirrors.	Brandy—all week—help her make friends. Roger—reinforce sharing.
Tuesday	Books—_Bodies_ by Barbara Brenner. Table toys—people puzzle. Music—hokey-pokey, bring in scale.	Footprint painting. Make weight and height chart	Denise and Carl—hokey-pokey. Jamal—puzzles.
Wednesday	Books—_Be a Bird, Be a Frog, Be a Tree._	Measure long bones, hip to knee, or wrist to elbow. Use a chicken bone as a unit of measurement.	Andrea—working on climbing apparatus, stand nearby.

Teacher Responsibilities: Both will talk about what bodies can do: eyes can see, hands pick up, feet and legs walk, etc. Be sensitive to the feelings of overweight, underweight, or particularly short or tall children when making height and weight charts. Appreciate each child exactly as she or he is!

Meet with your planning team (aide, co-teacher, parent) in your room to develop a weekly plan. Use the form below.

Weekly Plan			
Week: _____		Special Focus (if any): _____	
DAY	**CHANGES IN ENVIRONMENT**	**SPECIAL ACTIVITIES**	**TARGET CHILDREN**
Monday			
Tuesday			
Wednesday			
Thursday			
Friday			

Teacher Responsibilities:

_____

_____

_____

For one week, use the plan you developed as a guide. Then answer the following questions.

How did children react to changes in the environment?

_____

_____

_____

How did children react to special activities?

_____

_____

_____

What did you accomplish with target children?

_____

_____

_____

What changes did you make in the plan?

_____

_____

_____

What would you do differently next time?

_____

_____

_____

Discuss your plan and your experiences in using it with your trainer and other members of your teaching team.

IV. Following Administrative Policies and Procedures

In this activity you will learn:

- to identify your center's administrative policies and procedures; and

- to complete management tasks according to a schedule.

As a teacher in a child development program, you are a part of a large system. Your role in this system includes coordinating with other teachers, with all center staff, with parents, and possibly with other offices or agencies in the community.

A center runs smoothly when administrative policies and procedures are understood and followed by center staff. These policies and procedures are outlined in the center handbooks. They usually address the following topics:

- hours of operation;

- acceptance/registration procedures;

- fees and service charges;

- safety requirements;

- medical and health requirements;

- fire prevention and evacuation procedures;

- policy on closing for bad weather;

- contingency plans for center use in emergencies;

- reporting accidents;

- use of consumable supplies and reporting needs for new supplies;

- reporting suspected child abuse and neglect;

- reporting maintenance needs for furniture and equipment; and

- discipline.

Teachers should be aware of these policies and procedures so that all staff follow the same regulations during the center's day-to-day operations. In addition, parents may seek answers to questions about discipline, accidents, or other issues. Teachers should know the procedures regarding such issues so they can provide parents with information or direct them to discuss an issue with a supervisor, when appropriate.

Types of Records

The center's policies and procedures also address the kinds of records and forms that clerical/administrative staff are required to collect or keep on file and the role teachers play in this management task. These records may include:

- physical examination reports;
- height/weight charts;
- observation and assessment reports;
- daily attendance reports;
- parent contact forms;
- contagious disease exposure forms;
- medical emergency consent forms;
- weekly plan outlines;
- field trip permission forms;
- food service reports;
- inventory records;
- supply request forms;
- staff time sheets; and
- staff leave request forms.

To follow the center's procedures for reporting and recordkeeping, you may find it helpful to keep a list of necessary reports and the date each is due. Some reports may be due daily or weekly. Others are completed when an incident occurs, such as an accident. Still others, such as inventory reports, are used once a year. Your role will vary according to the reporting task. Some information, such as observation and assessment reports for children, may be collected and reviewed periodically by teachers. Other reports, such as a summary of a parent conference led by another staff member, may be completed by others but kept on file in case other people need to review the information.

Finally, your role includes not sharing with anyone, other than those who also care for your group, any confidential information. Maintaining confidentiality is a basic part of being a professional teacher.

In this learning activity you will review your center's administrative policies and procedures for completing various kinds of reports. Then you will complete a report schedule indicating when these reports are due and what teachers' responsibilities are with regard to completing these forms. First read the example of a report schedule on the next page.

Report Schedule
(Example)

REPORT	TEACHER'S RESPONSIBILITY	DATE DUE
Observation and assessment	*Complete daily recordings, record assessment information on observation and assessment report*	*Review with supervisor on last Friday of each month*
Attendance	*Record attendance for group*	*Every Friday*
Time sheet	*Fill in hours worked each day*	*Every Friday*
Supply requisition	*Request consumable supplies when inventory is low*	*15th of each month*
Annual leave request	*Request leave*	*Two weeks prior to date for which leave is requested*
Contagious disease exposure	*Complete form when parent notifies teacher of child's illness*	*By 6:00 p. m. on the day parent notifies me of illness*
Inventory	*Record quantities of equipment, toys, and consumable supplies*	*May 30*

Report Schedule

Now complete the schedule below for reports you must complete in your program and note your responsibilities for completing them.

REPORT	TEACHER'S RESPONSIBILITY	DATE DUE

Discuss this schedule with your trainer. Review and follow your center's administrative policies and procedures throughout the year.

Summarizing Your Progress

You have now completed all of the learning activities for this module. Whether you are an experienced teacher or a new one, this module has probably helped you develop new managerial skills. Before you go on, take a few minutes to summarize what you've learned.

- Turn back to Learning Activity II, Individualizing Your Program. Review the recordings completed for the children in your group. Why are they examples of objective and accurate recordings? How did you use this information to individualize your program for these children? Was this information included in your weekly plans for your group?

- Next, review your responses to the pre-training assessment for this module. Write a summary of what you learned and list the skills you developed or improved.

_____

_____

_____

_____

_____

_____

_____

_____

_____

If there are topics you would like to learn more about, you will find recommended readings listed in the orientation, which can be found in Volume I.

Your final step in this module is to complete the knowledge and competency assessments. Let your trainer know when you are ready to schedule the assessments. After you have successfully completed these assessments, you will be ready to start a new module. Congratulations on your progress so far, and good luck with your next module.

Answer Sheets

Being an Effective Manager

Observing and Recording Information About Each Child's Growth and Development

1. **How did Mr. Lopez use a regular activity to gather objective and accurate information about Eric?**

   He recorded what Eric did and said during a food preparation activity.

2. **What are three things Mr. Lopez learned about Eric?**

   a. Eric can make a choice.

   b. He can hold a knife and use it for spreading, with assistance.

   c. He can form a simple phrase.

   d. He can complete a task.

   e. He can eat finger foods.

   f. He likes crunchy peanut butter.

   g. He is open to suggestions.

Working as a Member of a Team to Plan an Individualized Program

1. **How did Ms. Kim use a team approach to planning?**

   She asked each teacher to prepare for a meeting by gathering information, to bring prepared copies of the planning and evaluation forms to the meeting, and to participate actively.

2. **How did the teachers use observation information for planning?**

   On the basis of what the children did during the week, the teachers developed plans to conduct activities and bring new materials outdoors to build on children's interests.

Following Administrative Policies, Practices, and Procedures

1. How did Ms. Williams stay informed about administrative policies and procedures?

She reviewed the staff handbook and discussed certain procedures with a colleague.

2. What tasks did Ms. Williams complete according to the center's policies?

She submitted a request for annual leave, filled out the field trip request form, and sent permission slips home to parents.

Glossary

Administrative policies and procedures	The systems outlined by the center's staff handbook and parent handbooks that ensure the smooth operation of the center.
Curriculum	The framework, based on a written plan, for the experiences children have with materials, each other, and teachers.
Individualized program	A program in which the environment and teachers' interactions with children are suited to each child's interests, strengths, and needs.
Objective recordings	Written information that includes only the facts about behaviors that are seen and heard.
Planning	The establishment of specific steps to accomplish program objectives.
Systematic observation	Consistent watching, listening to, and recording of what children say and do, according to a particular method.

Module 13
Professionalism

What Is a Professional and Why Is a Commitment to Professionalism Important?

A professional is a person who uses specialized knowledge and skills to do a job or provide a service. As an early childhood teacher, you are a member of an important profession. You work with children during a time when they are developing more quickly than they will at any other period in their lives. You help shape children's views about learning and the world around them. The care you provide influences how children feel about themselves. If you build children's self-esteem during these early years, they will be more likely to succeed in life.

Professionalism for teachers means providing care based on your knowledge of what children do and what they need to grow and develop. It also means taking advantage of opportunities to learn more about children and yourself and to develop new skills that will make you more competent.

Your professional skills also support families. When parents have confidence in the reliable, high-quality care you and your colleagues provide, they can feel better about themselves as parents. Their own job performance also is improved because they know their children are well cared for at the center. And the information and insights you share with parents about their children promote a sense of teamwork.

When you need a service (such as medical or legal advice, or electrical repair), you look for a professional business or individual who can meet your needs. You choose professionals because you want:

- the needed service;

- specialized knowledge;

- a commitment to quality;

- dependability; and

- effectiveness.

In all these areas, teachers make unique professional contributions. They provide:

- the needed service—a high-quality child development program;

- specialized knowledge—an understanding of how children grow and develop and of how to meet their needs appropriately;

- a commitment to quality—providing a developmentally appropriate program in a safe and healthy environment;

- dependability—providing a service on a regular basis; and

- effectiveness—providing a program that helps children build cognitive and creative skills and develop self-discipline and self-esteem.

Lilian Katz, an early childhood educator, has studied how teachers grow professionally. She suggests that they pass through four different stages of professional development, each of which is briefly described below.

Stage One: Survival

Teachers are new and often insecure. They devote most of their attention to learning the center's routines and performing tasks as assigned. If you are at this stage, orientation, training, and experience will help you move to stage two, consolidation.

Stage Two: Consolidation

Teachers become more confident and begin to look beyond simply completing the daily routines. They seek new ways to accomplish routine tasks and to handle problems. If you are at this stage, you will find it useful to spend time with other teachers exchanging ideas and feelings. Conversations, group meetings, training sessions, and open discussions will help you grow and move to stage three, renewal.

Stage Three: Renewal

After a year or two on the job, teachers begin to be bored with the day's routines. Often their interest drops and enthusiasm falls. Teachers in this stage need a renewal—new challenges. If you are at this stage, you should try to attend conferences and workshops, join professional organizations, or pursue a special interest. These professional activities will provide needed stimulation and help you move to stage four, maturity.

Stage Four: Maturity

Teachers at this stage are committed professionals. They understand the need to seek new ideas and skills. They continue to grow professionally. If you are a mature teacher you can be a model for new teachers. You might also seek new challenges as a supervisor, trainer, or center administrator.

Teaching is a profession that requires many different kinds of skills. In your work you fulfill the roles of educator, child development specialist, health care advisor, and nutritionist. Your work is important to the children you care for, their families, and the community.

Maintaining a commitment to professionalism has several positive results. First, it builds your self-esteem. You feel proud when you learn new skills, acquire knowledge, and become more competent. The sense of success you experience as you become a competent teacher is rewarding and fulfilling.

Second, when you provide professional care, you are helping children grow, learn, and develop to their full potential. And third, your professional behavior helps the field of early childhood education. As you and others provide high-quality programs for children, you build respect for the profession, which can result in more recognition for the important service you provide.

Teaching is not just a job—it's a profession. While you help children to grow and develop, you can enjoy your work, do the best job you can, and continue to grow and advance as a teacher and as a person.

Maintaining a commitment to professionalism means:

- continually assessing one's own performance;

- continuing to learn about caring for children; and

- applying professional ethics at all times.

Listed below are examples of how teachers maintain a commitment to professionalism.

Continually Assessing One's Own Performance

Here are some examples of what teachers can do.

- Identify areas where performance could be improved. "I can't figure out how to help Johnnie learn to use his words instead of hitting other children. Perhaps this article will help me."

- Know how to judge their own competence in a certain area. "I'm not really providing enough art experiences for the children. I'll talk with one of the other teachers to get some ideas."

- Compare their own performance against professional standards and guidelines. "I know that I should never leave a class of children unsupervised. I'll wait until the aide returns before I go to the supply room."

- Participate in professional organizations and/or professional activities. "I think I will attend this conference to learn more about advocacy."

Continuing to Learn About Caring for Children

Here are some examples of what teachers can do.

- Keep current about procedures and guidelines concerning child development. "I have a few free moments. I'll review this new policy on reporting suspected incidents of child abuse."

- Keep informed of the latest early childhood practices. "I'd like to attend that workshop next weekend. I can share the information at the next staff meeting."

- Apply knowledge and skills on the job. "Helping Sara learn to use the potty was much easier after I read *Toilet Learning*. The ideas in the book really worked."

- Talk with colleagues about child development and child care. "I think I'll try to take my break with Ms. Williams today. Maybe she has some suggestions on how we can prepare the children for the field trip."

Applying Professional Ethics at All Times

Here are some examples of what teachers can do.

- Maintain respect and confidentiality for each child. "The files that we keep on each child are confidential, Mrs. Robinson. Arnisha's file will be kept in our locked cabinet. Only the teachers, the center director, and you and her father are allowed to read your child's file."

- Be dependable and reliable in performing their duties and responsibilities. "Boy, I'm tired this morning, but I won't call in sick, because I know those kids need me."

- Show no personal bias against children because of culture, background, or gender. "Boys and girls both can play in the woodworking area. You must wait, Jamal, until one of the other children leaves, and then you can play there."

- Speak out against practices that are not developmentally appropriate. "We don't want to force Tanya to learn to read before she's ready, Mr. Grisson. Very few children are ready at age four."

- Stand up for parts of the program that you believe are appropriate for the children. "Dramatic play helps the children make sense of the world, Mrs. Grundy. They will still learn the difference between make-believe and fibbing."

- Support the center director and other administrative staff by avoiding gossip. "I know you're upset, Ms. Frilles, but if you don't agree with your performance appraisal, you really should discuss it with the center director. Why don't you make an appointment to talk with her next week?"

- Show support for other teachers when they need assistance. "I'd be happy to help you re-arrange your room, Mr. Lopez. Just let me know when you're ready."

Maintaining a Commitment to Professionalism

In the following situations, teachers are maintaining a commitment to professionalism as they care for preschool children. As you read each one, think about what the teachers are doing and why. Then answer the questions that follow.

Continually Assessing One's Own Performance

Ms. Kim sinks down into her chair to think at the end of a long day. The morning started out smoothly, but by late afternoon everything was crazy. Clean and dirty clothes were mixed together. Parents had complained earlier in the week that their children had on someone else's clothes. Today she spent ten minutes helping Joseph find his hat and gloves. The gloves were found with Matthew's coat. The hat was near the block corner, where she had left it when they came in from outdoors. "This cannot go on," she said to herself. "I have to get more organized. Mr. Lopez always seems so organized. Maybe he can give me some pointers. My supervisor can give me some suggestions, too."

1. How did Ms. Kim assess her own performance?

_____

_____

_____

2. What did she decide to do with the results of her self-assessment?

_____

_____

_____

Continuing to Learn About Caring for Children

Mr. Lopez completed a self-assessment for preschool teachers and worked with his supervisor, Ms. Lee, to identify three areas where he could improve his skills. They discussed what might be reasonable goals. Mr. Lopez decided that he would review a module on learning environments (one of the three areas) during the following month and attend the in-service training session on the same topic. Ms. Lee also scheduled a visit to Mr. Lopez's room so that she could observe and offer suggestions on how the environment could be improved. They planned to meet again in a month to discuss progress on the plan and how Mr. Lopez's skills had improved.

1. **How did Mr. Lopez decide what knowledge and skills he should work to improve?**

_____

_____

_____

2. **How did Mr. Lopez plan to expand his existing knowledge and skills?**

_____

_____

_____

Applying Professional Ethics at All Times

Mrs. Johnson, a parent, arrived to pick up her child, Dora, from the center. When she walked in, Dora was building with the unit blocks. A second child, Joshua, was acting like a parachutist. He was about to jump from the bookshelf. Ms. Williams said, "Hello, Mrs. Johnson. Excuse me a moment," and turned immediately to Joshua. "Joshua," she said, "I know you like being a parachutist, but it is not safe for you to jump from this shelf. Let me help you down. You can jump near the pillows where it is safe." When she came back, Mrs. Johnson said: "Boy, he's wild, isn't he?" Ms. Williams responded, "Joshua really enjoys role playing. He has a great imagination. Now, let me tell you about Dora's day."

1. **How did Ms. Williams maintain professional ethics in talking to Mrs. Johnson?**

_____

_____

_____

2. **How did Ms. Williams interact with Joshua in a professional manner?**

_____

_____

_____

Compare your answers with those on the answer sheet at the end of this module. If your answers are different, discuss them with your trainer. There may be more than one good answer. As you complete the other modules in this training program, you will become more competent in caring for young children. Enhanced knowledge and skills will increase your level of professionalism. This module addresses other areas that can help you stay committed to being a professional teacher.

The Early Childhood Profession and You

Many of us feel that an early childhood program is "a great place to work." We feel our work is important to the young children and families we work with each day.

As professionals, we are continually reflecting on our feelings about working with young children, expanding our knowledge base, and developing positive relations with parents and each other. Despite the importance of our work, the early childhood profession does not always receive the status and recognition it deserves.

All of these factors may contribute to how you feel about your career in the early childhood field. Consider the following questions:

How do you feel about being an early childhood teacher?

_____

_____

_____

_____

Why did you choose this profession?

_____

_____

_____

_____

What do you like best?

_____

_____

_____

_____

What would you like to change?

_____

_____

_____

_____

What can you do to begin bringing about these changes?

_____

_____

_____

_____

Answer these questions and discuss them with your trainer and a group of other staff members.

When you have finished this overview section, you should complete the pre-training assessment. Refer to the glossary at the end of the module if you need definitions for the terms that are used.

Pre-Training Assessment

Listed below are the skills that teachers use to maintain their commitment to professionalism. Think about whether you do these things regularly, sometimes, or not enough. Place a check in one of the columns on the right for each skill listed. Then discuss your answers with your trainer.

SKILL	I DO THIS REGULARLY	I DO THIS SOMETIMES	I DON'T DO THIS ENOUGH
CONTINUALLY ASSESSING ONE'S OWN PERFORMANCE			
1. Knowing how to judge my competence in a certain area.			
2. Comparing my performance against the center's procedures and guidelines.			
3. Comparing my performance against the recognized standards of the early childhood profession.			
4. Applying my unique skills and experiences to my work as a teacher.			
CONTINUING TO LEARN ABOUT CARING FOR CHILDREN			
5. Participating in professional early childhood education organizations.			
6. Reading books or articles about child development and early childhood education practices.			
7. Talking with or observing other teachers to learn more about child development.			

SKILL	I DO THIS REGULARLY	I DO THIS SOMETIMES	I DON'T DO THIS ENOUGH
8. Participating in training offered by the center or other groups.			
APPLYING PROFESSIONAL ETHICS AT ALL TIMES 9. Keeping information about children and their families confidential.			
10. Carrying out my duties in a dependable and reliable way.			
11. Speaking out when child care practices are not appropriate.			
12. Supporting early childhood education practices that are developmentally appropriate.			
13. Showing no personal bias against any child in my care.			

Review your responses, then list three to five skills you would like to improve or topics you would like to learn more about. When you finish this module, you will list examples of your new or improved knowledge and skills.

_____
_____
_____
_____
_____
_____

Now begin the learning activities for Module 13, Professionalism.

I. Assessing Yourself

In this activity you will learn:

- to recognize your unique skills and abilities; and

- to use the profession's standards to assess your own competence.

Each teacher, just like each child, is a unique person with special interests and strengths. You bring your own interests and skills to your profession, and you share them with the children you care for. One teacher may share a love for music with children; another may share a love for the outdoors. In this way everyone benefits. The children pick up on a teacher's enthusiasm and learn to appreciate something new. In turn, the teachers are able to use their special interests on the job, which makes working more satisfying and fun.

What are you really good at? What do you most enjoy? What do you like best about your job? What would you like to change? These are all questions that teachers can ask themselves. They will help you focus on what makes you unique and what special qualities you bring to your profession.

Begin this learning activity by reading "Being Curious About Yourself" and "Carol Hillman: Gardener, Naturalist, Teacher" on the following pages. The first reading will help you think about yourself; the second tells how one teacher brought her special interests and abilities to the classroom.

Next, use the form that follows the readings to record your responses to questions about how you feel about being a teacher. Take time to think about what you really want to say.

Being Curious About Yourself[1]

Who are you? What do you care about? Why are you here? What interests you about children? What gives you pleasure in being with them? Which of your interests do you enjoy sharing with them? What are your goals for them?

Does all this seem obvious—of course you know about yourself? In fact, most of us keep growing in self-understanding, and we learn in the same way we learn about other people—by observing and reflecting on our observations. Why did I get so mad when Marta dropped a cup yesterday? It was an accident. Did it trigger something from my own past that had very little to do with the present situation? Why do I find it so hard to like Jorge? I catch myself being almost mean to him—sarcastic, in a way that just isn't appropriate with little kids. Why do I do that?

Sometimes a friend or colleague can help us think through our self-observations if we're willing to share them. It can be uncomfortable, learning more about ourselves, especially about the parts of ourselves we really don't like. Some people go to therapists to get help with this process, to have someone who can listen thoughtfully to their questions about themselves.

What do you like to do with children? Sing, cook, go on walks, pet animals, have conversations, watch them playing, snuggle, comb hair, and wash faces? Do you get to do what you like to do on your job? If not, could you? If you're a caregiver spending every day with children, it's important that you have many opportunities to be a decision maker, to say, "This is what I want to do next." Not at the children's expense, but in response to both your needs and theirs. If caregivers are contented and growing, children are more likely to be contented and growing too.

Which describes you better: You like parenting children; you like teaching children; you like playing with children? Competence in child care may be based on any of these enjoyments. Parenting is being responsible, taking good care of children, appreciating their growth; if you're experienced as a parent, that may be the role you fall into naturally in child care. Teaching implies particular interest in children's thinking and problem solving, in what they know and understand—and in helping them learn. Playing with children implies being in touch with the child in yourself.

What kind of learner are you? How do you learn best? Different people learn by reading, by taking classes, by observing children's behavior, by discussing their experiences with colleagues and friends, by going to conferences and workshops, by trying things for themselves and seeing what happens. Which of these things work for you? Does your center encourage you to keep learning and give you credit for what you do? A child care center is a *living place* for children and adults. It should be a good place to live together and learn together about the world. What are you learning at your work? What risks are you taking?

---

[1]Reprinted with permission from Elizabeth Jones, "The Elephant's Child as Caregiver," *Beginnings* (Redmond, WA: Exchange Press, 1986), p. 10.

Carol Hillman: Gardener, Naturalist, Teacher[2]

I believe deeply that what you are outside of school affects what you are in school. I have a farm in Massachusetts that has for many years been a resource to me and to the children in my classroom.

There I grow things, looking after the whole process myself. I like having the knowledge that I can grow vegetables or flowers without relying on chemicals. The flowers are just as important as the edible things. I pick and dry many of them, making everlasting bouquets from them. The whole process gives me a feeling of self-sufficiency and a kind of calmness.

Those feelings translate to the classroom in ways that you might not suspect. I come to the classroom with a keen sense of the pleasure it can be to do with what you have, without having to go out and buy things. I try to show the children those same pleasures. We make bird feeders from cups and chenille-wrapped wire. They take the feeders home and have a season's worth of birds coming and going. For me, that is much better than robots, superheroes, or transformers.

Growing things takes attention—you are constantly watching what needs water, what needs thinning, what can be picked. I want to communicate that awareness to children. Every morning we have a meeting, and I ask them what they notice that is different. Almost every day we go outdoors, not just to a playground, but to the woods that surround us on practically all sides. I want the children to become investigators in the natural world: I want them to be curious about the stream, the trees, and the leaves on the ground.

Something else is fed by growing things—my aesthetic sense, a love for beautiful arrangements, shapes, and colors. Many years ago, on my first job after college, I worked at an art gallery in New York City and learned, among other things, how to hang an exhibition. Since then, I have carried with me the importance of placement, whether I am placing blocks on a shelf or plants in a garden.

That, too, carries over to the classroom. The blocks, the baskets of parquetry blocks, the puzzles and pegboards must each stand apart to command their own space and importance. What I am after is a sense of order, not a strict cleanliness—children need messiness, too.

But beyond that sense of order, my experiences in gardens and the wider outdoors have given me a taste for naturally beautiful things. Rather than stickers or predrawn forms, the children in my classes make collages from shells and sand, sweetgum pods, the bright orange berries of bittersweet vines, acorns, and pine cones.

Outside my garden, the most important part of my life as a part-time naturalist is raising monarch butterflies. For a number of years, I've worked with Dr. Fred Urquart of Toronto, who was trying to locate the hidden spot where monarchs migrate during the winter months.

---

[2]Reprinted with permission from Carol Hillman, "Teachers and Then Some: Profiles of Three Teachers," *Beginnings* (Redmond, WA: Exchange Press, 1986), pp. 21-22.

I've been a part of that search by raising, tagging, and releasing butterflies. Only a few years ago, after a lifetime of tracking the butterflies marked by many people such as myself, Urquart was able to locate the monarch's wintering spot high in the mountains near Mexico City. I have a whole portion of my garden devoted to milkweed, which is the sole food source for monarchs. I find the small caterpillars on the plants and take them into school. During the first few weeks of school each year, the children and I watch the whole metamorphosis—from caterpillar, through chrysalis, to full butterfly. We keep the monarchs in a huge butterfly case for a few days after they emerge. Then, on warm, blue sky days, children take turns holding and releasing the monarchs into the air. It is probably a moment they won't forget.

Taking a Look At Yourself

I think I'm really good at:

_____

_____

_____

I really enjoy:

_____

_____

_____

I can share my interests and skills with children in the following ways:

_____

_____

_____

I would like to be better at:

_____

_____

_____

I would like to know more about:

_____

_____

_____

Discuss your responses with two colleagues. Have they learned anything new about you? Do they see things that you did not see? Use the space below to write what you learned from doing this exercise.

_____

_____

_____

_____

Standards of the Child Care Profession

Every profession sets standards for performance. Your center has defined administrative policies and procedures. In addition, the child care profession has several statements of standards. You should become familiar with all of them. These standards are not intended to restrict you. Good teachers are always prepared to adjust daily routines to meet individual children's needs and interests. These standards act as guides. In using them, you, other early childhood professionals, and parents can confirm that you are providing quality care.

Several documents are accepted by the early childhood profession as indicators of professional work. Reviewing these documents can help you evaluate your performance.

- The *Child Development Associate (CDA) Competency Standards* define 13 skill areas needed by early childhood teachers. Teachers who master the skill areas can earn a credential that is based on performance with children rather than on formal training. The competency standards also serve as guidelines for teachers who are not seeking a CDA credential but want to improve their child care skills.

- The *Center Accreditation Program* (CAP) is an accreditation process conducted by the National Association for the Education of Young Children (NAEYC). It is the first nationally recognized program to accredit early childhood centers. CAP has criteria for high-quality early childhood programs in 10 categories. Centers are accredited through a six-step process that includes self-study, a validation visit, and a final team review.

- The statement on *Developmentally Appropriate Practice,* developed by NAEYC, gives guidelines for the kinds of practices that are suitable for children at particular ages and stages of development. Appropriate activities and teaching practices are outlined for children from infancy through age eight.

Reviewing these documents and completing the self-assessments for each of the self-instructional modules should give you a comprehensive picture of your skills and capabilities. This review will also identify areas you need to know more about and skills you need to develop or improve.

Obtain a copy of NAEYC's *Developmentally Appropriate Practice* statement and write a paragraph about one aspect that is particularly meaningful to you. Discuss how this statement relates to what you do in your classroom.

_____
_____
_____
_____
_____
_____
_____
_____
_____
_____
_____
_____
_____
_____
_____
_____

Discuss your statement with your trainer.

II. Continuing to Learn About Caring for Children

In this activity you will learn:

- to continue to expand your knowledge and skills; and

- to make short- and long-range professional development plans.

No matter how many years you've been a teacher or how much you already know, it is important to continue to learn more about your profession. This is true for a number of reasons.

- **There is always new information to be learned**. Professionals need to keep up with the latest developments in the field. New research often leads to new, more effective strategies for working with children. Learning and growth are ongoing for the child care professional.

- **Continual learning makes you an active, thinking person**. Teachers who also are always learning new things are more interesting people and are more likely to inspire the children in their care. If you enjoy learning, you are more likely to make others enjoy it, too. Teachers who keep learning always have new ideas to bring to the center.

- **You care about children**. Each article or book you read, and every discussion or conference you participate in, may give you new insights or help you resolve nagging problems. Suppose, for example, that a child with special needs joins your group. You may seek to learn new ways to meet this child's needs. Because you care about all children, you are always alert for new and helpful information relating to their development.

- **You want to grow professionally**. A commitment to continue learning can lead to improved performance. Learning can not only result in an increased feeling of confidence but may also lead to more responsibility, a higher position, and more pay.

How can teachers continue growing and learning? In addition to participating in this self-instructional training program, there are many other ways you can continue learning. You might:

- join professional organizations;

- read books and articles;

- network with other professionals in the field;

- observe other teachers; and

- take advantage of training opportunities.

13

Joining Professional Organizations

Professional organizations help you keep up to date on the latest information and current issues in the profession. Many have local affiliates that meet regularly. These organizations offer newsletters, books, brochures, and other publications with useful information and helpful tips. At their conferences attendees can meet others with similar interests and concerns.

The following are descriptions of the major professional organizations in the child care profession.

Association for Childhood Education International (ACEI)
11141 Georgia Avenue, Suite 200
Wheaton, MD 20902
(301) 942-2443

ACEI, established in 1892, is represented in all 50 states and in many nations abroad. The Association addresses the care and education of children from birth through adolescence.

Child Care Employee Project (CCEP)
P.O. Box 5603
Berkeley, CA 94705
(415) 653-9889

CCEP is a nonprofit advocacy organization working to improve the wages, status, and working conditions of the child care profession. Organized in 1977 by child care workers, CCEP provides assistance to child care providers, parents, policymakers, and the media on issues that affect the child care workforce. A quarterly newsletter and a wide variety of materials on child care employee issues are available from CCEP.

Council for Early Childhood Professional Recognition
1341 G Street, N.W., Suite 400
Washington, DC 20005
(800) 424-4310
(202) 265-9090

The Council is the national credentialing program for early childhood educators. Its goal is to improve the quality of early childhood programs by assessing, improving, and recognizing the skills of education staff in child care settings. The Council awards the Child Development Associate (CDA) credential, the nationally recognized credential for child care workers.

National Association for the Education of Young Children (NAEYC)
1509 16th Street, N.W.
Washington, DC 20036
(202) 232-8777 or (800) 424-2460

With more than 60,000 members, NAEYC is the largest early childhood professional organization in this country. This group publishes *Young Children*, an early childhood journal of ideas, findings, and issues in child care. NAEYC also publishes books, posters, and other media materials on child care issues. NAEYC's annual national conference offers the early childhood professional training on a range of important topics. The conference is also a wonderful opportunity to meet other teachers as well as writers and researchers in the field.

NAEYC has 360 affiliate groups working locally, statewide, and regionally on behalf of young children. The main office can tell you about the group nearest you.

National Black Child Development Institute (NBCDI)
1023 15th St., NW, Suite 600
Washington, DC 20005
(202) 387-1281

NBCDI is a group that advocates on behalf of the growth and development of black children. It organizes and trains networks of members to voice concerns regarding policies that affect black children and their families. NBCDI sponsors an annual conference that focuses on critical issues in child care development, education, foster care and adoption, and health. NBCDI also publishes the *Black Child Advocate*, a quarterly newsletter.

National Institute for Hispanic Children and Families
2000 Rosemont Avenue NW
Washington, DC 20010
(202) 265-9885

This group considers the child care needs of Latino children and analyzes how those needs compare with the needs of other children. The group also reviews and assesses legislation affecting Latino children and their families.

Southern Early Childhood Association (SECA)
P.O. Box 56130
Little Rock, AR 72215
(501) 663-0353

SECA comprises early childhood educators, teachers, administrators, researchers, teacher trainers, and parents in the United States and abroad. The group provides a voice on local, state, and federal issues affecting young children. An annual conference is held to exchange information and ideas. SECA also publishes materials on the latest issues in child development and early education. Publications include *Dimensions* (a quarterly journal), *The Portfolio and Its Use,* and *Developmentally Appropriate Assessment of Young Chidren.* SECA has 13 state groups.

Reading Books and Articles

Books and articles help you expand your knowledge and skills. You can review articles or chapters in a book during lunch or at home. A list of helpful resources can be found at the end of each module. You can also borrow materials from the public library in your community.

Networking

Networking is spending time with people who perform similar tasks to share ideas, information, and experiences. It is a good way to find solutions to problems, gain new knowledge, or help colleagues cope with difficult situations. You can network with one other person or with a group. Group networks can include other child care professionals, in the local community or in the state. Meetings can be very informal, perhaps after work or on a Saturday. They can also be formal, with speakers and a detailed agenda. What is important is that teachers meet, share ideas, and get support in coping with the demands of their jobs.

Observing Other Teachers

You can learn a lot by visiting the room of another teacher, either in your center or at another child care program. Because each teacher is unique, you can observe others and learn new approaches to solving discipline problems, managing a transition time, or coping with feeding three hungry children at one time.

Participating in Training

Training is another way to keep up to date in the child care field and develop new skills. You can attend courses offered by community groups. County extension agencies offer nutrition courses, and public school adult-education programs offer courses on a wide range of topics. College or university courses may also be an option.

Your center provided this self-instructional training for all teachers. As you complete each module, your knowledge of child development and child care will grow.

Begin this learning activity by reviewing your answers on page 339, "Taking a Look at Yourself." Pick one item from your responses to "I would like to be better at" or "I would like to know more about." Consider the sources of assistance available to you: the public library, workshops, professional organizations, your supervisor, and other colleagues. Identify what specific resources can help you with the task or topic you have selected. Use the form on the next page to list what you find.

Continuing to Learn About Caring for Children

I want to improve or learn more about:

_____

_____

_____

_____

_____

_____

_____

_____

_____

_____

_____

Resources I can use:

SOURCE	CONTACT PERSON
Public Library	
Workshops	
Professional organization	
Supervisor/colleagues	

Making Plans for Continued Learning

Now that you have identified resources to help you in an area you want to work on, you need to plan how and when to use those resources. When you develop a plan, you clarify what you want to achieve—your goal—and how you will go about achieving it. With a written plan in front of you, you feel like you're already making progress. And you are! Knowing where you're going and how you're going to get there makes it easier to take each step and to recognize your goal when you reach it. As you take each step and check it off on your plan, you can visualize your movement toward your goal.

You can improve your skills in the following ways:

- Take advantage of opportunities that come your way. Attend workshops and training offered by your center or other groups.

- Use other teachers as resources and offer yourself to them as a resource. Consult your supervisor about theoretical issues and practical concerns. Share your ideas with other teachers.

- Review how you manage your time. If you look closely at how you spend each day, you may find some time-wasting activities. Finding ways to do things faster or better may leave extra time for reading, studying, and reassessing how you are doing in your work.

- Set specific goals for yourself. Try to do something on a regular basis to fulfill them.

In Learning Activity I, Assessing Yourself, you identified tasks you would like to improve. You also identified tasks that you're good at. The chart you just completed helped you think about resources that are readily available to you. Use the results of these two activities to make plans for your professional development. For the short term you may want to focus on tasks you think most need improving. For the long term you may want to build on an area you are strong in and become even more skilled—so that you can share your competence with others while you increase your self-confidence.

In this learning activity you will make some short- and long-range plans for yourself. Then you will identify possible barriers and decide how to overcome them. Read the example on the following page and fill out the chart that follows.

Plans for Professional Development
(Example)

Short-Range Plans

What would I like to do right away to improve my skills?

- *Take a course on how to guide children's behavior.*

- *Learn more activities for children to do outside.*

- *Complete Module 8, Self.*

What barriers might hinder me from completing these plans?

- *It's hard to find time to complete the activities and still care for all the children.*

- *I can't find any resources on the reasons for children's behavior.*

What can I do to overcome these barriers?

- *I can talk with other teachers about trading some responsibilities so we can all have more time to work on the modules.*

- *I'll send away to NAEYC for two brochures: "Helping Children Learn Self-Control" and "Love and Learn: Discipline for Young Children."*

Long-Range Plans

What would I like to be doing a year from now?

- *Begin working on a degree in early childhood education.*

- *Join one professional association.*

- *Complete the self-instructional modules.*

What barriers might hinder me from completing these plans?

- *I have no money to attend school.*

- *My spouse may transfer to a new place before I finish.*

What can I do to overcome these barriers?

- *I can take one or two courses at a time rather than a full load.*

- *I can find out about loans that might be available for going to school.*

- *I can find names of colleges and universities where I might transfer credits if I relocate.*

Plans for Professional Development

Short-Range Plans

What would I like to do right away to improve my skills?

_____

_____

_____

_____

What barriers might hinder me from completing these plans?

_____

_____

_____

_____

What can I do to overcome these barriers?

_____

_____

_____

_____

Long-Range Plans

What would I like to be doing a year from now?

_____

_____

_____

_____

What barriers might hinder me from completing these plans?

_____

_____

_____

_____

What can I do to overcome these barriers?

_____

_____

_____

_____

Discuss your plans with your trainer. What barriers can you overcome? Agree on an overall plan to achieve your goals, both short and long term.

III. Applying Professional Ethics at All Times

In this activity you will learn:

- what it means to act in a professional manner; and

- to identify professional behavior.

As discussed in Learning Activities I and II, being a professional involves assessing one's knowledge and skills and continually building on them. But professionalism is more than having expertise. It has to do with how you apply your knowledge and skills daily as you work with parents, children, and staff. It means doing your job to the best of your ability. And it involves your actions in the child care setting and in the community.

Professionals need to do what is right rather than what is easy. Practicing professionals are committed to doing what is best for all children in their care, on every occasion. Here are some examples.

ETHICS OF TEACHING	PROFESSIONAL BEHAVIOR	UNPROFESSIONAL BEHAVIOR
Maintaining confidentiality about children and their families. Avoiding talking to other parents about a particular child, particularly in front of that child.	Discussing a child's problem confidentially with another teacher or the supervisor and trying to identify ways to help the child. "Ms Kim, sometimes Mrs. Gabriel brings Tommy to the center in dirty clothes. We need to discuss the situation with our supervisor."	Talking about a child in front of the child or with a parent other than the child's. "Did you see what that child was wearing? I'm glad you don't dress your child in rags."
Being honest, dependable, and reliable in performing duties. Being regular in attendance and performance. Coming to work on time, returning from breaks on time, and performing duties on schedule.	Arriving at work every day on time and performing assigned duties. "I'll be ready to go home just as soon as I finish wiping down these tables."	Calling in sick unnecessarily, arriving late, or not doing assigned duties. Paying more attention to adults in the center than to children. "You'll have to watch these kids yourself. I have to go call my girlfriend."

ETHICS OF TEACHING	PROFESSIONAL BEHAVIOR	UNPROFESSIONAL BEHAVIOR
Treating parents with respect, even during difficult situations.	Talking to a parent who always comes late about the problem this causes and discussing possible solutions. "Mrs. Lowell, our center closes at 6:30 p.m. If you can't get here by 6:30, could someone else pick up Jennifer?"	Getting angry at a parent who is late and demanding that he or she do better. Talking to other parents or acquaintances outside the center about parents. "This is the third time you've been late this week. Don't you know I need to go home too?"
Treating each child with respect, regardless of gender, culture, or background. Treating each child as an individual; avoiding comparisons.	Comforting a child who is hurt or upset. Including activities and materials that reflect the cultures and backgrounds of all children.	Teasing children if they cry. Asking one child to behave just like another child. "Why can't you play nicely like Timothy does?"
Making sure activities, practices, and routines are developmentally appropriate.	Talking with parents about appropriate activities for their child's stages of development.	Making all children do the same activities or meeting all children's needs on a strict schedule. "Wake up, Damian, it's time for everyone to eat. You've been sleeping long enough."
Providing a good model for learning and for language and communication skills. Using standard grammar and sentence structure. Never using profanities in front of children.	Using standard pronunciation. Using complete sentences when talking with children. "Free play is over now. It's time for everyone to pick up the toys."	Using non-standard grammar, slang, or profanity with children. "No more time for play. Pick up them toys now."

352

ETHICS OF TEACHING	PROFESSIONAL BEHAVIOR	UNPROFESSIONAL BEHAVIOR
Dressing to do the job. Being conscious of dress, grooming, and hygiene.	Wearing comfortable clean clothes so that you can play with and care for children: clothes you can sit on the floor in, bend and lift in, and move quickly in, when necessary. "I like your new outfit, Mrs. Carter. It looks comfortable and it's very flattering."	Wearing clothes that hinder movement and that you have to worry about. "You'll have to ask Ms. Peterson to help you. I can't walk on the grass in these heels."
Recording information appropriately.	Keeping good records to aid in making accurate reports to parents and the supervisor. "Lori's mother said she really likes our recordkeeping center. She can look on the chart and see what Lori's day was like."	Not taking the time to record needed information because it's too much trouble. "No one ever reads these accident reports. I'm not wasting my time filling one out."
Advocating on behalf of children, families, and others. Letting others know the importance of child care work.	Joining a professional organization. "I'm really glad I joined NAEYC. Their materials really help me be a better teacher."	Belittling child care work as "only babysitting." "As soon as I can I'm going to get myself a real job."

In this activity you will list examples of how your behavior conforms to ethics of teaching. Then you will read several case studies and identify what a professional early childhood educator should do in each situation.

ETHICS OF TEACHING	EXAMPLES OF YOUR OWN PROFESSIONAL BEHAVIOR
Maintaining confidentiality about children and their families. Avoiding talking to other parents about a particular child, especially in front of that child.	
Being honest, dependable, and reliable in performing duties. Being regular in attendance and performance. Coming to work on time, returning from breaks on time, and performing duties on schedule.	
Treating parents with respect even during difficult situations.	
Treating each child with respect, regardless of gender, culture, or background. Treating each child as an individual; avoiding comparisons.	

PROFESSIONALISM

ETHICS OF TEACHING	EXAMPLES OF YOUR OWN PROFESSIONAL BEHAVIOR
Making sure activities, practices, and routines are developmentally appropriate.	
Providing a good model for learning and for language and communication skills. Using good grammar and sentence structure. Never using profanities in front of children.	
Dressing to do the job. Being conscious of dress, grooming, and hygiene.	
Recording information appropriately.	
Advocating on behalf of children, families, and others. Letting others know the importance of child care work.	

Ethical Case Studies[3]

The following situations were published by the National Association for the Education of Young Children. After reading each one, write down what you think a good early childhood educator would do. Then plan a time to discuss your responses with your trainer and a group of colleagues.

1. Case Study: The Abused Child

Mary Lou, a two-year-old in your school, is showing the classic signs of abuse: multiple bruises, frequent black eyes, and psychological withdrawal. Her mother, a high-strung woman, says she falls a lot, but nobody at the center has noticed this. Her father twice seemed to be drunk when he picked Mary Lou up. The law says you must report suspicions of abuse to the Children's Protective Office. But in your experience, when the authorities get involved they are usually unable to remove the child from the home or improve the family's behavior. Sometimes the families simply disappear, or things become worse for the children.

What should a good early childhood educator do?

_____

_____

_____

_____

2. Case Study: The Working Mother

Timothy's mother has asked you not to allow her four-year-old son to nap in the afternoon. She says, "Whenever he naps he stays up until 10:00 at night. I have to get up at 5:00 in the morning to go to work. I am not getting enough sleep." Along with the rest of the children, Timothy takes a one-hour nap almost every day. He seems to need it in order to stay in good spirits in the afternoon.

What should a good early childhood educator do?

_____

_____

_____

_____

---

[3]Case studies reprinted with permission from Stephanie Feeney, "Ethical Case Studies for NAEYC Reader Response," *Young Children* (Washington, DC: National Association for the Education of Young Children, May 1987), pp. 24-25.

356

3. Case Study: The Aggressive Child

Eric is a large and extremely active four-year-old who often frightens and hurts other children. You have discussed this repeatedly with the director, who is sympathetic but unable to help. The parents listen but feel that the behavior is typical for boys his age. They won't get counseling. A preschool specialist from the Department of Mental Health has observed the child, but her recommendations have not helped either. Meanwhile Eric terrorizes other children and parents are starting to complain. You are becoming stressed and tired, and your patience is wearing thin. You and your co-teacher are spending so much time dealing with Eric that you are worried the other children are not getting the attention they need.

What should a good early childhood educator do?

_____

_____

_____

_____

4. Case Study: The "Academic" Preschool

Heather has just gone back to school to get her Child Development Associate credential. She has been assigned as your trainee. She has taught at a preschool for several years, is happy there, and receives a good salary. When you have observed her, you have seen three- and four-year-olds using workbooks for long periods of time. The daily program includes repetitious drill on letters, numbers, shapes, and colors. Children are regularly being "taught" the alphabet and rote counting to 100. You have also noticed that most interactions are initiated by adults and that children have few opportunities to interact with materials.

You mention to Heather that you do not think the school's curriculum is appropriate for preschool children. She replies that she had a similar reaction when she began working there, but the director and other teachers assured her there was no problem with the curriculum. They told her that this is the way they have always taught at the school. The parents are very satisfied with it.

What should a good early childhood educator do?

_____

_____

_____

_____

When you have completed these case studies, plan a time to discuss your responses with your trainer and other teachers. These are difficult situations to handle, and it will help you to discuss your ideas with others.

IV. Becoming an Advocate for Children and Families

In this activity you will learn:

- to recognize the importance of being involved in advocacy for children and families; and

- to become involved in advocacy efforts.

Early childhood educators are directly affected by local and national policies and programs for children and families. Therefore, becoming an advocate on behalf of high-quality programs for children and families is part of being a professional.

Advocacy is working for change. This often means taking the opportunity to speak out on issues that may be affecting the children and families in your program or on issues that affect your own working conditions.

How You Can Become an Advocate[4]

A first step in becoming an early childhood advocate is to understand the importance of advocacy. This means recognizing how public and private policies affect children's lives and accepting that children need a strong voice to ensure that the programs they attend support their development. Advocates must ask themselves: "What can I do to ensure adequate attention to children's needs by policymakers, elected officials, administrators, schools, businesses, and other groups?" Answering this question, however, requires making a commitment to act.

Advocacy efforts try to improve the circumstances of children's lives so they get what they need to grow to their full potential. Early childhood educators are especially well-informed on this issue from both theory and practice. Early childhood advocates commit themselves to sharing this knowledge with others. They act on what they know; they move beyond good intentions and take action. Advocates overcome the fear of becoming involved. They realize that children's problems are a collective responsibility. They take the critical, transforming step from concern to action.

As early childhood educators, we expand our commitment to children, families, and our profession when we act on our beliefs and share our knowledge with others. Early childhood educators can contribute to advocacy in six ways.

---

[4]Adapted with permission from Stacie G. Goffin and Joan Lombardi, *Speaking Out: Early Childhood Advocacy* (Washington, DC: National Association for the Education of Young Children, 1988), pp. 2-5.

Contribution #1: Sharing Our Knowledge

Our beliefs and knowledge are based on an understanding of child development, the practice of early childhood education, and relationships with parents. Therefore, we can make important contributions to policy debates about the developmental needs of children and the characteristics of safe and nurturing early childhood environments. This is our professional knowledge base. We need to assume responsibility for sharing these understandings with parents, policy makers, and other decision makers. We can help decision makers focus on the role of policy in enhancing children's development. In these ways, our advocacy efforts can become a catalyst for change.

Contribution #2: Sharing Our Professional Experiences

We work with children and their families daily. We experience firsthand the impact of changing circumstances—such as unemployment, lack of child care, inappropriate curricula, and conflicts between work and family—before decision makers are informed that these issues are "new trends." When children and families in our programs receive services from public and private agencies, we are firsthand observers and monitors of whether children's needs are being met. As a result, we have the opportunity—and a professional responsibility—to share the personal stories that give meaning to group statistics. Without sharing confidential information, we can describe how policies affect children and families.

Personal experiences help us become more persuasive. We live these stories in our day-to-day work with children and families.

Contribution #3: Redefining the "Bottom Line" for Children

The debate about programs for young children is often tied to other policy issues such as welfare, job training, and teenage pregnancy. Funding for children's programs is often seen as an investment directed toward children's future productivity. Joining children's issues with broader political issues and social concerns is an effective political technique. These strategies can expand our base of support and help frame children's issues in ways consistent with many of society's accepted values.

Our unique perspectives on children, however, also enable us to speak out for children's inherent "worth." We know that childhood is a meaningful time for development in its own right. If policies for children and families are made solely on the basis of "return on investment," children will suffer when investors seek a higher return or decide to pull out of the "market." Early childhood educators must remember that these investment strategies are means to achieve a desired end. They must not become so effective that they undermine the "bottom line" of early childhood advocacy—encouraging policies that promote children's development.

Contribution #4: Standing Up for Our Profession

Early childhood is growing as a profession. We know how important our jobs are to children and their families. Therefore, we must speak out on behalf of caregiving and early childhood education as a profession and for the special expertise needed to be a professional.

Many people are unaware that early childhood education has a distinctive, professional knowledge base. We know that the quality of early childhood programs depends upon the training and compensation of the staff providing the care and education. Early educators know firsthand about the impact of low wages, high staff turnover, burnout, and inadequately trained staff and administrators. We are obligated to share these stories, too.

Advocacy efforts on behalf of our profession are most effective when we emphasize the benefits of our work for children and families. We must begin to exercise our power to speak out on issues that affect our profession.

Contribution #5: Involving Parents

Our daily interactions with parents provide many opportunities for us to share our common concerns and goals for children's well-being. We have a unique opportunity to help parents recognize their power as children's primary advocates—for both their own and another's children.

Parents can be especially effective advocates on behalf of their children. Parents represent a critical consumer voice. By involving parents, we can dramatically expand the constituency speaking out for children.

Contribution #6: Expanding the Constituency for Children

Early childhood educators have important linkages with public school administrators and teachers, health care providers, religious organizations, and many other professional and volunteer groups. These interactions provide natural opportunities to inform others about the developmental needs of children, appropriate teaching practices, and the supports families need to strengthen themselves. We can act as catalysts to help others understand children's needs as our collective responsibility and our shared future.

In this activity you will identify advocacy steps that you feel you can take and develop a plan to become involved. First read "Actions Early Childhood Educators Can Take," then answer the questions that follow the reading.

Actions Early Childhood Educators Can Take[5]

You can choose from many courses of action once you make a commitment to become an advocate for children, their families, and your profession. Here are a few of the choices:

- Share ideas for appropriate practice with other teachers and parents (instead of just observing disapprovingly).

- Explain to administrators why dittos are inappropriate learning tools for young children (rather than using them and feeling resentful that you have to practice your profession in ways that are inconsistent with its knowledge base).

- Explain to parents why children learn best through play (instead of bemoaning that parents are pushing their children or giving in and teaching with inappropriate methods and materials).

- Write a letter to the editor of a newspaper or magazine to respond to an article or letter (instead of just complaining about how other people don't understand the needs of children, their families, or their caregivers).

- Write to your state or federal legislators about a pending issue and share your experiences as a way to point out needs (rather than just assuming someone else will write).

- Meet someone new who is interested in early childhood education and ask her or him to join a professional group such as NAEYC, NBCDI, SACUS, or ACEI (instead of just wondering why the person isn't involved).

- Ask a friend to go with you to a legislator's town meeting (instead of staying home because you don't want to go alone).

- Volunteer to represent your professional group in a coalition to speak out on the educational needs of young children (instead of waiting to be asked or declining because you've never done it before).

- Agree to serve on a legislative telephone tree (rather than refusing because "my phone call won't matter anyway").

- Work and learn with others to develop a position statement on a critical issue (instead of saying "I don't really know much about this topic").

- Volunteer to speak at a school board meeting about NAEYC's position statement *Developmentally Appropriate Practice in Early Childhood Programs Serving Children from Birth Through Age 8* (Bredekamp, 1987) (instead of resigning yourself to the fact that your school system doesn't understand much about early childhood education).

---

[5]Reprinted with permission from Stacie G. Goffin and Joan Lombardi, *Speaking Out: Early Childhood Advocacy* (Washington, DC: National Association for the Education of Young Children, 1988), pp. 14-15.

• Conduct a local or state survey of salaries in early childhood programs (instead of ignoring the issue because no one has the facts).

• Persuade colleagues that it is important to work toward accreditation from the National Academy of Early Childhood Programs (rather than assuming no one wants to improve the program).

A Plan to Become an Advocate

Which activity listed in the reading is of most interest to you?

_____

_____

_____

_____

_____

Why is it often difficult to speak out on these issues?

_____

_____

_____

_____

_____

How do you think you could become more involved in speaking out for young children, families, and the profession?

_____

_____

_____

_____

_____

Discuss your responses with your trainer.

V. Taking Care of Yourself

In this activity you will learn:

- to recognize the importance of taking care of yourself; and

- to take care of yourself physically, emotionally, socially, and intellectually.

Although your first responsibility as a teacher is to take care of the needs of children, you also have a responsibility to take care of yourself. All you have to give is yourself—your caring, your energy, and your commitment. You cannot do this when you are not at your best. To teach young children, you need to be in good physical and emotional health. You also need to feel that you are appreciated, meaningfully connected to others, intellectually stimulated, and performing a job worth doing.

Taking care of yourself means considering your needs and well-being in four areas: physical, emotional, social, and intellectual.

Your Physical Well-Being

Health is very important to a person who teaches young children. Without physical stamina, good health, and a good diet, a teacher is not adequately prepared to work with young children for long hours every day. Physical well-being is influenced by three key factors: good diet, adequate rest, and regular exercise. Taking care of your physical well-being means being sure you eat foods that are good for you, get enough rest, and exercise several times a week.

Your Emotional Well-Being

The way you feel about yourself, your work, and the world affects how you interact with the children and adults around you. The more positive you feel about yourself, the better you will be able to care for young children. When you start to feel worried or depressed, it is good to talk with family and friends about your concerns.

Your Social Well-Being

Having people to talk to is essential for survival. A trusted person with whom to share your joys, frustrations, and ideas can be very important in determining how you feel about yourself as a person and as a teacher. The person may be a colleague, spouse, relative, or friend. What is important is that you have someone (at least one, but preferably several people) with whom you can exchange ideas, feelings, resources, and moral support.

Your Intellectual Well-Being

Most adults enjoy learning something new and being challenged. Like children, adults need to continue to explore, experiment, and learn. Your learning can be about job-related issues such as child development and about other topics as well.

In this learning activity you will assess how well you are taking care of yourself. Record your activities for two days. For Day 1 record your activities for today. Review your answers, note areas where you could take better care of yourself, and try to improve your schedule tomorrow. Record that schedule under Day 2.

	DAY 1	DAY 2
Physical Well-Being		
Did I eat three balanced meals?	_____	_____
How much sleep did I get? (Is that average?)	_____	_____
Did I get any exercise?	_____	_____
Emotional Well-Being		
Did I have a generally positive outlook?	_____	_____
Did I take a few moments to relax after a stressful situation?	_____	_____
Social Well-Being		
Did I spend time with someone I care about?	_____	_____
Did I talk through a day's problem with a friend or colleague?	_____	_____
Intellectual Well-Being		
Did I read anything for information or interest—a book, an article, the newspaper?	_____	_____
Did I learn something new?	_____	_____

Discuss this activity with your trainer and make a commitment to take good care of yourself. Use the space below to note what actions you will take.

I will do the following things to take care of myself:

_____

_____

_____

_____

_____

Summarizing Your Progress

You have now completed all of the learning activities for this module. Whether you are an experienced teacher or a new one, this module has probably helped you maintain a commitment to professionalism. Before you go on, review your responses to the pre-training assessment for this module. Write a summary of what you learned and list the skills you developed or improved.

If there are topics you would like to know more about, you will find recommended readings listed in the orientation, which can be found in Volume I.

Your final step in this module is to complete the knowledge and competency assessments. Let your trainer know when you are ready to schedule the assessment. After you have successfully completed the assessment, you will be ready to start a new module. Congratulations on your progress so far, and good luck with your next module.

Answer Sheet

Maintaining a Commitment to Professionalism

Continually Assessing Your Own Performance

1. **How did Ms. Kim assess her own performance?**

   a. She thought about how the day had progressed.

   b. She considered feedback from parents.

   c. She thought about how she felt about the day's events.

2. **What did she decide to do with the results of her self-assessment?**

   a. She decided to become more organized.

   b. She decided to talk to Mr. Lopez, another teacher, to get some pointers.

   c. She decided to talk to her supervisor to get some suggestions.

Continuing to Learn About Caring for Children

1. **How did Mr. Lopez decide what knowledge and skills he should work to improve?**

   a. He completed a self-assessment.

   b. He talked with Ms. Lee, his supervisor, to identify areas for improvement.

   c. He set specific goals.

2. **How did Mr. Lopez plan to expand his existing knowledge and skills?**

   a. He selected a module to review.

   b. He planned to attend in-service training.

   c. He planned an observation and feedback visit from Ms. Lee.

   d. He scheduled a follow-up meeting with Ms. Lee.

Applying Professional Ethics at All Times

1. **How did Ms. Williams maintain professional ethics in talking to Mrs. Johnson?**

    a. She greeted the parent politely when she arrived.

    b. She responded to Mrs. Johnson's comments in a positive way.

    c. She maintained confidentiality by not discussing Joshua's behavior with another parent.

2. **How did Ms. Williams interact with Joshua in a professional manner?**

    a. She acted quickly to ensure Joshua's safety.

    b. She used positive guidance techniques to redirect Joshua to a safe place for jumping.

Glossary

Competence	A skill or ability to do something well.
Ethics	A set of principles, standards, or guidelines that direct acceptable behavior—what is right or good rather than quickest or easiest.
Job description	The official written statement describing a teacher's job.
Maintaining confidentiality	Sharing information only with people who have a right to know.
Networking	Spending time with people who perform similar tasks to share ideas, information, and experiences.
Professionalism	A commitment to gaining and maintaining knowledge and skills in a particular field, and to using that knowledge and those skills to provide the highest-quality services possible.
Professional behavior	The consistent, complete application of knowledge and skills.

NOTES

NOTES

NOTES

NOTES

NOTES

NOTES

NOTES

NOTES

NOTES

NOTES